NELE GÜLCK

DER BAUM DES PARADIESES

THE TREE OF PARADISE

DIE SAMMLUNG VON ALF TROJAN

THE COLLECTION OF ALF TROJAN

KERBER ART

EIN FICHTENBAUM STEHT EINSAM
IM NORDEN AUF KAHLER HÖH.
IHN SCHLÄFERT; MIT WEISSER DECKE
UMHÜLLEN IHN EIS UND SCHNEE.

ER TRÄUMT VON EINER PALME,
DIE, FERN IM MORGENLAND,
EINSAM UND SCHWEIGEND TRAUERT
AUF BRENNENDER FELSENWAND.

HEINRICH HEINE

THERE STANDS A LONELY PINE-TREE
IN THE NORTH, ON A BARREN HEIGHT;
HE SLEEPS WHILE THE ICE AND SNOW FLAKES
SWATHE HIM IN FOLDS OF WHITE.

HE DREAMETH OF A PALM-TREE
FAR IN THE SUNRISE-LAND,
LONELY AND SILENT LONGING
ON HER BURNING ROCK FACE.

HEINRICH HEINE

SABINE DANEK

DIE SÜDSEE IM WOHNZIMMERSCHRANK

Es begann mit Schmetterlingen. Die trug Alf Trojan am Revers. Kleine flatterhafte Dinge, die jede Blüte befruchten wollen, wie seine Freundin Tasch fand. Das war Anfang der Siebzigerjahre und als ihre Beziehung ernster wurde, tauschte der angehende Arzt die Schmetterlings-Broschen gegen eine Palme ein. Knallig und aus Plexiglas war sie, erstanden auf dem Portobello-Flohmarkt in London – und in den nächsten 40 Jahren kamen mehr als 1500 weitere Palmenobjekte hinzu.

Palmenhemden und Palmenleuchter, Modellbau-Palmen und Palmenstifte, Schwämme in Palmenform, Emaille-Eimerchen mit Palmen darauf oder Schneekugeln mit Palmen darin. Unter ihnen schippert ein Bötchen entlang, tanzt ein verliebtes Paar oder grinst ein Weihnachtsmann.

Ein Konzept beim Sammeln verfolgte Alf Trojan nicht. Es ging einzig um die Liebe zum Motiv – und darum, dass die einzelnen Stücke nicht allzu groß waren. Schnell kamen Souvenirs von Freunden, Kollegen und Verwandten hinzu, Bierkühler aus Australien, Tischsets aus Marrakesch, eine Palmenflöte aus Peru oder nordisches Treibholz mit Palmenmalerei. Später auch selbstgebastelte Palmen der Nichten. Ein Geschenk für Alf Trojan zu finden, war nie ein Problem. Fuhr Tasch, die mittlerweile seine Frau war, nach Frankfurt, übernachtete sie im Hotel Palmenhof, aß im Palmengarten und brachte Alf von ihren Reisen Shampoofläschchen und Speisekarten mit.

Man muss das Sammeln in sich haben, um es mit so viel Leidenschaft wie Alf Trojan zu betreiben, mit so viel Ausdauer und Akribie. Seinen Spleen nennt er es selbst. Seine Frau, von Beruf Psychotherapeutin, vermutet, dass er damit frühkindliche Erfahrungen verarbeitet. Einige Freunde meinen, Palmen hätten etwas Phallisches. Was immer es ist, es entstand aus einer tiefen Sehnsucht nach dem Süden und nach fernen Ländern, der er bis heute auf zahlreichen Reisen nachgeht, vom Jemen bis Jamaika, von den Kanaren bis nach Indien.

Denn wo Palmen sind, ist das Glück nicht weit. Sanft wiegen sie sich im Sommerwind, sind von Wellen umspült. Leuchten vor hellblauem Himmel oder sind in das Rot der untergehenden Sonne getaucht. Sieht man Bilder von Palmen, hört man fast das Meeresrauschen und die Klänge von Ukulelen im Hintergrund.

Alf Trojans Ehe ist bis heute glücklich. Von seiner Palmen-Sammlung aber hat er sich vor Kurzem getrennt. Das Arbeitszimmer war laut Tasch „ein einziger Palmenwahnsinn“. Die Palmen lagen in Schränken, waren in Kisten untergebracht, im Ankleidezimmer hingen Hunderte Palmenanstecker an Stoffbändern, der Flur war mit Palmenbildern plakatiert, im Gästebadezimmer türmten sich Palmenseifen. Nur mit echten Palmen hat es nie geklappt. Die blieben kümmerlich oder sind eingegangen.

Im Winter 2017/2018 überließ Alf Trojan seine Palmensammlung der Hanseatischen Materialverwaltung, einem gemeinnützigen Requisitenfundus im Hamburger Oberhafen. Krumm geschmolzene Kerzen, Palmen in einen Tischläufer eingewebt oder auf zarte Kaffeetassen gemalt, angestaubte Teddybären im Miniaturliegestuhl unter Palmen, der Achtzigerjahre-Raumduft „Lukiluft Südseezauber" – an einigen Stellen ist das Paradies auch etwas in die Jahre gekommen. Zerknickt und angeschlagen so manches Teil, das Wasser der Schneekugeln verdunstet.

Klein wirken die Palmenobjekte vor den riesigen Kulissen und Möbeln, die sonst in der Materialverwaltung zu finden sind. Umso größer sind die Träume und Sehnsüchte, die sie verströmen, die Klischees und der Kitsch, mit denen sie überladen sind.

Die Palmenmotive selbst verweisen bereits über sich hinaus auf das „Island in the Sun", auf kollektive Sehnsüchte und Ideale. Gleichzeitig zeigen sie in ihrer Gesamtheit als Sammlung, wie das Bild der Palme sich von den Siebzigerjahren bis heute verändert hat. Und schließlich fügt ihr Abbild weitere Ebenen hinzu: Mit dem Blick auf das Einzelstück und auf unverstellte Details zeigt es, wie Fernweh im Taschenformat endet, wie ein Sehnsuchtsmotiv zur Massenware wird oder zum Take-away wie in den wunderschönen Palmenszenarien, die liebevoll in eine Muschel hineingeschnitzt sind. Dabei erzählen die Dinge nicht nur von Palmen, Sehnsüchten und Südseezauber, sondern vor allem auch vom Sammeln selbst.

Alf Trojan versteht sich nicht so sehr als Sammler. Er verbringt keine Zeit damit, Palmenobjekte zu suchen, die Geschichte seiner Lieblingsstücke zu recherchieren oder überhaupt viel darüber zu reden. Er findet Palmen. Er ist umgeben von Palmen. Je länger er mit Palmen zu tun hat, desto schönere Palmen finden ihren Weg zu ihm. Wie selbstverständlich sind sie Teil seines Alltags geworden. Und weil diese leidenschaftliche Verbindung nicht einfach abriss, als er seine Sammlung aufgab, behielt er seine liebsten Palmen, und wird auch regelmäßig rückfällig, wenn er auf ein besonders schönes Stück stößt. Für ihn ist „das Palmensehen nicht vorbei".

SABINE DANEK

THE SOUTH SEAS IN THE LIVING ROOM CABINET

It began with butterflies. Which Alf Trojan wore on his lapel. Flighty little things trying to fertilize every flower as his girlfriend Tasch described them. It was the beginning of the 1970s and as their relationship became more serious, the prospective doctor swapped his butterfly brooch for a palm. It was made of plexiglass and it is garish, purchased at London's Portobello Market – and over the next 40 years more than 1.500 palm themed objects were added. Palm shirts and palm lamps, model palms and palm pens, palm-shaped sponges, enamel buckets with palms on or snow globes with palms inside, under which little boats sailed along, lovers danced or a Santa Claus grinned.

Alf Trojan did not follow any concept in his collecting. It was all about his love of the motif – and that all the individual pieces not be too big. Souvenirs came quickly from friends, colleagues and relatives; beer coolers from Australia, table sets from Marrakesh, a palm flute from Peru, even palm motifs painted on driftwood found on northern beaches. Later his nieces made him palm items themselves. Finding a gift for Alf Trojan was never a problem. Tasch, in the meantime, had become his wife and when in Frankfurt, she stayed overnight in the Hotel Palmenhof, ate in the Palm Gardens and took her travel shampoo bottles and menu back home for Alf.

One has to be a born collector to be able to collect with as much passion, stamina and meticulous care as Alf Trojan. He, himself, dubs it his quirk. His wife, a psychotherapist, conjectures that he is processing early childhood experiences. A few friends feel the palms have something phallic about them. Whatever it is, it comes from a deep longing for the South and distant lands, that to this day he continues to pursue, having made numerous journeys already from the Yemen to Jamaica and from the Canaries to India. For where the palms are, happiness is never far away. They gently sway in the summer wind and the waves wash around them. Gleaming against a light blue sky or steeped in the red of a setting sun. Upon seeing pictures of palms, one can almost hear the sea and the sound of the ukulele in the background.

His marriage to Tasch is happy to this day. But he parted with his palm collection recently. The study was, according to Tasch "like a one-off palm tree madness".

The palms, stored in cupboards, were housed in cardboard boxes, in the dressing room hundreds of palm badges hung on strips of fabric, the corridor was plastered with palm pictures, the guest bathroom towered with bars of palm soap. Only real palm trees failed to thrive, remaining puny or withering away.

In winter 2017/2018 Alf Trojan has left his collection to the Hanseatische Materialverwaltung, a non-profit prop warehouse in

Hamburg's Oberhafen area. Twisted melted candles, palms woven into a table runner or painted onto delicate coffee cups, dusty teddy bears on miniature sun beds under palms and an 1980s air freshener "Lukiluft South Sea Magic" – in some places, however, the paradise has grown a little long in the tooth. Some items are tattered and battered, a few of the snow globes' water has long since evaporated.

The objects appear small against the huge scenery and furniture, usually to be found in the Hanseatische Materialverwaltung. But the dreams and the longings they emit, the clichés and kitsch with which they are charged is huge.

The palm motif itself, already refers to beyond that "Island in the Sun", to collective longings and ideals. Simultaneously, in their entirety as a collection, they show how the image of the palm has changed from the 1970s up to the present day. Finally, the images add other levels: in the gaze at the individual piece and its raw details, it is revealed how wanderlust in pocket format ceases, how a motif of longing becomes a mass-produced item or becomes a take-away as in the beautiful palm scenarios, so lovingly cut into a shell. And in so doing they not only recall the longing and magic of the South Seas but also tell, most significantly, of the act of collecting.

Hereby, Alf Trojan himself does not really think of himself as a collector. He did not spend any time searching for palm objects or researching the history of his favorite objects or even to talk that much about them. He finds palms. He is surrounded by palms. The longer he had to do with palms, the more beautiful the palms were that found their way to him. How taken for granted they became a part of his everyday life. As this passionate connection did not end when relinquishing his collection, he kept his most beloved palms, and he also regularly relapses when he comes across a particularly beautiful piece. "For him the seeing of palms is not over".

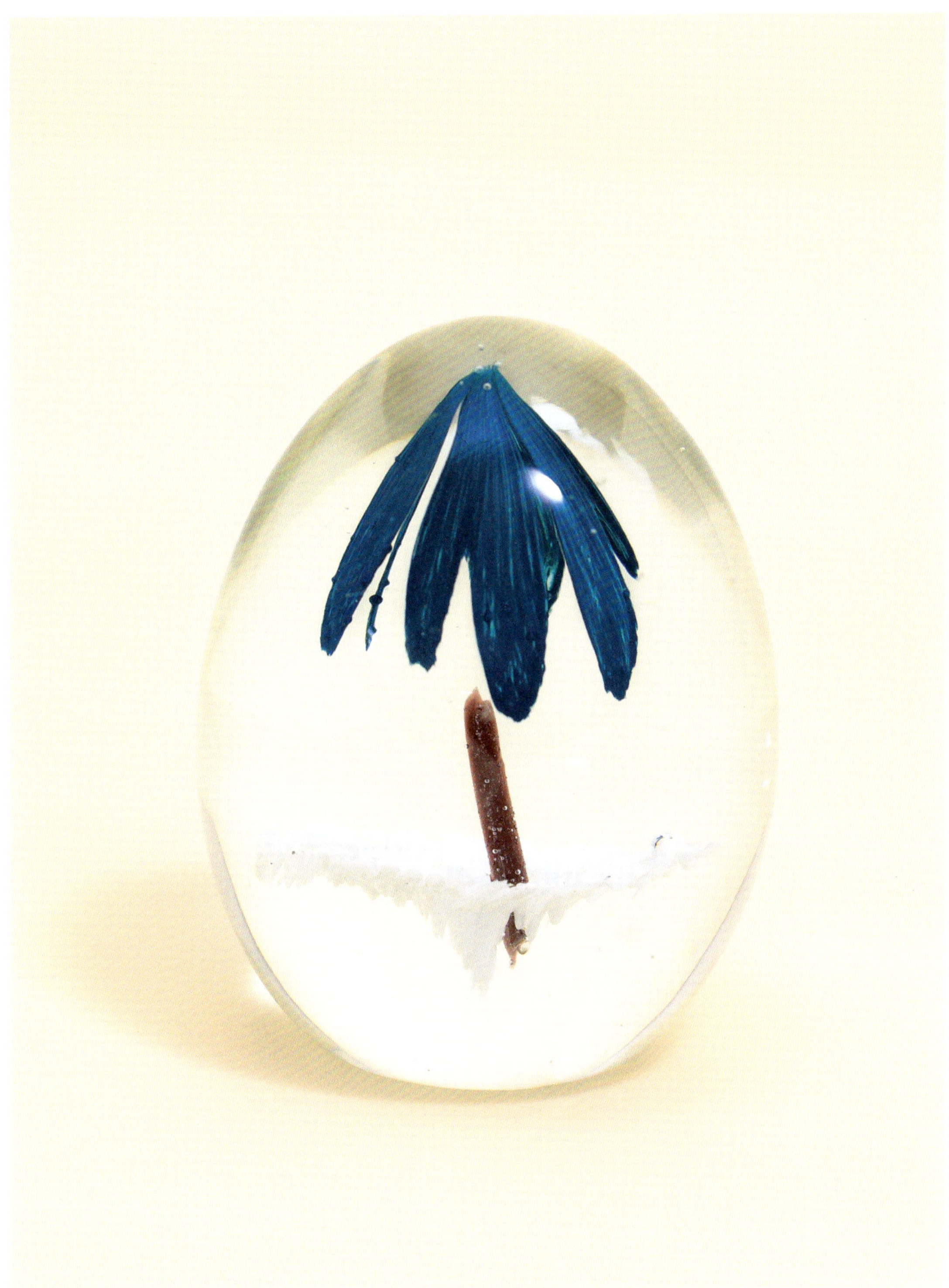

01
Briefbeschwerer Glas, Kunstharz, 9 × 7 × 7 cm, undatiert; in Besitz von Alf Trojan
Paperweight glass, synthetic resin, 3.54 × 2.76 × 2.76 in, undated; property of Alf Trojan

02
Handgewebter Läufer Schafswolle, handgefärbt, 60 × 32 cm, 1999/ Marktstand Marokko; leichte Gebrauchsspuren
Handwoven runner sheep wool, hand dyed, 23.62 × 12.59 in, 1999/ market stall Morocco; slight signs of wear

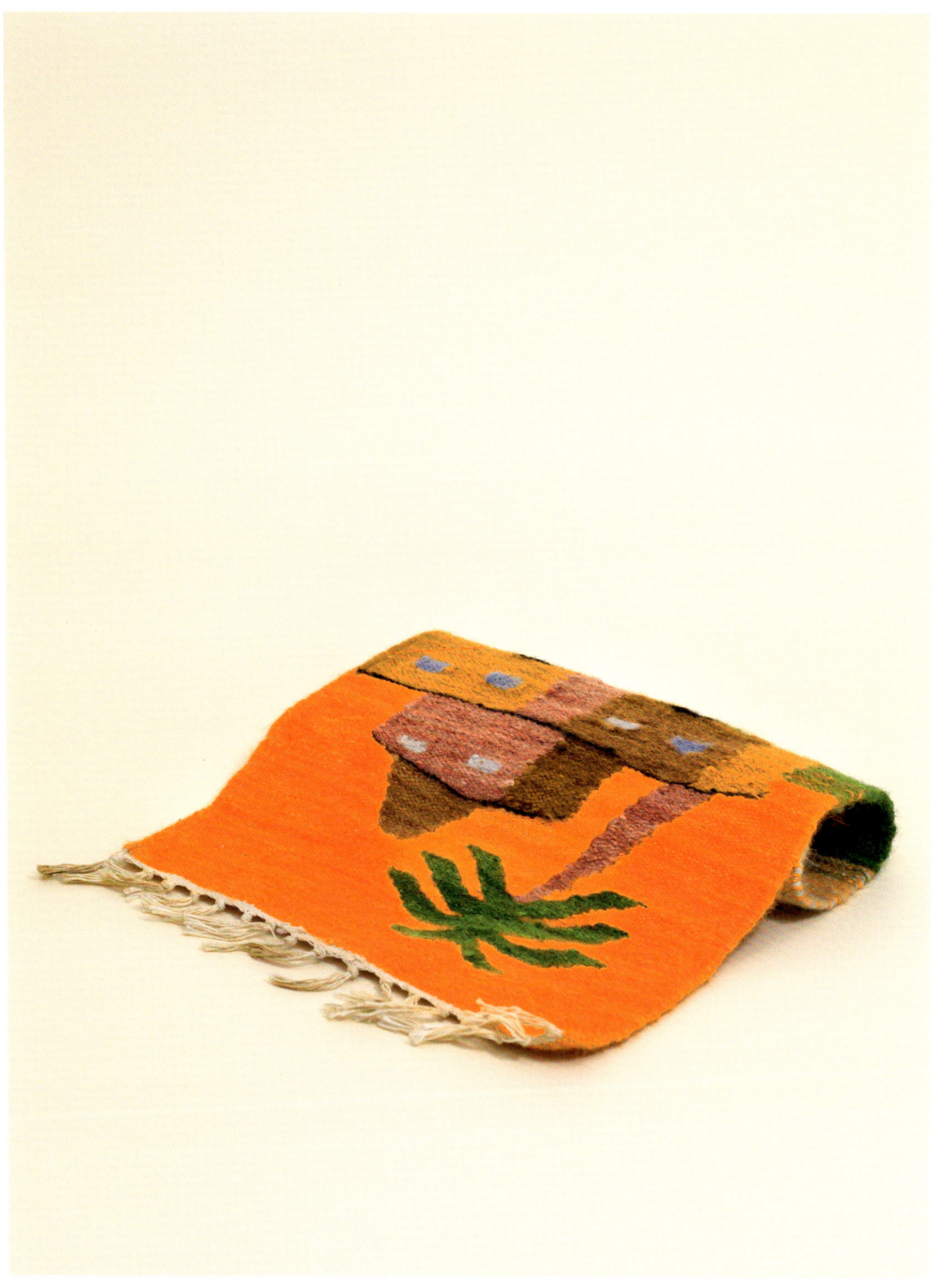

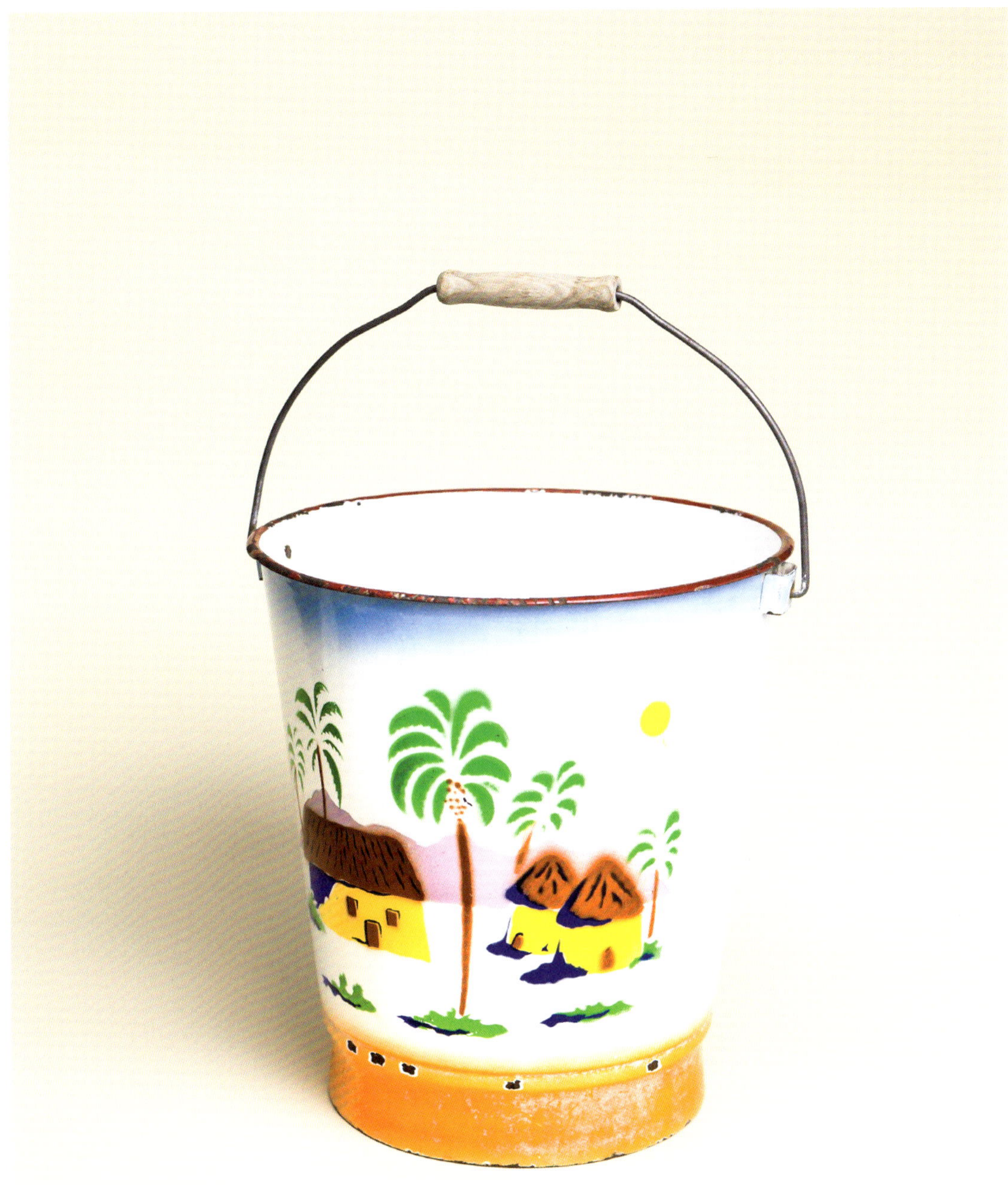

03
Putzeimer handbemalt, Emaille, Holz, 32 × 29 × 27,5 cm, 1994/Flohmarkt Brandenburg; Roststellen
Cleaning bucket hand-painted, enamel, wood, 12.59 × 11.41 × 10.82 in, 1994/fleamarket Brandenburg; rust spots

04
Aufblasbare Palme Polyvinyl, 18,3 × 17 × 9 cm, undatiert; Flecken
Inflatable palm tree polyvinyl, 7.2 × 6.69 × 3.54 in, undated; stains

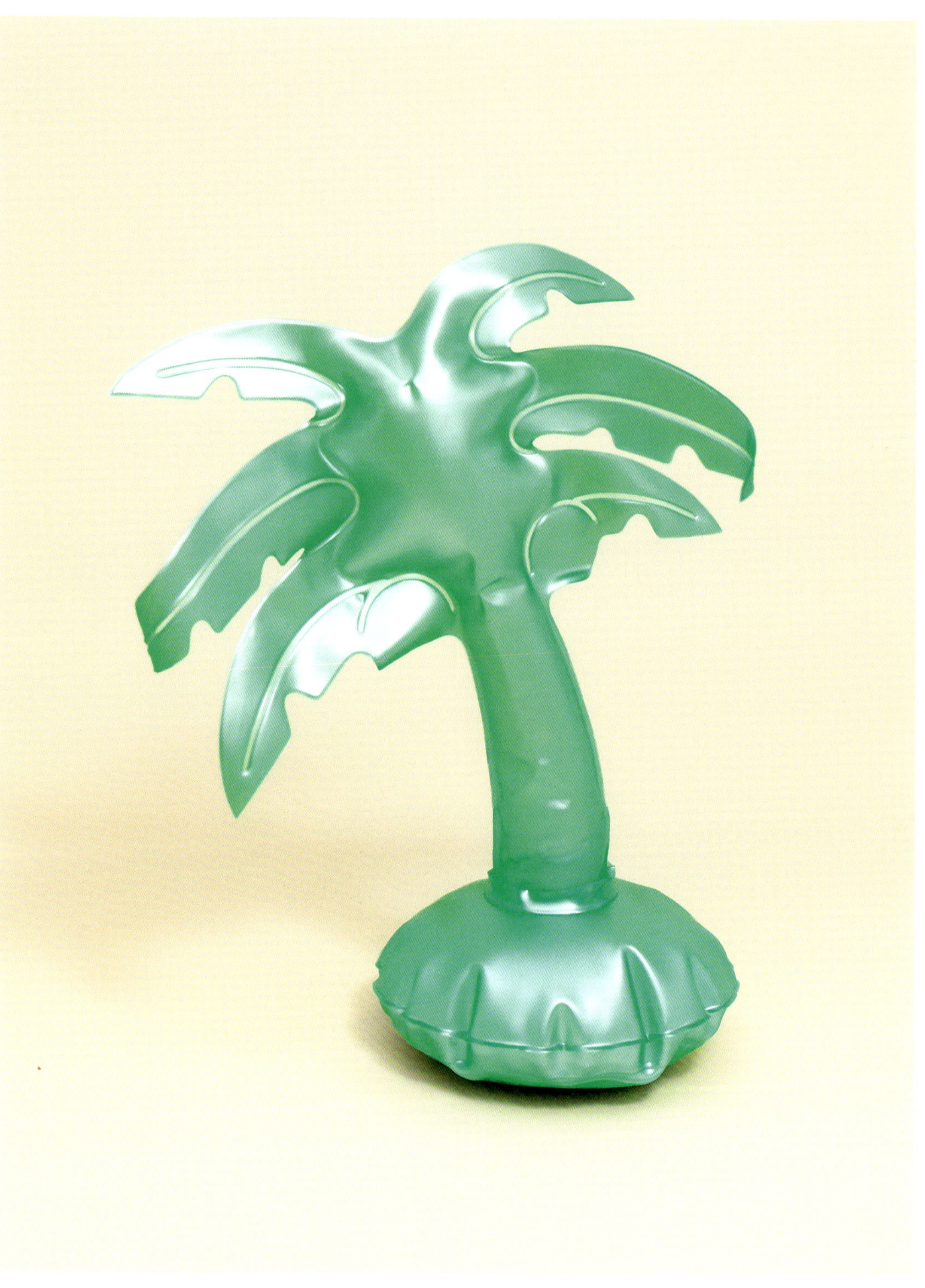

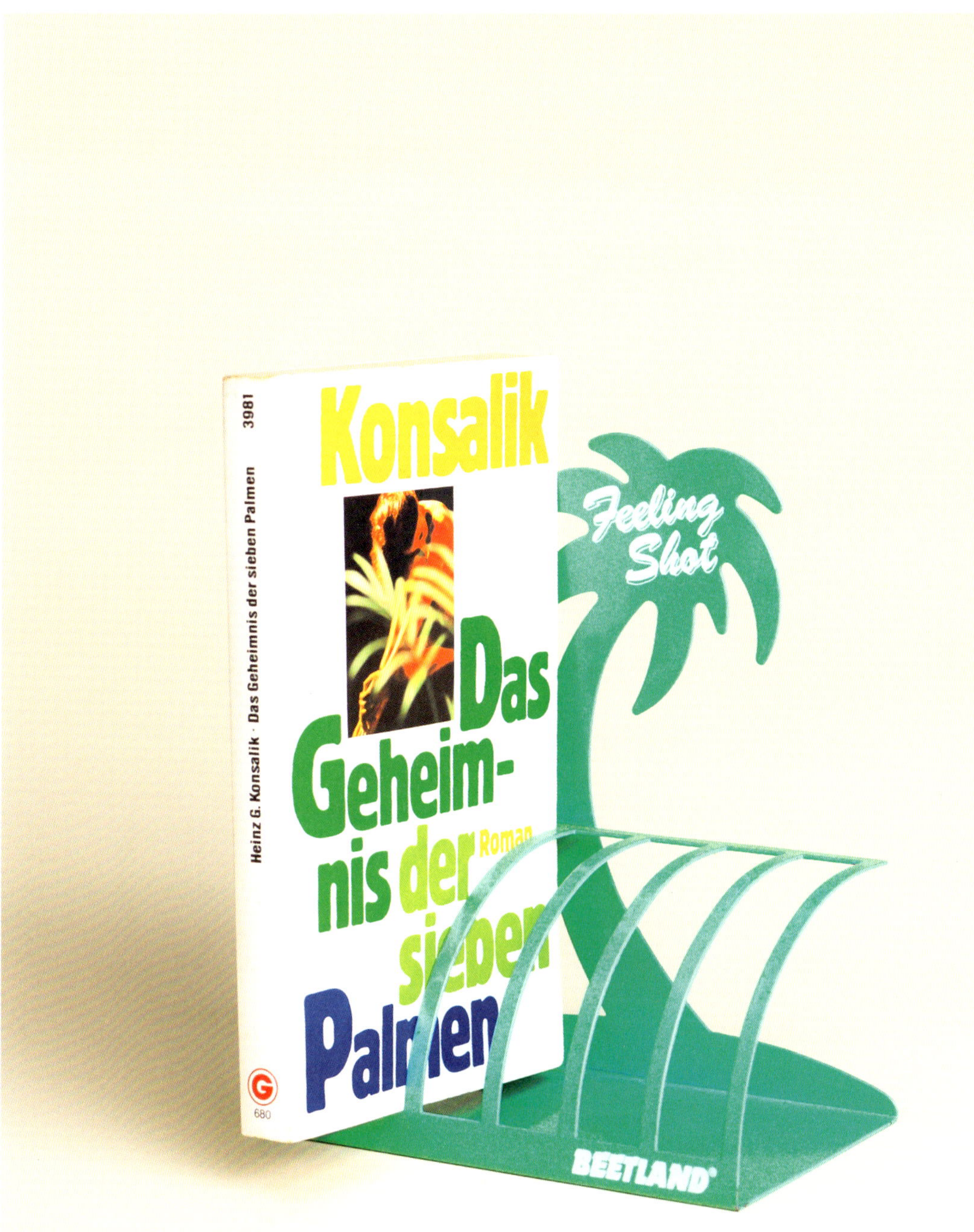

05–06
Toastständer „Beetland“
(made in Japan), Aluminium,
16,7 × 4 × 8,3 cm, undatiert;
leichte Kratzer
Toast rack "Beetland"
(made in Japan), aluminum,
6.57 × 5.51 × 3.26 in, undated;
slight scratches

Taschenbuch „Das Geheimnis der sieben Palmen“
von Heinz Günther Konsalik,
Goldmann Verlag, 1981,
285 Seiten, 18,2 × 11,4 × 2,2 cm,
1982/Buchhandlung Berlin
Paperback "Das Geheimnis der sieben Palmen"
by Heinz Günther Konsalik,
Goldmann Publishing, 1981,
285 pages, 7.16 × 4.48 × 0.86 in,
1982/bookstore Berlin

07
Handgeschnitzter Tischkalender
Holz, 16,5 × 21,2 × 4,8 cm, 1986/
Bali; Gebrauchsspuren
Hand-carved table calendar
wood, 6.49 × 8.34 × 1.88 in, 1986/
Bali; slight signs of wear

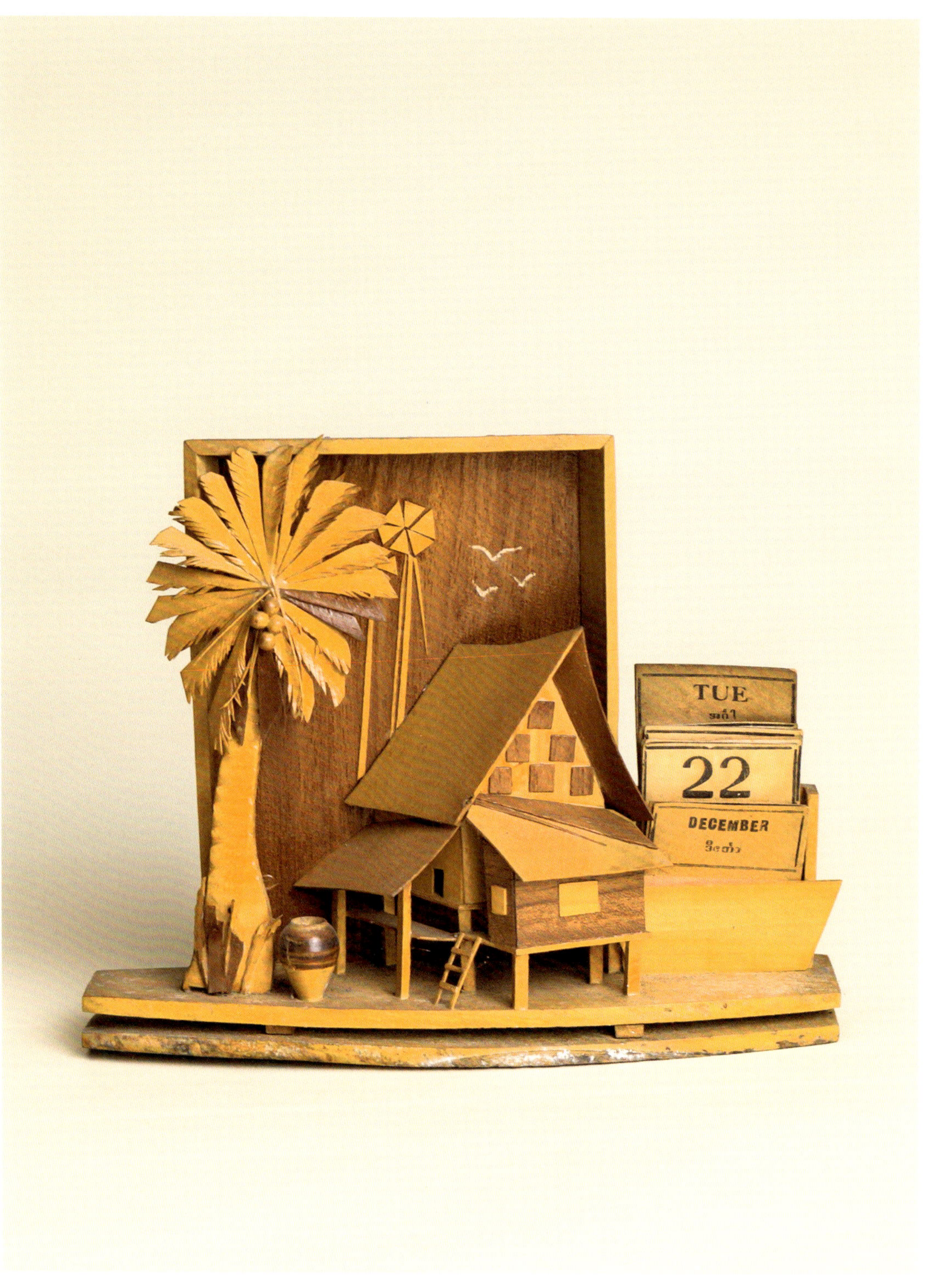

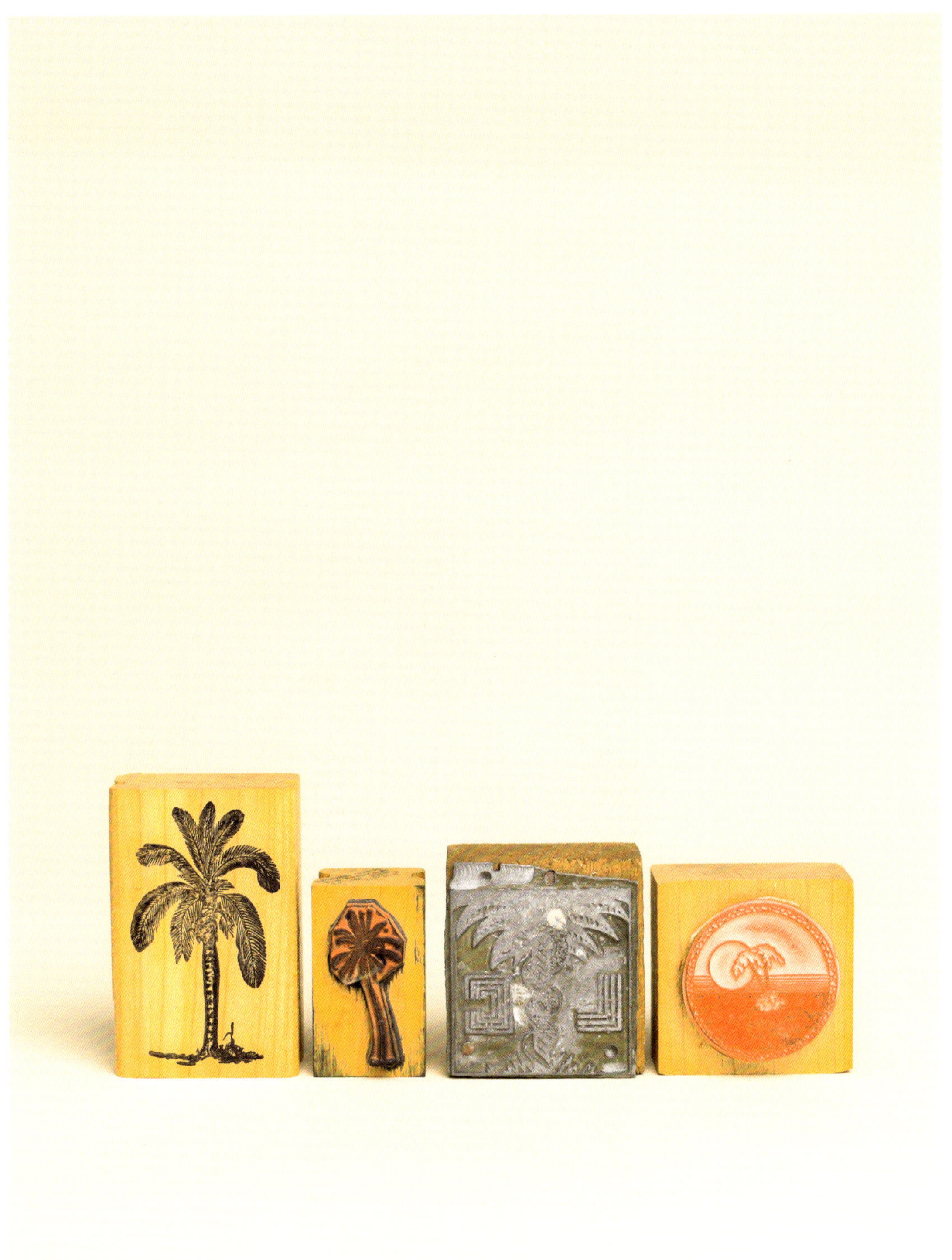

08–11
Stempel Holz, Gummi,
5,8 × 3,7 × 2,4 cm, 1978/Kalifornien;
wie neu
Rubber stamp wood, rubber,
2.28 × 1.45 × 0.94 in, 1978/California;
like new

Stempel Holz, Gummi,
3,8 × 2,3 × 2,1 cm, 1978/Kalifornien;
gut erhalten
Rubber stamp wood, rubber,
1.49 × 0.9 × 0.82 in, 1978/California;
in good condition

Stempel Holz, Metall,
4,2 × 4,2 × 2,4 cm, undatiert;
angebrochen
Rubber stamp wood, rubber,
1.65 × 1.65 × 0.94 in, undated;
slightly cracked

Stempel Holz, Gummi,
3,8 × 3,8 × 2,8 cm, 2001/Paris;
wie neu
Rubber stamp wood, rubber,
1.49 × 1.49 × 1.1 in, 2001/Paris;
like new

12
Dekopalme zum Auffächern mit Büroklammer, Papier, 34 × 20,4 cm, 2005; Geschenk eines Nachbarn, regelmäßig als Geburtstagsdekoration genutzt, leicht geknickt
Decorative palm tree foldable with paper clip, paper, 13.38 × 8.03 in, 2005; present from a neighbor, regularly used as birthday decoration, slightly bent

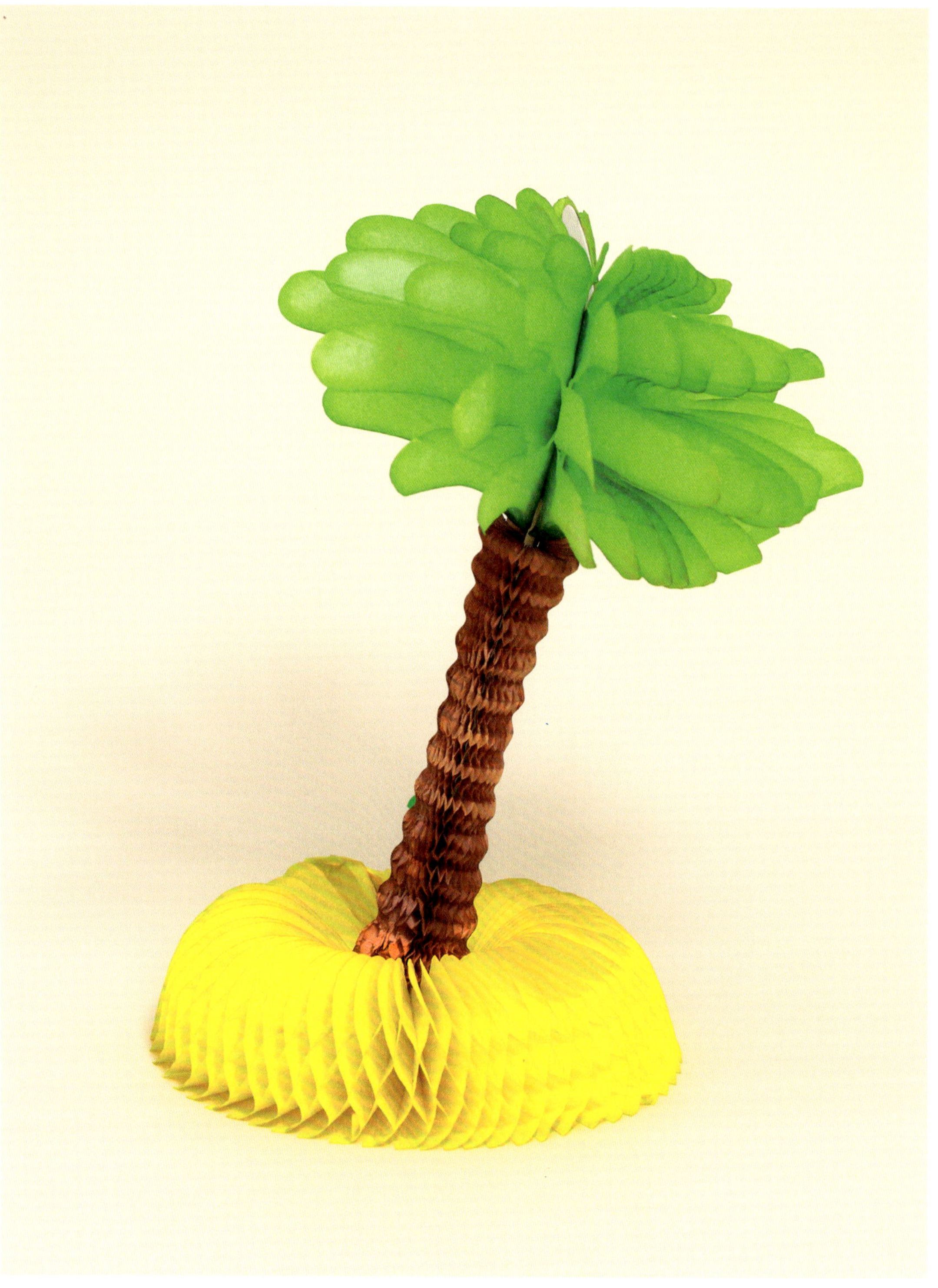

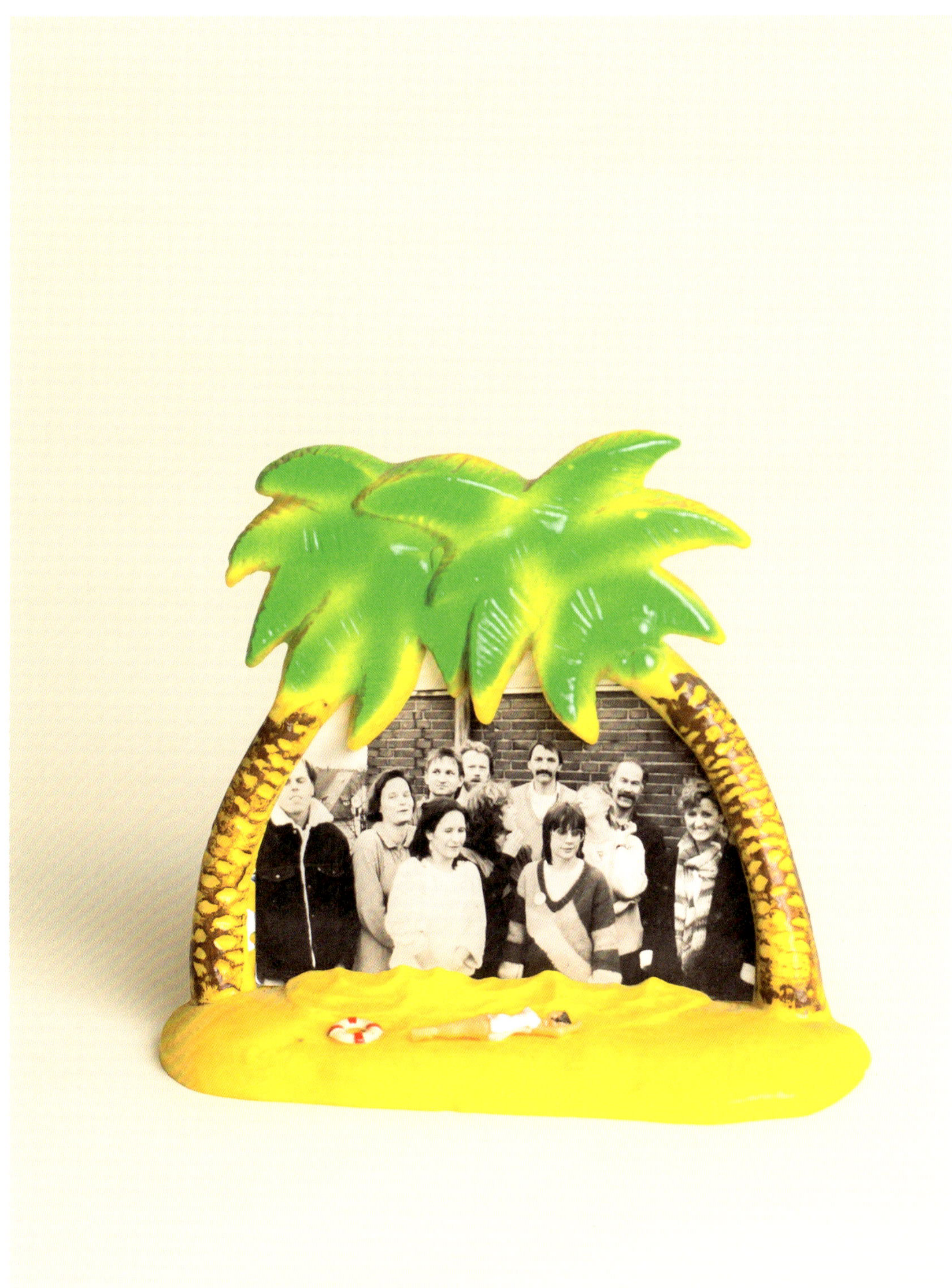

13
Bilderwechselrahmen mit Fotografie Kunststoff, 14 × 17 × 5 cm, 1984; Geschenk von KollegenInnen eines Forschungsprojekts zu Gesundheitsselbsthilfegruppen (Foto, 2. v. r.: Alf Trojan), in Besitz von Alf Trojan
Changeable picture frame with photograph plastic, 5.51 × 6.69 × 1.96 in, 1984; present from colleagues from a research project on self-help health groups (photograph, 2nd from right: Alf Trojan), property of Alf Trojan

14
Radio von „Stanley Day“
(batteriebetrieben), Kunststoff,
18,6 × 29,8 × 21,2 cm, 1987/
Geschenkboutique Hamburg-Eppendorf; stark verstaubt
Radio by “Stanley Day”
(battery run), plastic,
7.32 × 11.73 × 8.34 in, 1987/
gift shop Hamburg-Eppendorf;
very dusty

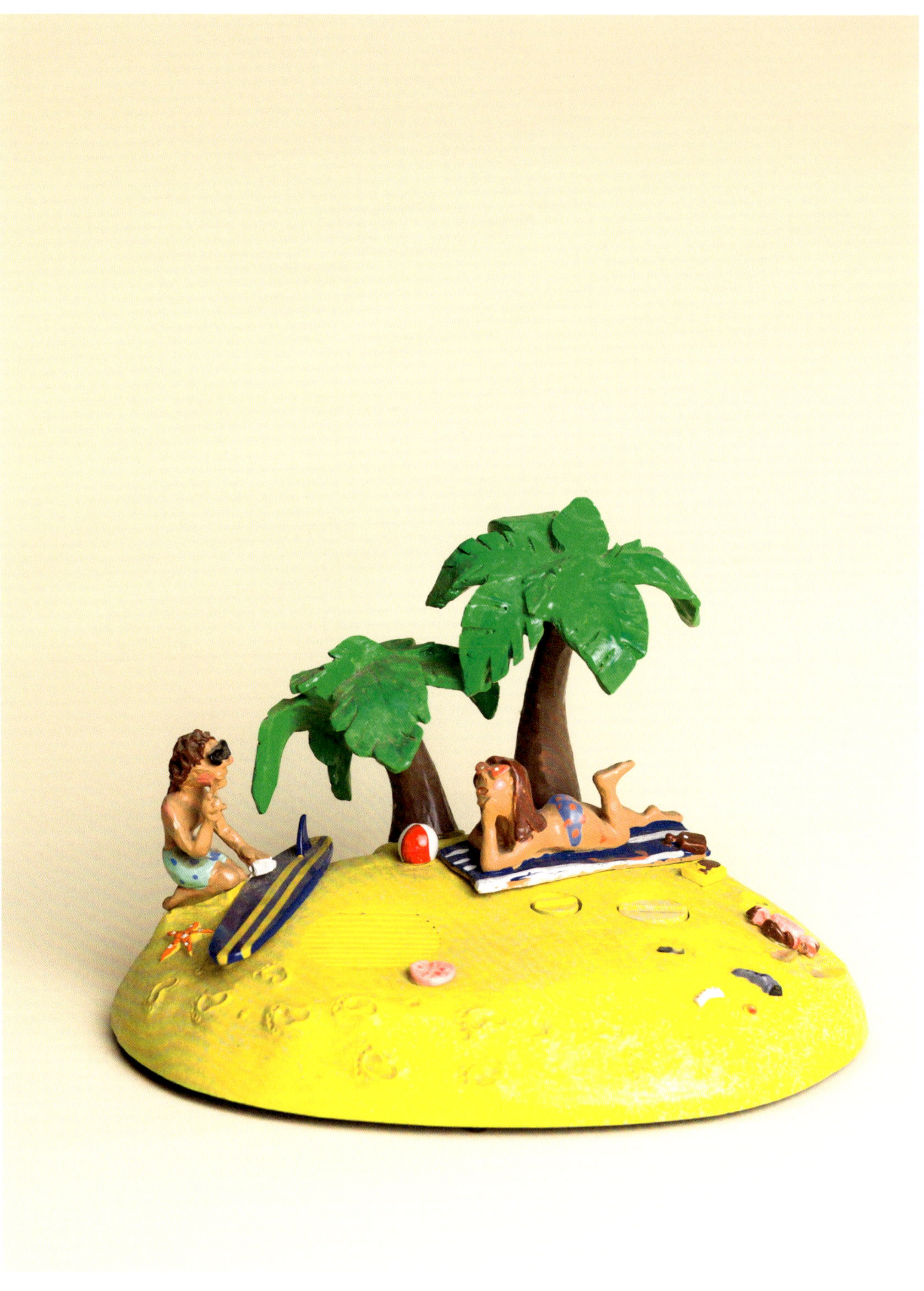

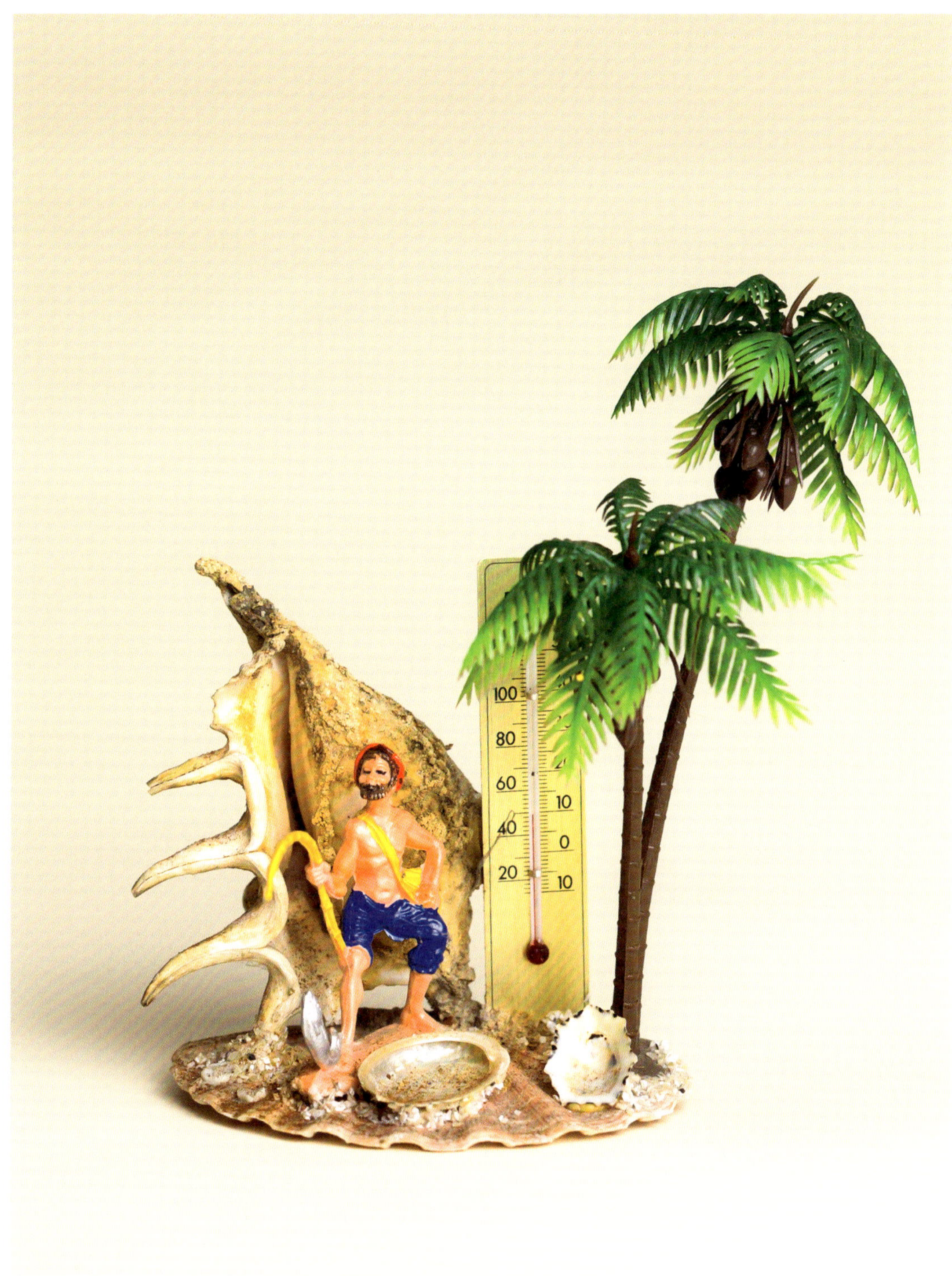

15

Thermometer (Handarbeit), Muscheln, Kunststoff, Sand, 18,2 × 17,2 × 1,3 cm, 1993/Argentinien; leichte Gebrauchsspuren

Thermometer (handmade), shells, plastic, sand, 7.16 × 6.77 × 4.44 in, 1993/Argentina; slight signs of wear

16
Stiftehalter mit zwei Kugelschreibern Kunststoff, Kunstrasen, 15,6 × 8,6 × 6,5 cm, 2013/Flohmarkt; wie neu
Pencil holder with two ballpoint pens plastic, artificial turf, 6.14 × 3.38 × 2.55 in, 2013/flea-market; like new

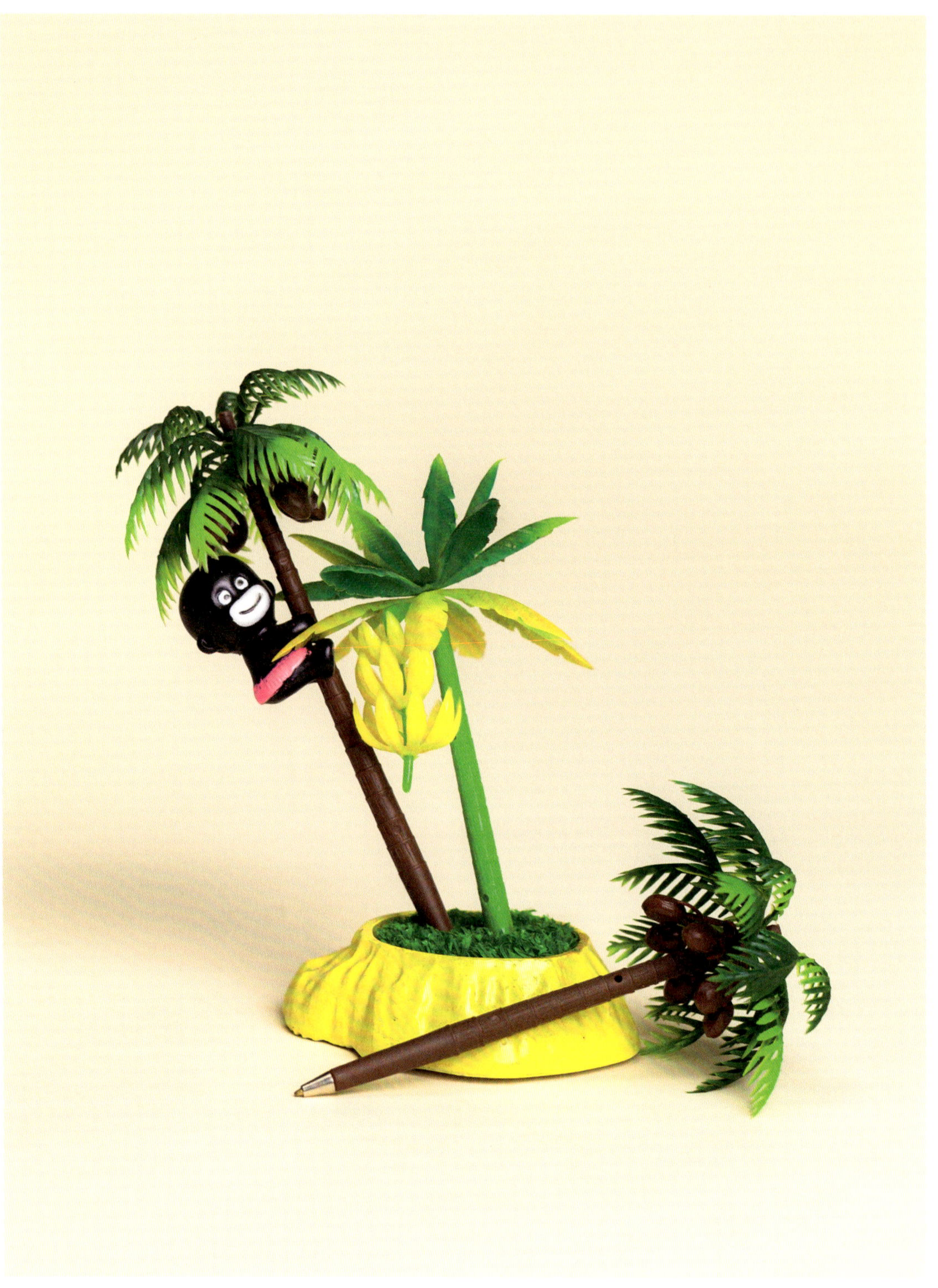

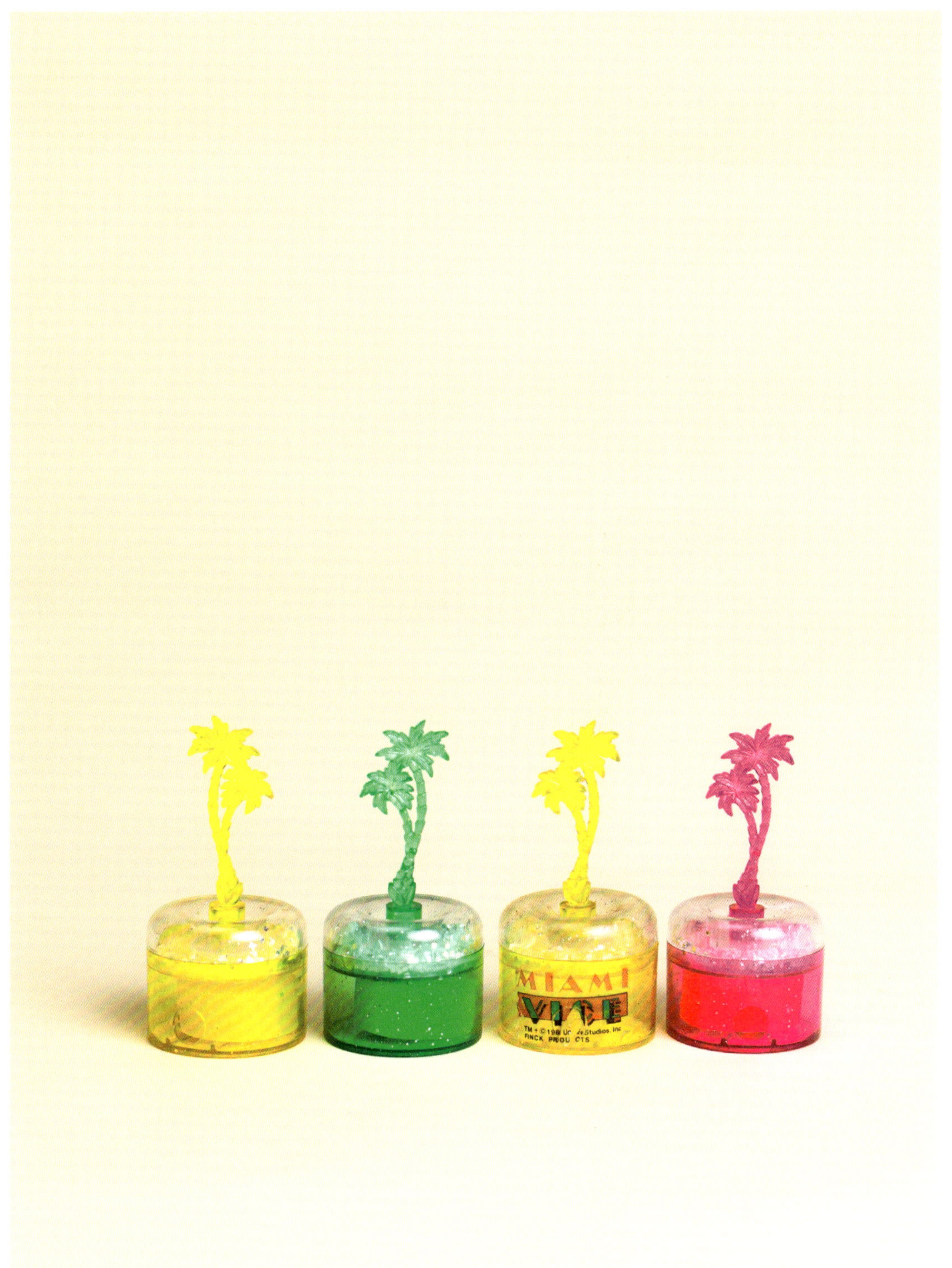

17–20
Vier Bleistiftanspitzer
„Miami Vice“ von den Universal Studios (gelb, grün, pink), Kunststoff, 8,8 × 4 × 2,1 cm, 1986/ Souvenirshop Hollywood; leichte Gebrauchsspuren
Four pencil sharpeners
“Miami Vice” from Universal Studios (yellow, green, pink), plastic, 3.46 × 1.57 × 0.82 in, 1986/ tourist shop Hollywood; slight signs of wear

21
Dekopalme (Unikat), Glas, 28,5 × 23,5 × 8,3 cm, 1992/ Flohmarkt Hamburg; ein gebrochener Palmenwedel
Decorative palm tree (unique object), glass, 11.22 × 9.25 × 7.2 in, 1992/fleamarket Hamburg; one broken palm frond

22
Kerze Wachs, 14,2 × 4,6 cm, undatiert; leicht gekrümmt
Candle wax, 5.59 × 5.74 in, undated; slightly bent

23
Puzzle 5-teilig, Holz, 9 × 7 × 1,2 cm, 2010/Flohmarkt; Farbe ausgeblichen
Jigsaw puzzle 5 pieces, wood, 3.54 × 2.75 × 0.47 in, 2010/fleamarket; faded colors

24–25
Spielzeugpalme Holz, bemalt, 20,3 × 11,2 × 2,9 cm, Flohmarkt; wie neu
Toy palm tree wood, painted, 7.99 × 4.52 × 1.14 in, fleamarket; like new

Spielzeugpalme Holz, bemalt, silberner Sternaufkleber, 19,6 × 11,5 × 2,4 cm, undatiert; Kleberspuren
Toy palm tree wood, painted, silver star-sticker, 7.71 × 4.52 × 0.94 × in, undated; traces of glue

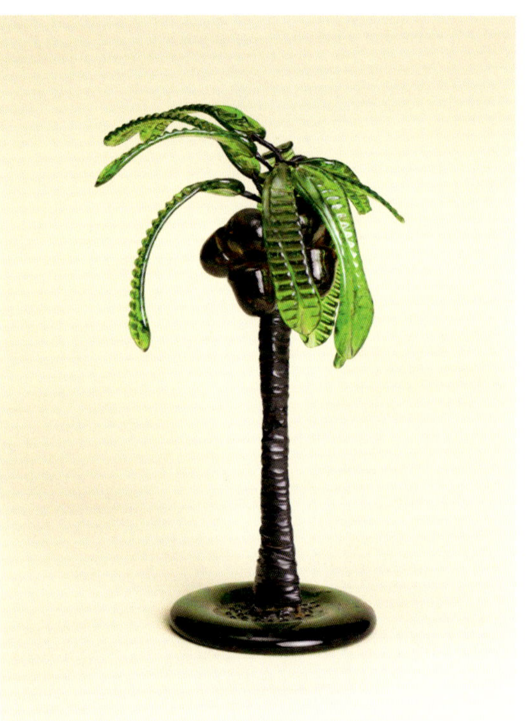

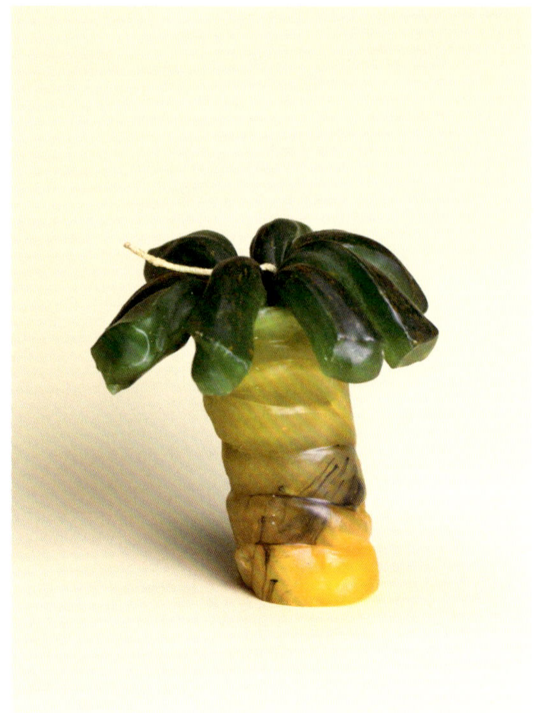

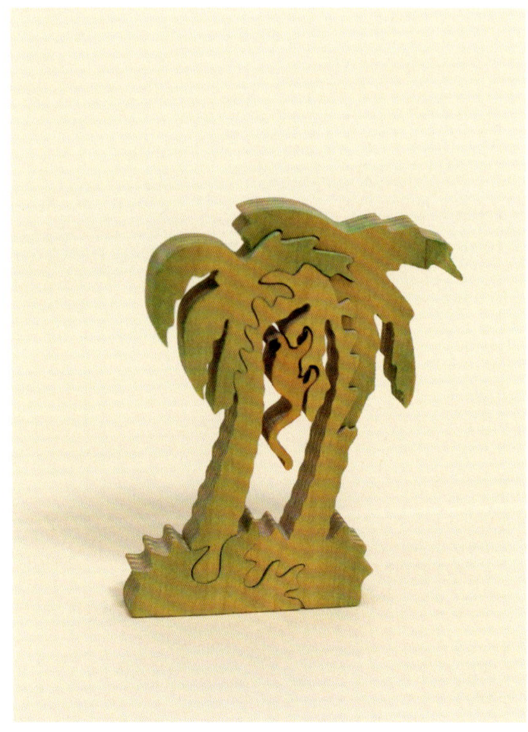

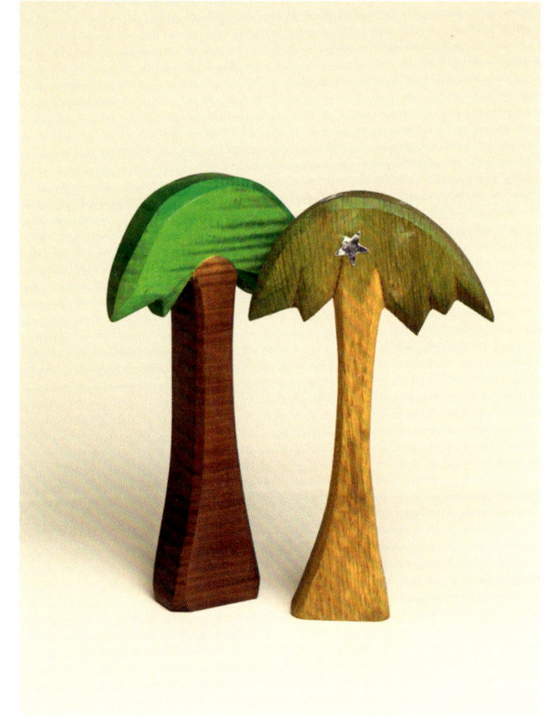

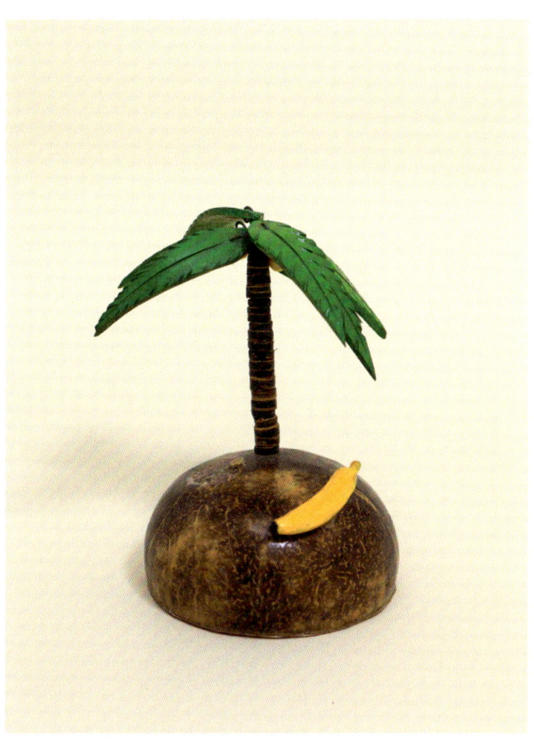

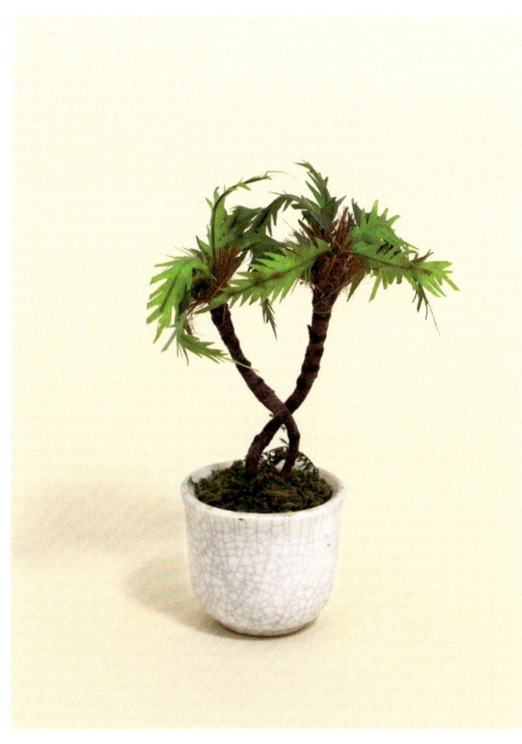

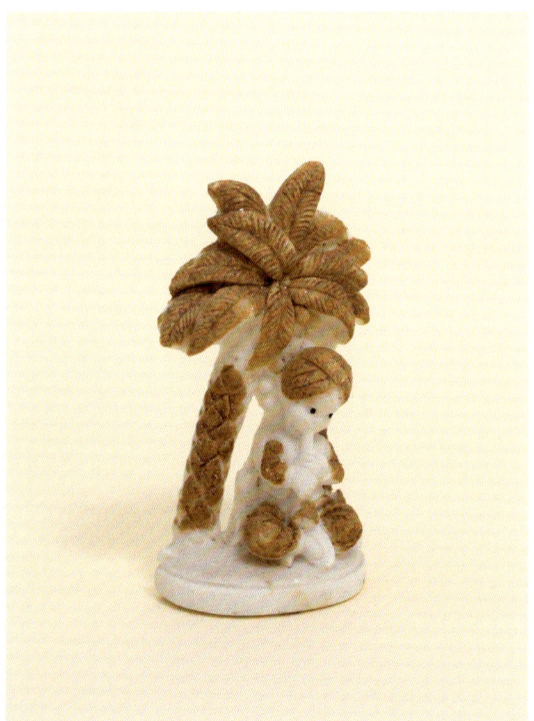

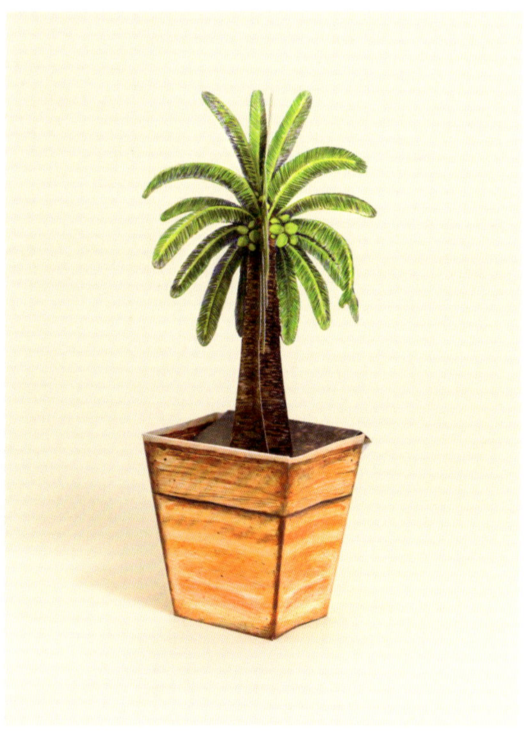

26
Dekopalme (Handarbeit), Kokosnuss, Holz, Draht, 15,2 × 9,8 cm, 1997/Philippinen; leichte Gebrauchsspuren
Decorative palm tree (handmade), coconut, wood, wire, 5.98 × 3.85 in, 1997/Philippines; slight signs of wear

27
Miniaturkunststoffpalme im Übertopf Keramik, Kunststoff, 12,9 × 10 × 4,9 cm, 2014/Flohmarkt; leichte Gebrauchsspuren
Miniature plastic palm tree with pot ceramic, plastic, 5.07 × 3.93 × 1.92 in, 2014/fleamarket; slight signs of wear

28
Dekopalme mit Engel
Kunststein, Glitzermineralien, 15,7 × 9 × 4,4 cm, 2007/Flohmarkt; zeigt über Farbveränderung das Raumklima an, leichte Gebrauchsspuren
Decorative palm tree with angel artificial stone, glitter minerals, 6.18 × 3.34 × 1.73 in, 2007/fleamarket; shows room climate through change of color, slight signs of wear

29
Postkarte zum Aufklappen
Pappe, 23,8 × 7,9 × 6,2 cm, undatiert; unbeschriebene Rückseite
Foldable postcard cardboard, 9.37 × 3.11 × 2.44 in, undated; back side left blank

30
Kaffeekanne Glas, Kunststoff, 16 × 12 cm, 2001/Flohmarkt Wendland; leichte Gebrauchsspuren
Coffee pot glass, plastic, 6.29 × 4.72 in, 2001/fleamarket Wendland; slight signs of wear

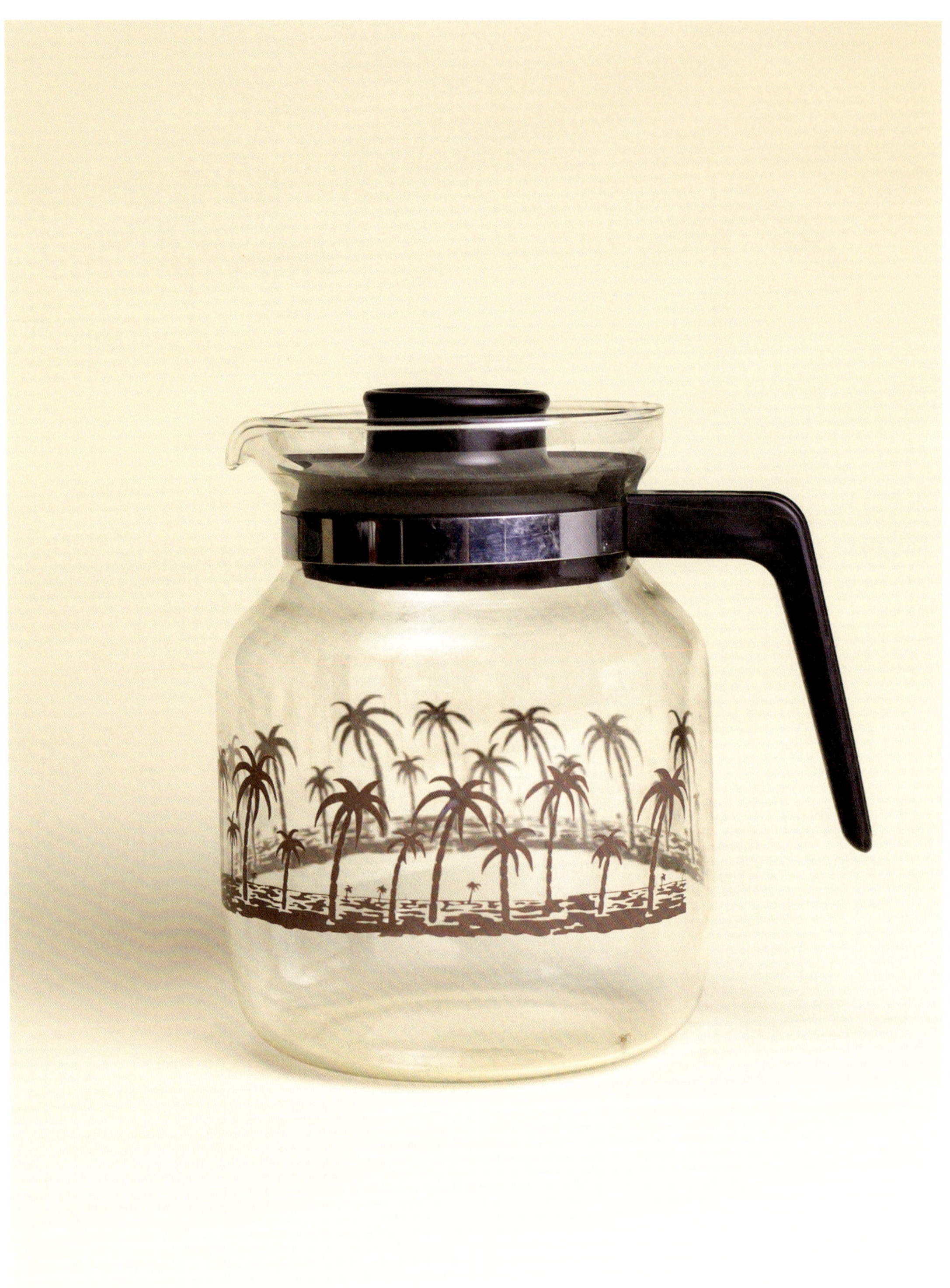

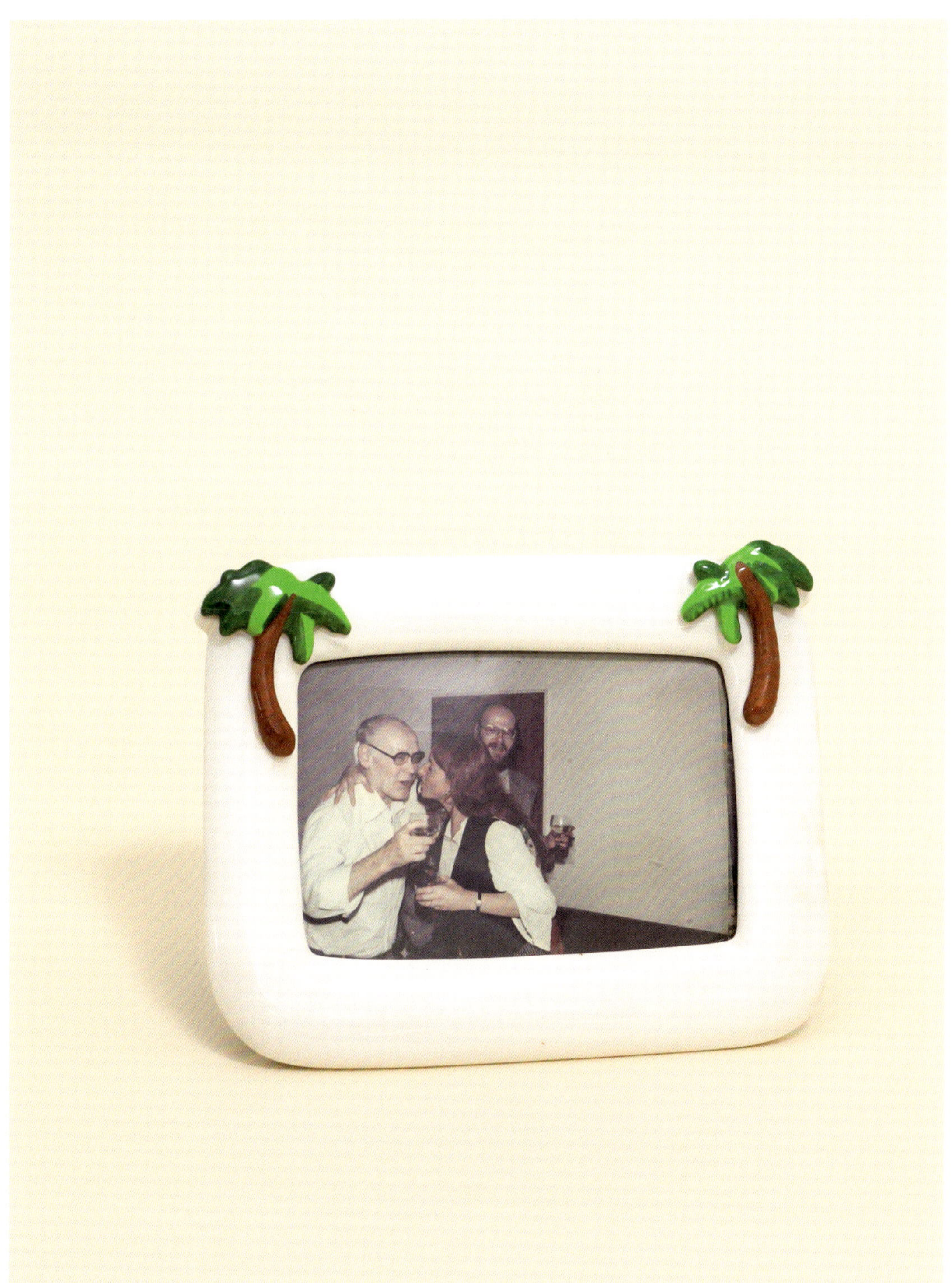

31
Bilderwechselrahmen mit Farbfotografie (Vater, Ehefrau und Bruder von Alf Trojan auf einem Familienfest Ende der Siebzigerjahre), Keramik, Glas, 13 × 16 cm, 1981/ Dänemark; in Besitz von Alf Trojan
Changeable picture frame with color photograph (father, wife and brother of Alf Trojan at a family reunion end of the 1970s), ceramic, glass, 5.11 × 6.29 in, 1981/Denmark; property of Alf Trojan

32

Yucca-Palme im Übertopf

Porzellan, 17 × 21 × 21 cm, undatiert; Yucca-Palme hat die Trockenheit des Sommers 2018 nicht überstanden, Übertopf in Besitz von Alf Trojan

Yucca plant in pot

porcelain, 6.69 × 8.26 × 8.26 in, undated; Yucca plant didn't survive the heatwave in summer 2018, pot property of Alf Trojan

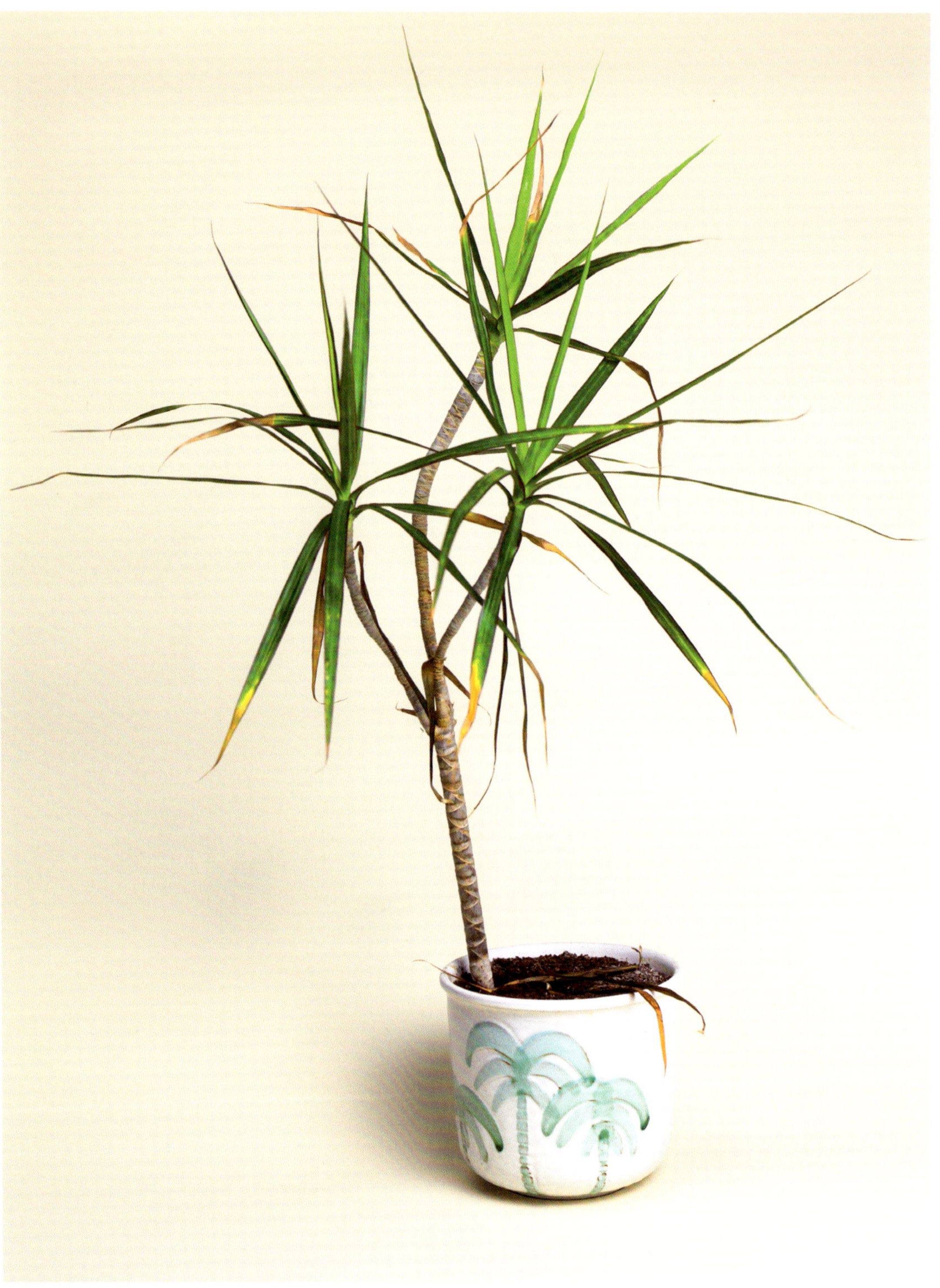

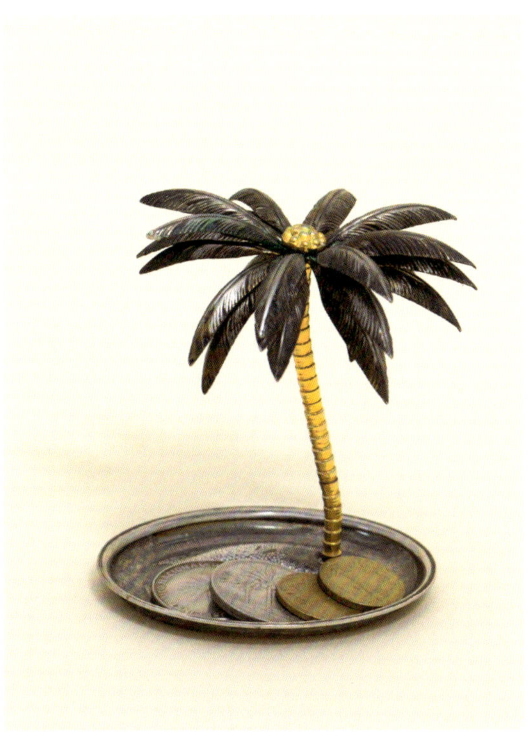

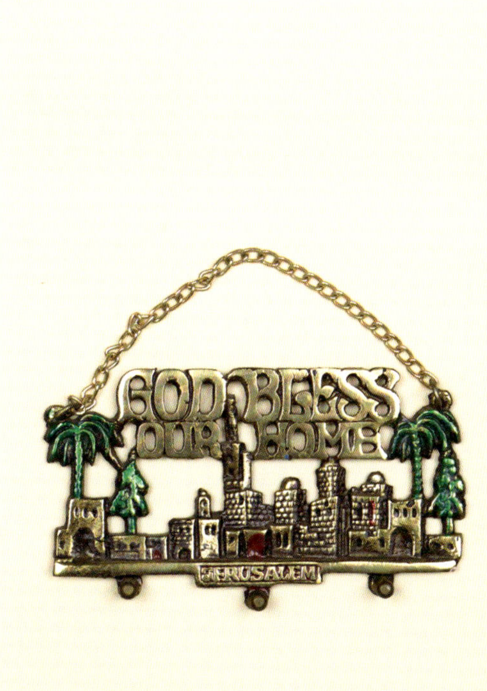

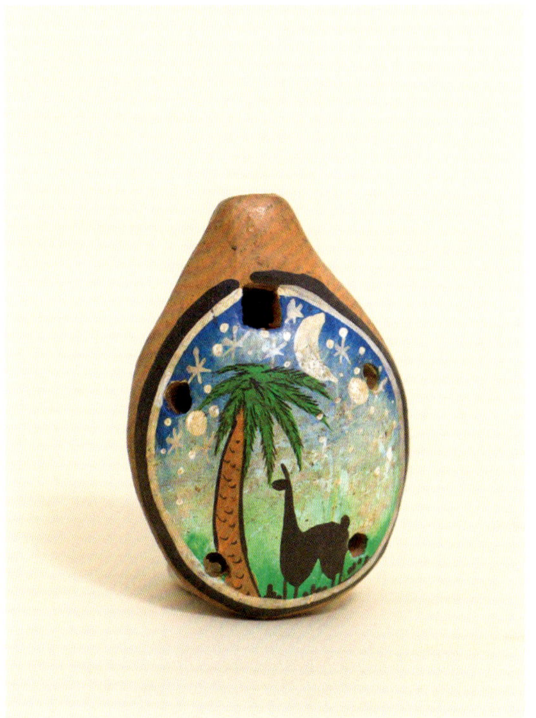

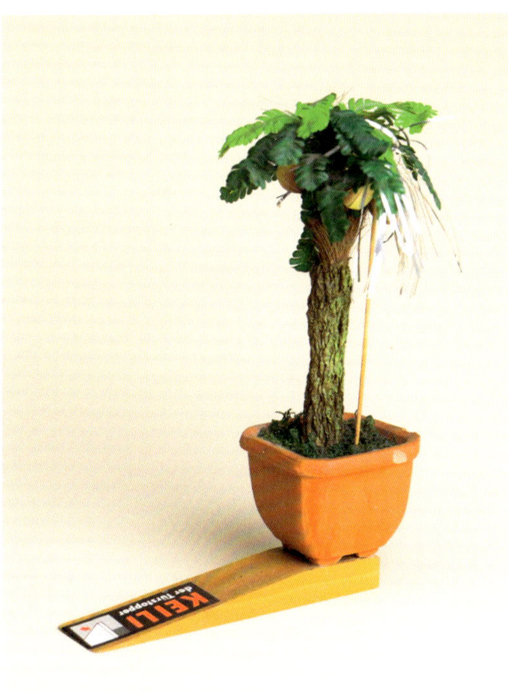

33–34
Münzschale versilbertes Messing, 9,3 × 8,7 × 8,2 cm, 1976/Indien; leichte Gebrauchsspuren
Bowl for coins silver-plated brass, 3.66 × 3.42 × 3.22 in, 1976/India; slight signs of wear

Vier internationale Münzen Kupfer, 2,5 × 2,5 cm/1,9 × 1,9 cm, undatiert; Wechselgeld von verschiedenen Auslandsreisen
Four international coins copper, 0.98 × 0.98 in/0.75 × 0.75 in, undated; change from various trips abroad

35
Schlüsselbrett Eisen, 6,8 × 12,5 × 1,6 cm, 2008/Souvenirladen Haifa
Key holder iron, 2.67 × 4.92 × 0.62 in, 2008/tourist shop Haifa

36
Handbemalte Flöte Ton, 5,2 × 4 × 1,8 cm, 1995/Touristenmarkt Peru; Gebrauchsspuren
Hand-painted flute clay, 2.04 × 1.57 × 0.7 in, 1995/tourist market Peru; signs of wear

37
Türstopper „Keili“ Kunststoff, Keramik, Holz, 24 × 8 × 16 cm, 2012/Flohmarkt; in Besitz von Alf Trojan
Doorstop “Keili” plastic, ceramic, wood, 9.44 × 3.14 x 6.29 in, 2012/fleamarket; property of Alf Trojan

38–39
Luftpostbrief mit zwei abgestempelten Briefmarken Papier, 11 × 22 cm, 1989/Brandeis University; Palmen-Briefmarke war Zufall, da der Absender nichts von Alf Trojans Sammelleidenschaft wusste, in Besitz von Alf Trojan
Airmail letter with two postmarked stamps paper, 4.33× 8.66 in, 1989/Brandeis University; Palm tree stamp was a coincidence, as the sender did not know about Alf Trojan's collector passion, property of Alf Trojan

Handbemalter Brieföffner Holz, 0,3 × 19 × 2 cm, 1991/ Mitbringsel aus Jamaika; wie neu
Hand-painted paper knife wood, 0.11 × 7.48 × 0.78 in, 1991/ souvenir from Jamaica; like new

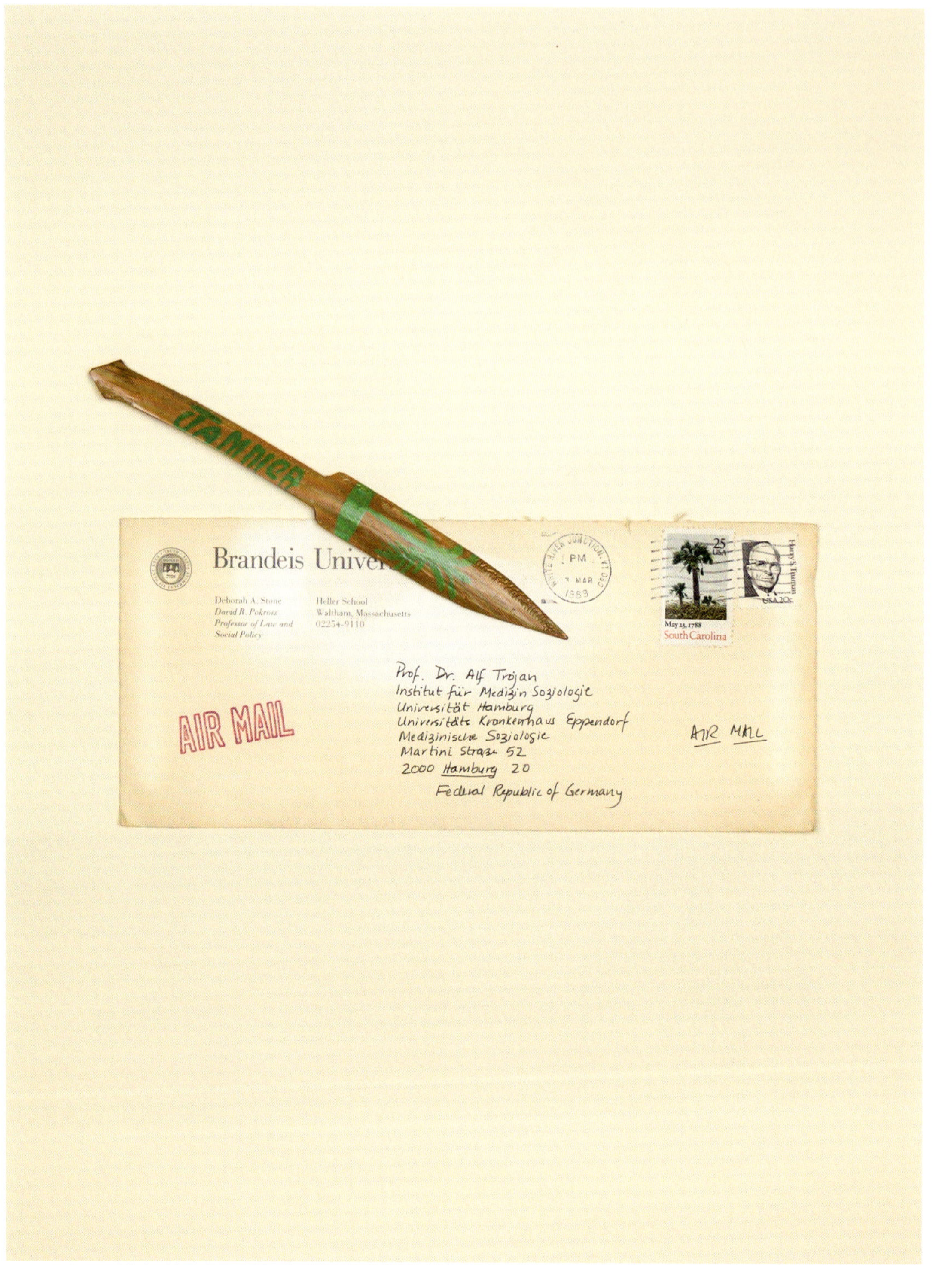

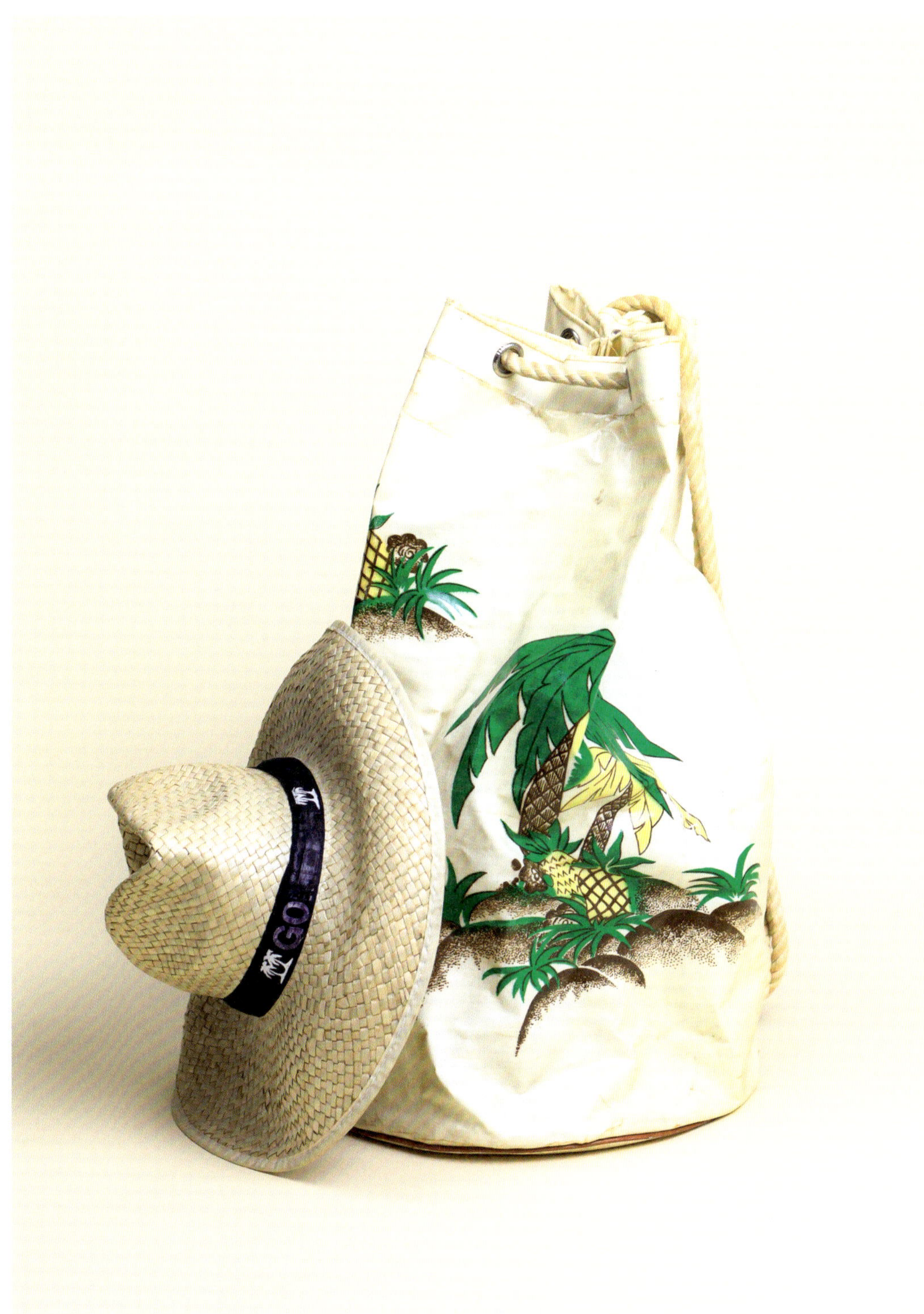

40–41
Hut Stroh, Baumwolle, 18 × 30 × 32 cm, 2004/Straßenstand La Gomera; Aufschrift „Gomera" teilweise geschwärzt, sehr häufig auf Reisen in Marokko benutzt
Hat straw, cotton, 7.08 × 11.81 × 12.59 in, 2004/roadside La Gomera; label "Gomera" partly blackened, very often used for trips to Morocco

Reisesack „Matchsack" von Giovanni Kunststoff, Baumwollkordel, 48,5 × 26,5 cm, 1977/Italien; starke Gebrauchsspuren, Flecken, als Tischtennis-Tasche genutzt
Travel bag "Matchsack" by Giovanni plastic, cotton cord, 19.09 × 10.43 in, 1977/Italy; heavy signs of wear, stains, used as ping-pong bag

42–80
Hangewebte Borte mit achtunddreißig Ansteckern
Wolle, 145 × 4,2 cm, undatiert; an fünf solchen Borten waren die insgesamt 262 Anstecker der Sammlung angebracht
Handwoven lace with thirty-eight pins wool, 57.08 × 1.65 in, undated; five of such laces altogether had 262 pins attached

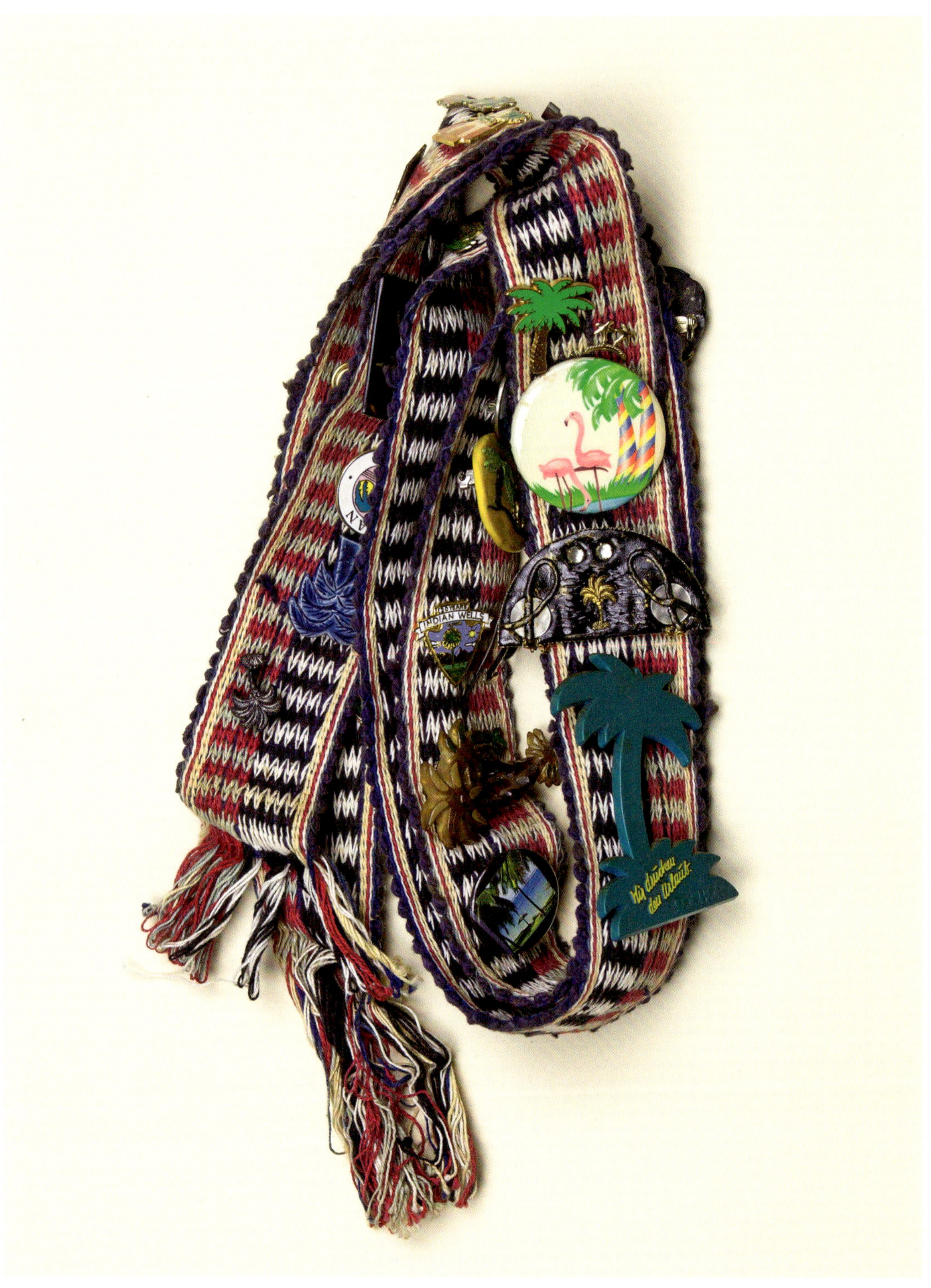

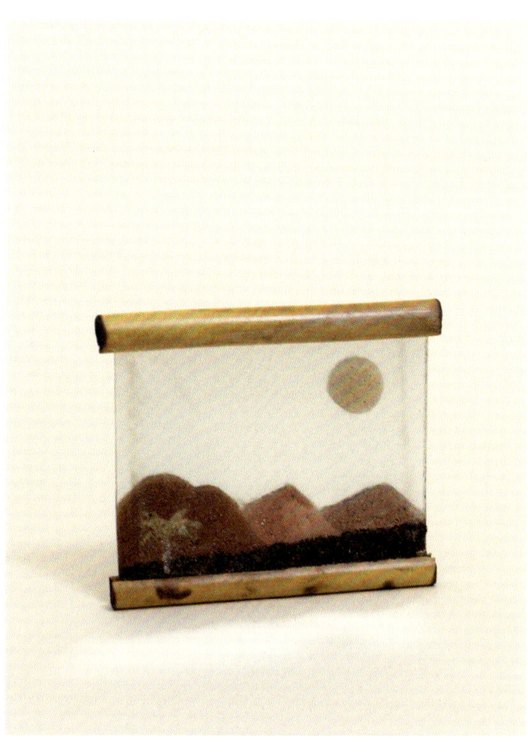

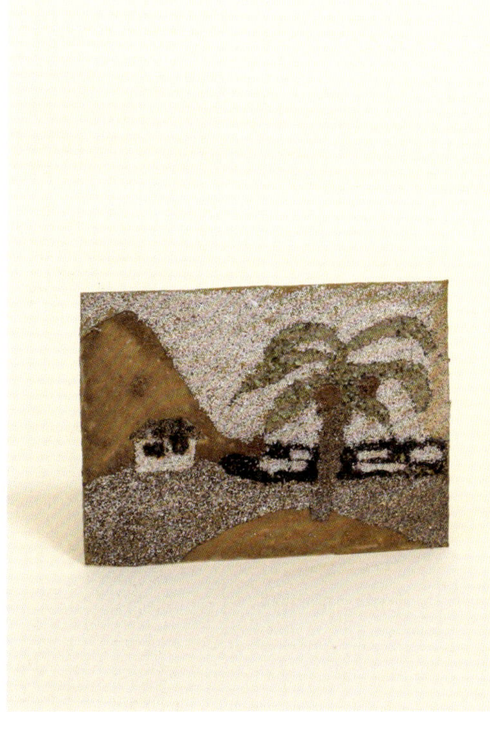

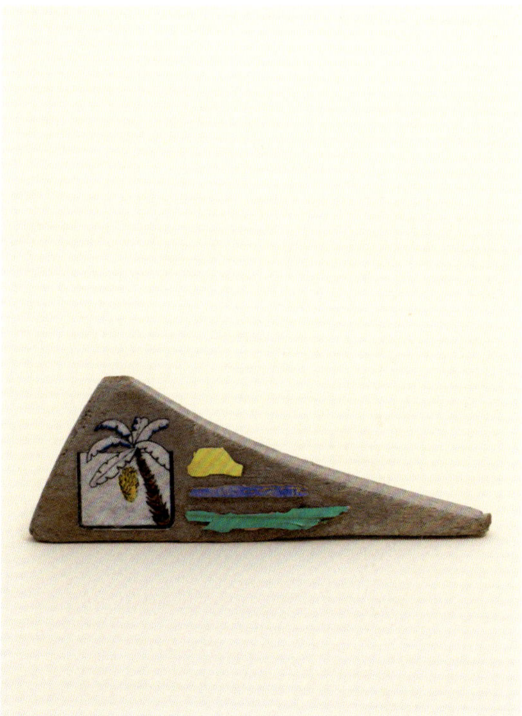

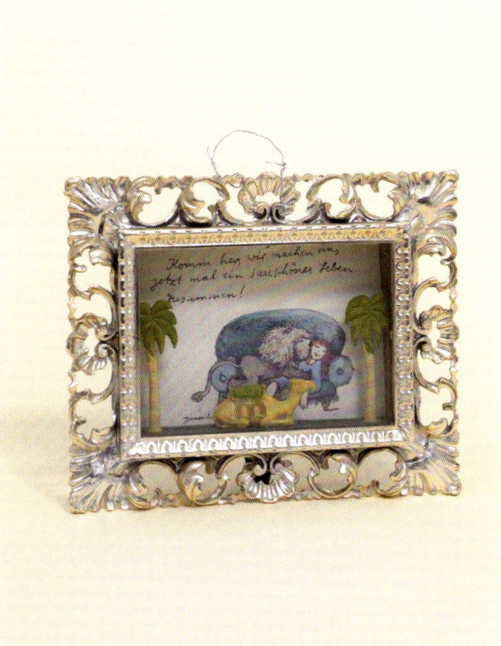

81
Kunsthandwerk Sand, Glas, Schilf, 9,3 × 10,4 × 1,1 cm, 1990/Souvenirshop Lanzarote
Arts and crafts object sand, glass, reed, 3.66 × 4.09 × 0.43 in, 1990/tourist shop Lanzarote

82
Kunstwerk Sand, Cornflakes-Verpackung, 14,2 × 10,4 cm, 1995/Straßenstand Lanzarote
Artwork sand, cornflakes packaging, 5.59 × 4.09 in, 1995/roadside Lanzarote

83
Treibholz Holz, 6,5 × 26 × 2,8 cm, 2000/El Medano, Teneriffa; von Alf Trojan handgeschnitzt, bemalt und mit Erinnerungsstücken beklebt, dient als Dekoration auf der Küchenfensterbank, in Besitz von Alf Trojan
Drift wood wood, 2.55 × 10.23 × 1.1 in, 2000/El Medano, Teneriffa; hand-carved by Alf Trojan, painted and decorated with souvenirs, in use as window sill decoration in kitchen, property of Alf Trojan

84
Beleuchtbarer Bilderrahmen mit Drahtaufhängung und Janosch-Postkarte „Komm, wir machen uns ein sauschönes Leben“, Kunststoff, Plexiglas, Postkarte, 17,5 × 22,5 × 4,4 cm, 1994/Flohmarkt; Geschenk des Sammlers an seine Frau zum 3. Hochzeitstag, in Besitz von Alf Trojan
Backlit picture frame with wire suspension and Janosch postcard “Come on, we'll make ourselves a ridiculously good life”, plastic, plexiglass, postcard, 6.88 × 8.85 × 1.73 in, 1994/fleamarket; 3rd wedding anniversary present from the collector to his wife, property of Alf Trojan

85
Sonnenbrille farbig beschichtetes Glas, Metall, 5,2 × 13,3 × 21,2 cm, 1997/USA; es gab insgesamt fünf Exemplare, vier hat der Sammler verschenkt, in Besitz von Alf Trojan
Sun glasses color-plated glass, metal, 2.04 × 5.23 × 8.3 in, 1997/USA; there were five pairs, four were given away by the collectors, property of Alf Trojan

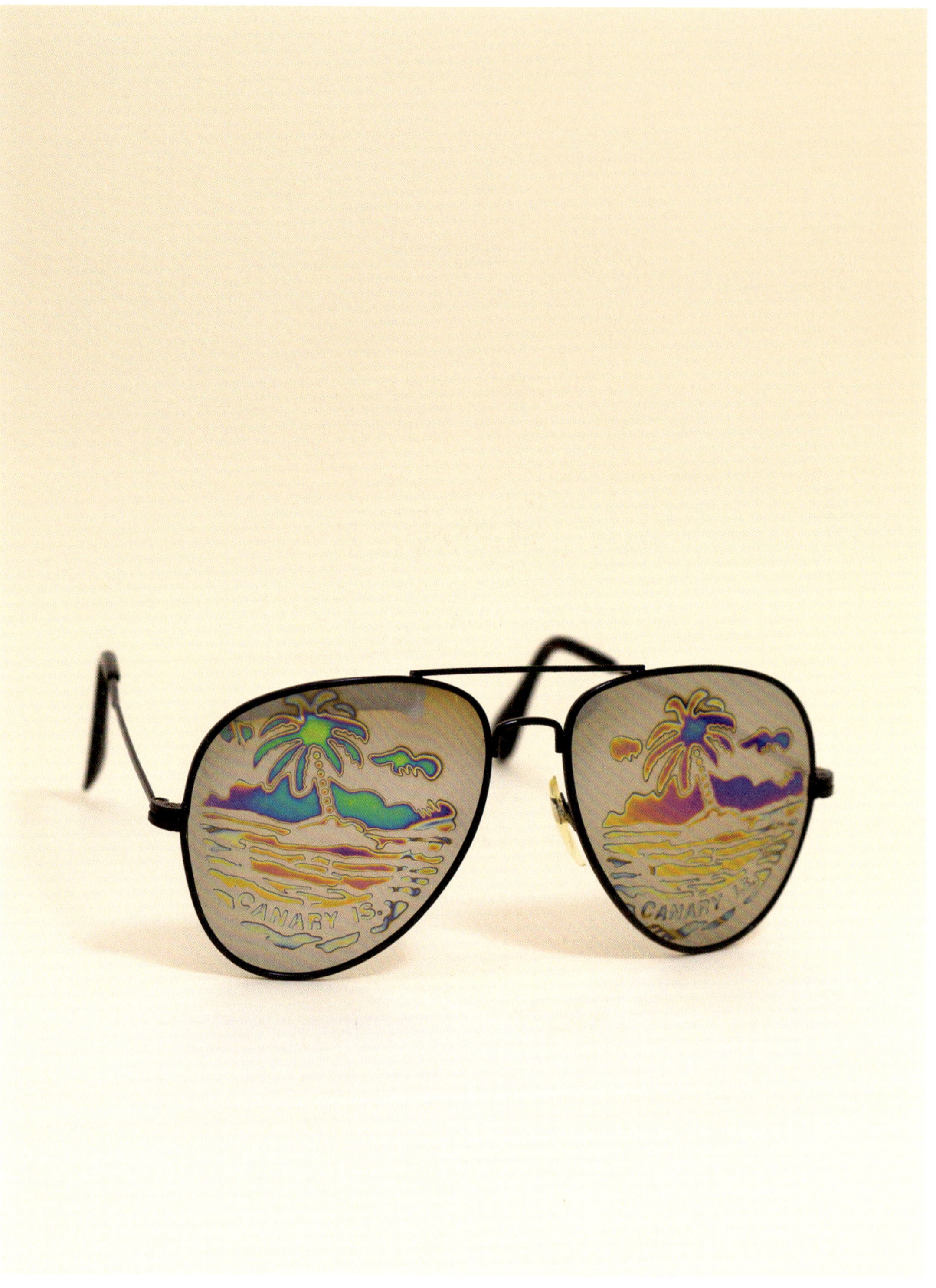

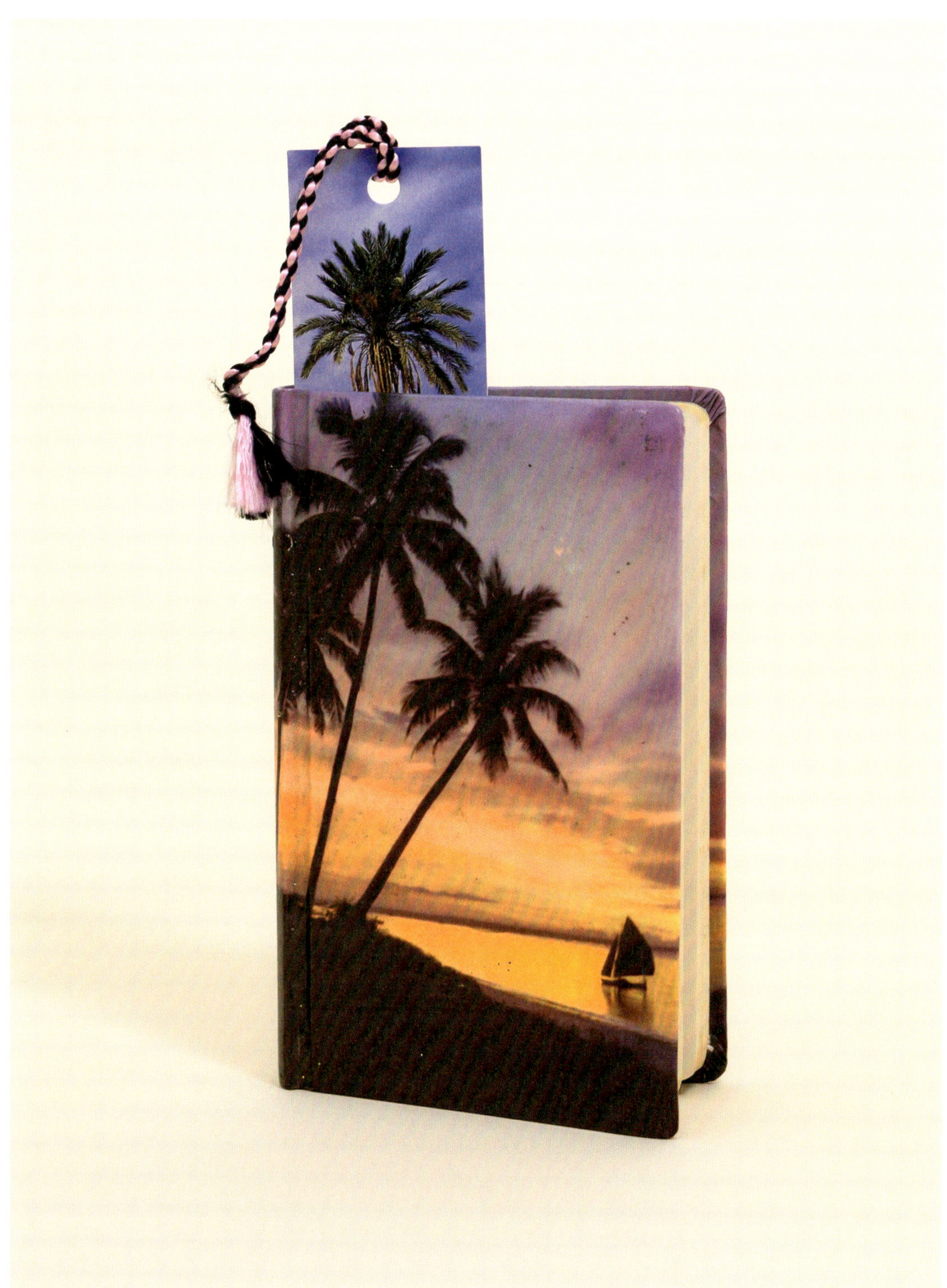

86–87
Notizbuch liniert, mit Adressverzeichnis (made in China), 14,9 × 10 × 0,6 cm, laminierter Karton, Papier, 1986; Geschenk der Ehe-frau, unbeschrieben, Seiten leicht vergilbt, in Besitz von Alf Trojan
Notebook lined, with address directory (made in China), 5.86 × 3.93 × 0.23 in, laminated cardboard, paper, 1986; present from wife, left blank, pages slightly gone yellow, property of Alf Trojan

Lesezeichen mit Bändchen Pappe, Polyester, 14,8 × 4,3 cm, 2016/Casablanca; Geschenk der Ehefrau, wie neu
Bookmark with string cardboard, polyester, 5.82 × 1.69 in, 2016/Casablanca; present from wife, like new

88–90
Spardose „Aloha lei Kuupo“ (made in Hawaii), Weißblech, 13,7 × 6,7 cm, 1995/Flohmarkt; leichte Gebrauchsspuren
Piggy bank “Aloha lei Kuupo” (made in Hawaii), tinplate, 5.39 × 2.63 in 1995/fleamarket; slight signs of wear

Spardose „Camel“ Tabak Metall, 7 × 5,4 cm, 1993/Flohmarkt London; Rostspuren
Piggy bank “Camel” tobacco metal, 2.75 × 2.12 in, 1993/fleamarket London; rust spots

Vier internationale Münzen und ein Geldschein Kupfer, Papier, 2,5 × 2,5 cm/1,9 × 1,9 cm/5 × 11 cm, undatiert; Wechselgeld von verschiedenen Auslandsreisen
Four international coins and bank note copper, paper, 0.98 × 0.98 in/0.75 × 0.75 in/1.97 x 4.33 in, undated; change from various trips abroad

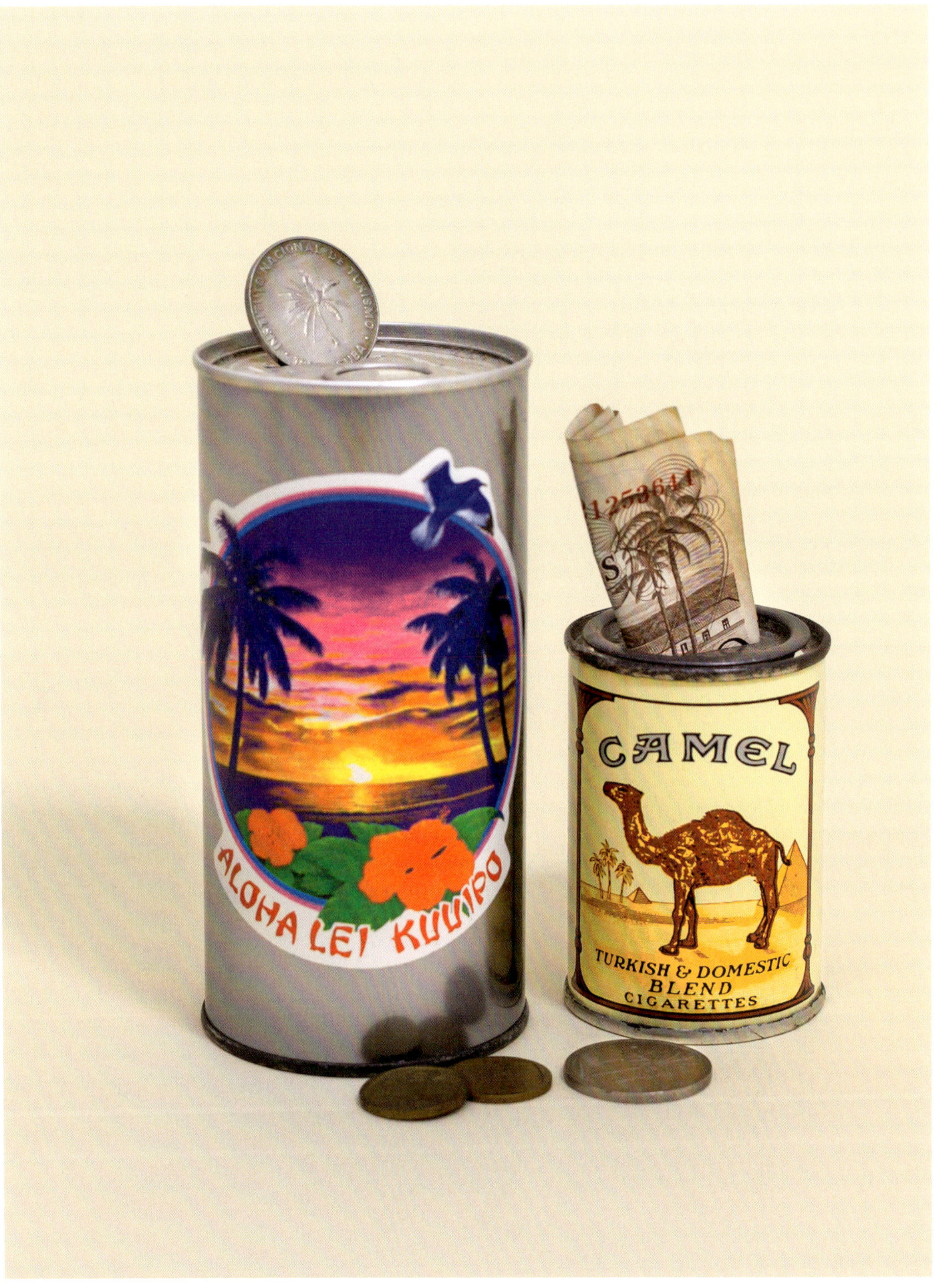

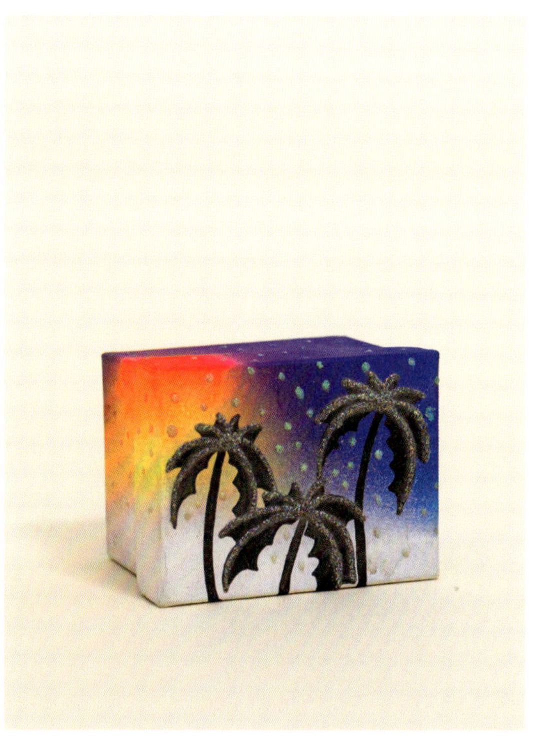

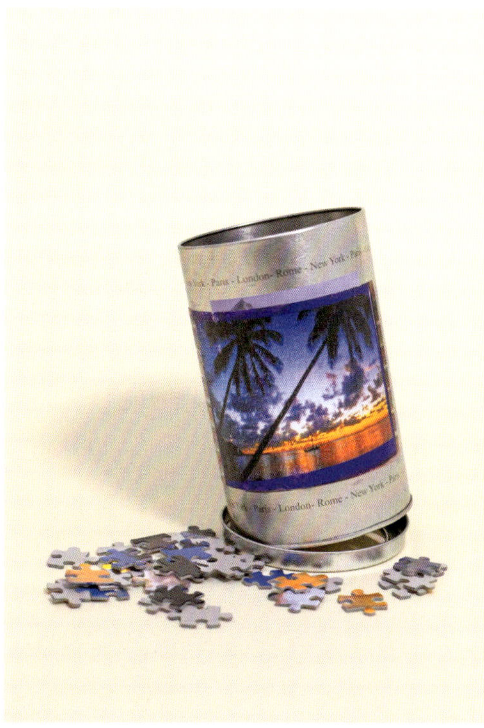

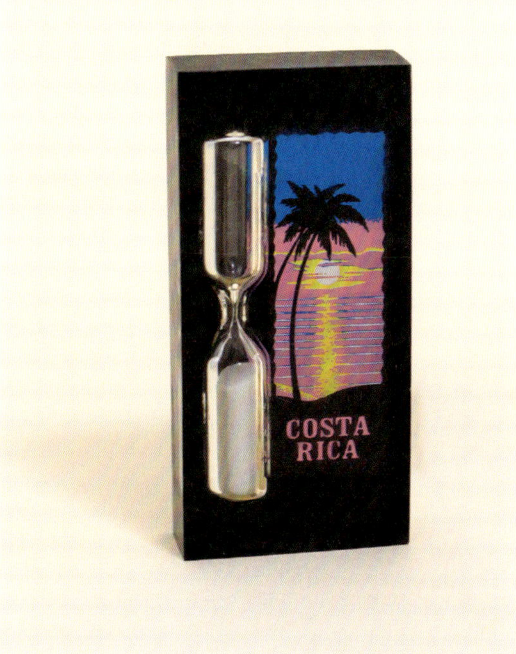

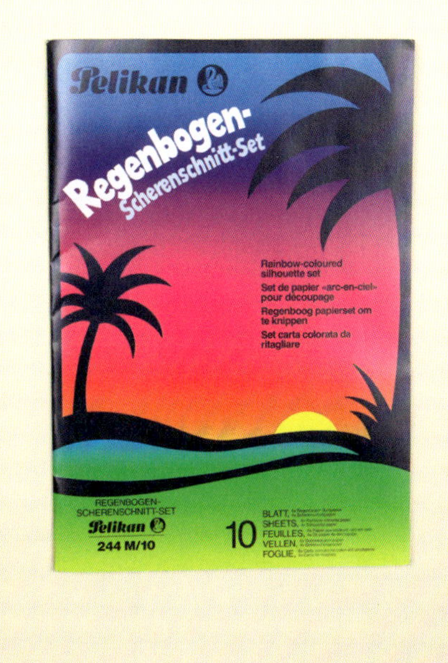

91
Pappschachtel mit Airbrush-technik und Glitzer verziert Karton, 6,3 × 8,4 × 6,5 cm, undatiert; diente als Geschenkverpackung für einen Palmenanstecker, sehr gut erhalten, in Besitz von Alf Trojan
Paper box with airbrush and glitter decoration cardboard, 2.48 × 3.3 × 2.55 in, undated; served as gift box for a palm tree pin, in very good condition, property of Alf Trojan

92
Puzzle „Paris – London – Rome – New York“ (82 Teile) in Metallbox, Aluminium, Karton, 15 × 9,5 cm, undatiert; in Besitz von Alf Trojan
Jigsaw puzzle "Paris – London – Rome – New York" (82 pieces) in metal box, aluminum, cardboard, 5.9 × 3.74 in, undated; property of Alf Trojan

93
Sanduhr „Costa Rica“ Kunstharz, Sand, Glas, 8,3 × 4 × 1 cm, 2007/Panama; leichte Gebrauchsspuren
Hourglass "Costa Rica" synthetic resin, sand, glass, 3.26 × 1.57 × 0.39 in, 2007/Panama; slight signs of wear

94
Regenbogen-Scherenschnitt-Set von Pelikan 10 Blatt Papier, 29,5 × 21 cm, Schreibwarenladen Hamburg; in Besitz von Alf Trojan
Rainbow papercut set by Pelikan 10 paper sheets, 11.61 × 8.26 in, stationery shop Hamburg, property of Alf Trojan

95–183
Sammelalbum mit Achtundachtizig Postkarten
(beschrieben und unbeschrieben), Karton, Papier, Palmenblätter, 30,2 × 35,8 × 3,8 cm, undatiert/ leichte Gebrauchsspuren
Scrapbook with eighty-eight postcards
(written and blank), cardboard, paper, palm leaves, 11.88 × 14.09 × 1.49 in, undated/ slight signs of wear

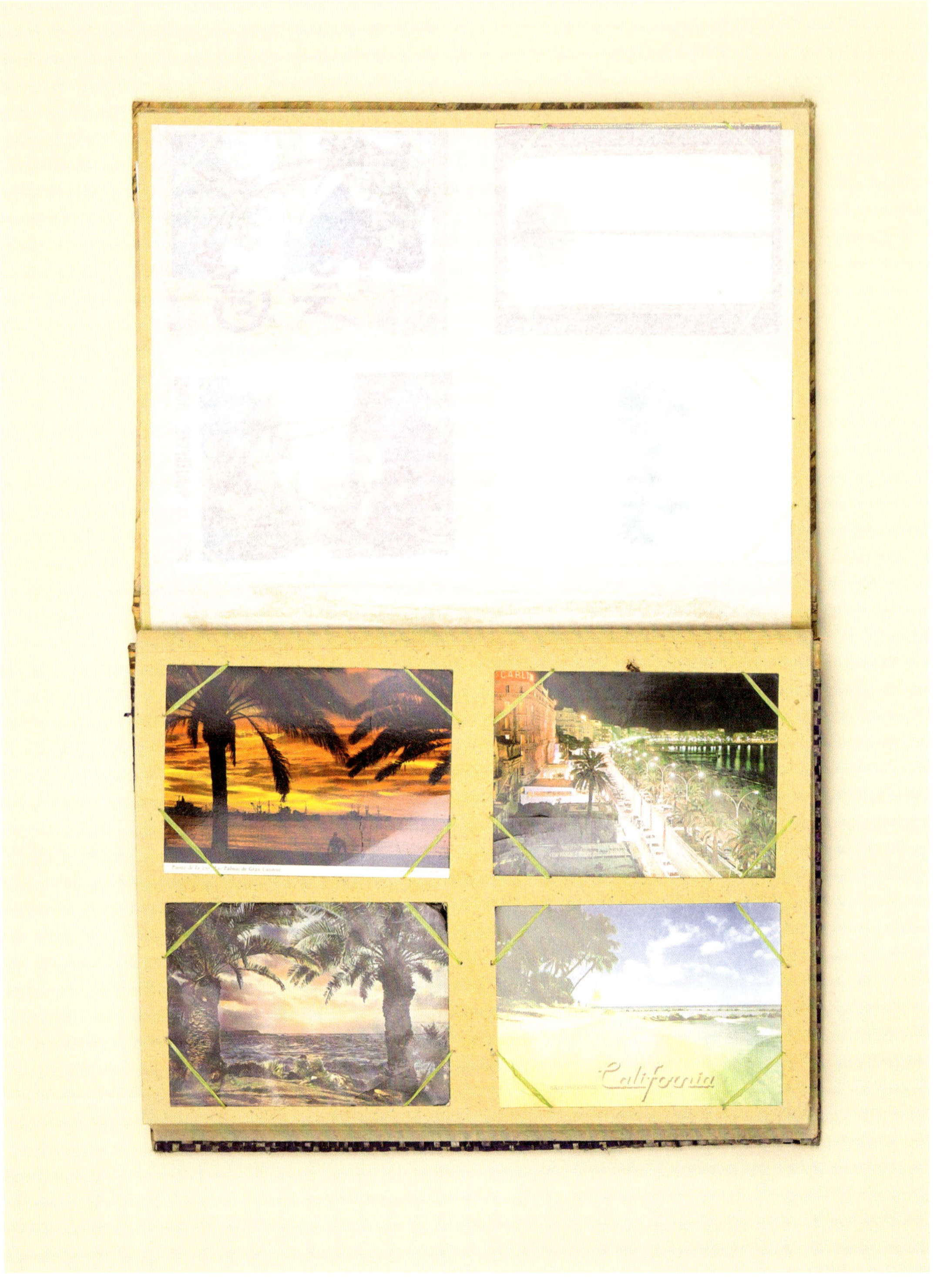

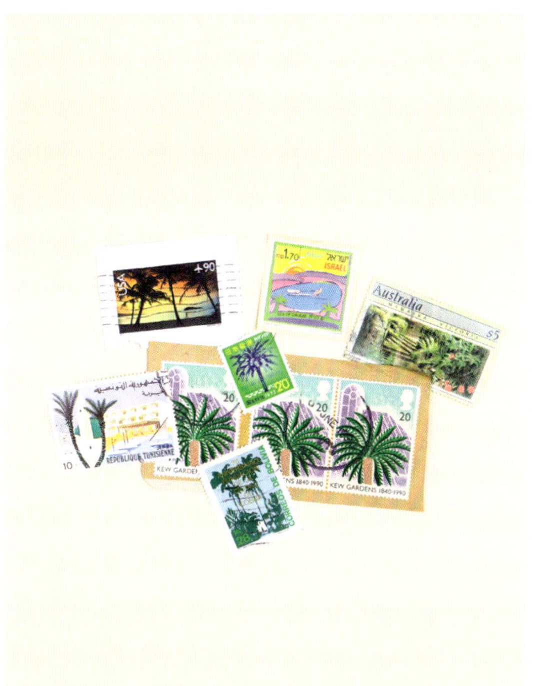

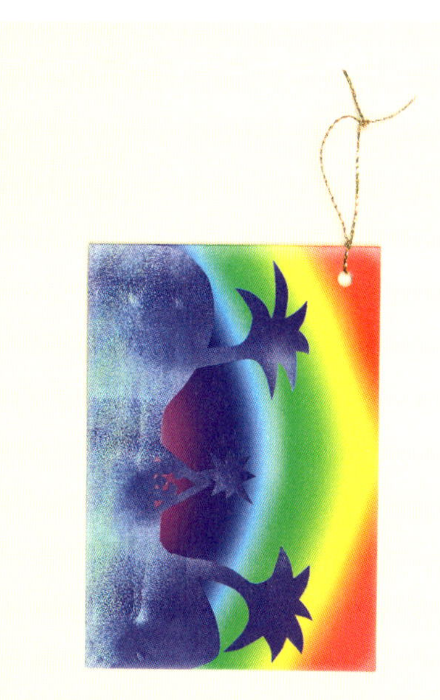

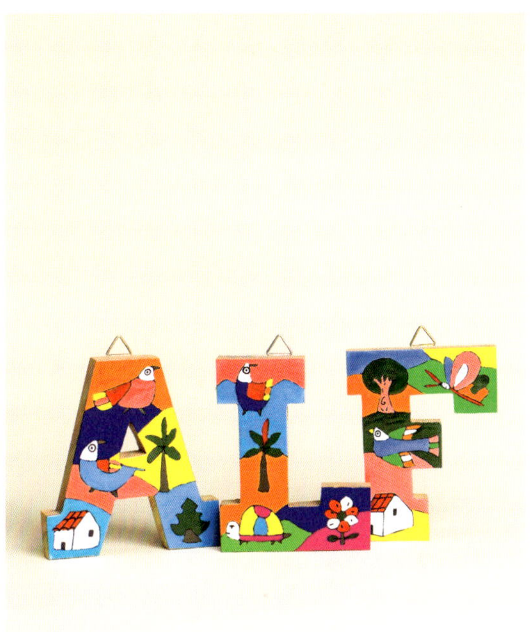

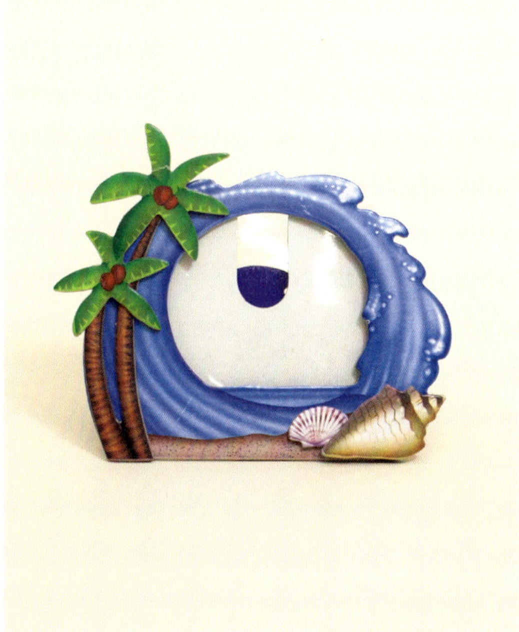

184–192
Neun abgestempelte Briefmarken
(USA, Israel, Australien, Tunesien, China, Bolivien, UK), teils auf Papier, verschiedene Größen, undatiert; durch Briefpost an den Sammler zusammengetragen, in Besitz von Alf Trojan
Nine postmarked stamps
(USA, Israel, Australia, Tunisia, China, Bolivia, UK), variously on paper, various sizes, undated; collected through mail, property of Alf Trojan

193
Postkarte als Geschenkanhänger
Handarbeit mit Airbrushtechnik, Papier, Metallkordel, 7 × 5,2 cm, undatiert; in Besitz von Alf Trojan
Postcard as gift tag
handmade with airbrush, paper, metal cord, 2.75 × 2.04 in, undated; property of Alf Trojan

194
Drei handbemalte Buchstaben
Holz, Draht, 22,5 × 10,8 × 1,5 cm, 2003/Mitbringsel aus Peru von einem Freund; in Besitz von Alf Trojan
Three hand-painted letters
wood, wire, 8.85 × 4.25 × 0.59 in, 2003/souvenir from Peru, from a friend; property of Alf Trojan

195
Wechselbilderrahmen
Pappe, Kunststofffolie, 14,5 × 17 × 4,6 cm, 1980/Taiwan; leichte Gebrauchsspuren
Interchangable picture frame
cardboard, plastic foil, 5.7 × 6.69 × 1.81 in, 1980/Taiwan; slight signs of wear

196
Schneekugel „Gran Canaria“
Kunststoff, Plexiglas, Wasser, Kunstschnee, 7,1 × 9 × 6,5 cm, 1984/ Souvenirshop Gran Canaria; vergilbt, etwas Wasser fehlt
Snow globe “Gran Canaria”
plastic, plexiglass, water, artificial snow, 2.79 × 3.54 × 2.55 in, 1984/ tourist shop Gran Canaria, gone yellow, some water missing

197
Schneekugel „I love Eilat“
Kunststoff, Plexiglas, Wasser, Kunstschnee, 6,3 × 7,5 × 3,1 cm, 1997/ Souvenirshop Israel; starke Gebrauchsspuren, ausgetrocknet
Snow globe “I love Eilat”
plastic, plexiglass, water, artificial snow, 2.48 × 2.95 × 1.22 in, 1997/ tourist shop Israel; heavy signs of wear, dried up

198
Schneekugel „Weihnachten“
Kunststoff, Plexiglas, Wasser, Kunstschnee, 5,5 × 7 × 5 cm, 2008/ Deutschland; etwas Wasser fehlt
Snow globe “Christmas” plastic, plexiglass, water, artificial snow, 2.16 × 2.75 × 1.96 in, 2008/ Germany; some water missing

199
Schneekugel „Flamingos“
Kunststoff, Plexiglas, Wasser, Kunstschnee, 5,5 × 7 × 5 cm, 2000/ Florida; leichte Gebrauchsspuren, etwas Wasser fehlt
Snow globe “Flamingos”
plastic, plexiglass, water, artificial snow, 2.16 × 2.75 × 1.96 in, 2000/ Florida; slight signs of wear, some water missing

200
Schneekugel „Cocktail“
Kunststoff, Plexiglas, Wasser, Kunstschnee, 5,5 × 7 × 5 cm, undatiert; starke Gebrauchsspuren, ausgetrocknet
Snow globe “Cocktail”
plastic, plexiglass, water, artificial snow, 2.16 × 2.75 × 1.96 in, undated; heavy signs of wear, dried up

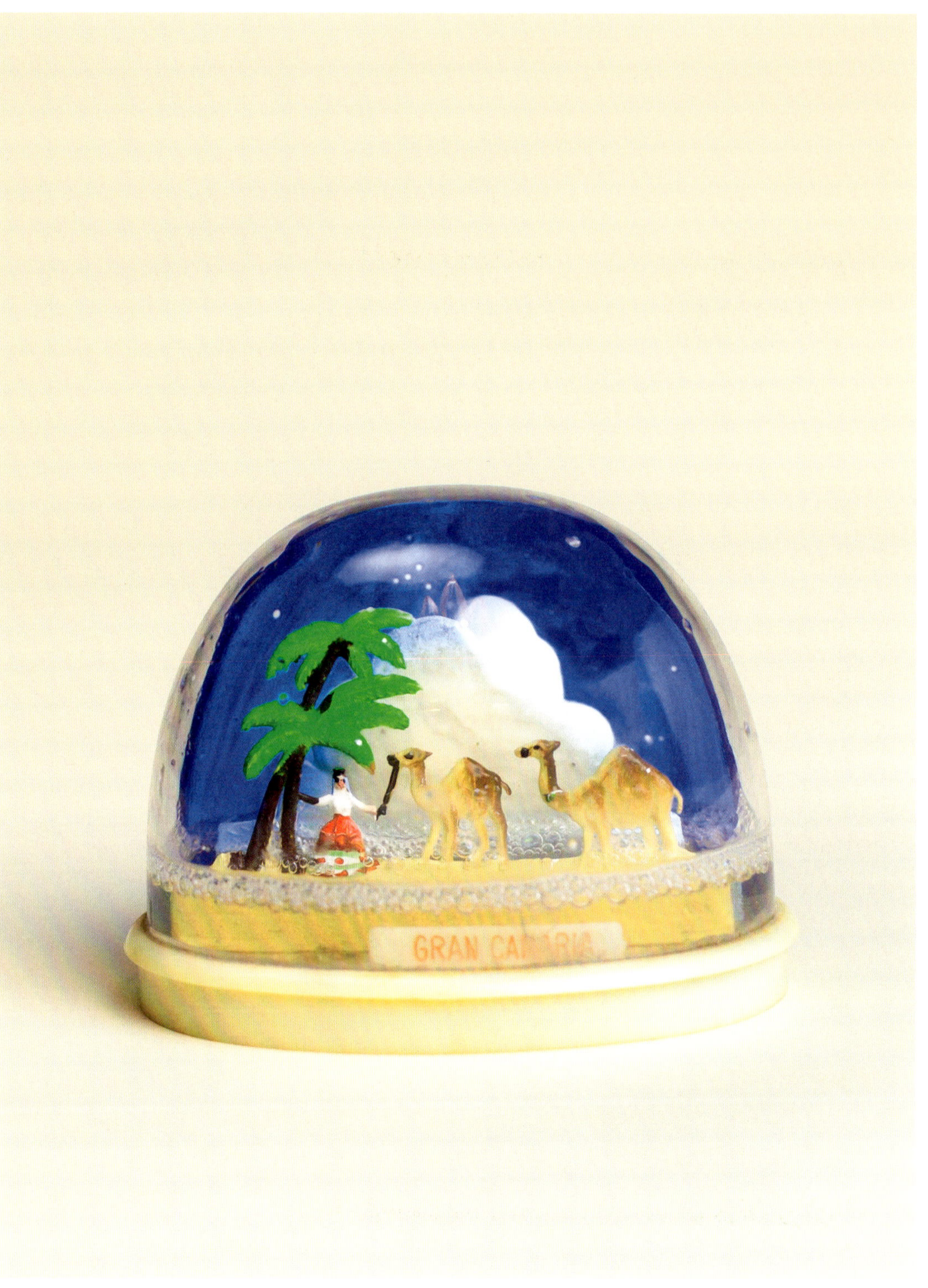

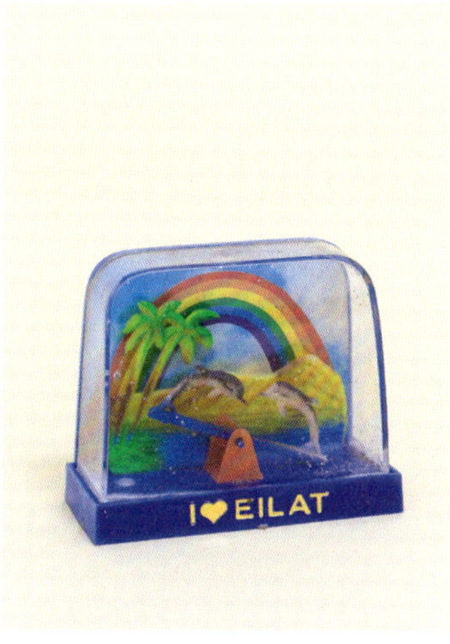

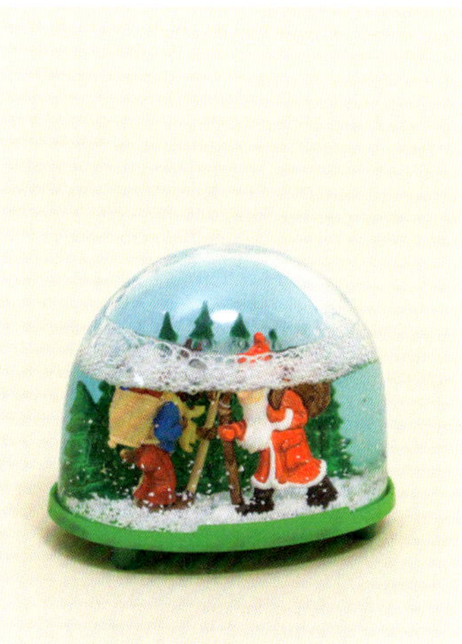

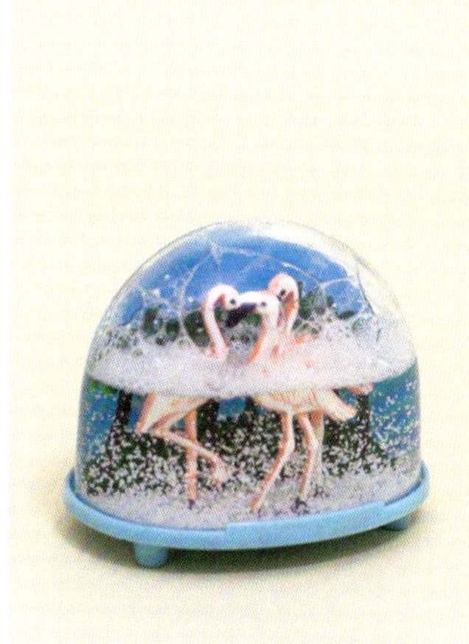

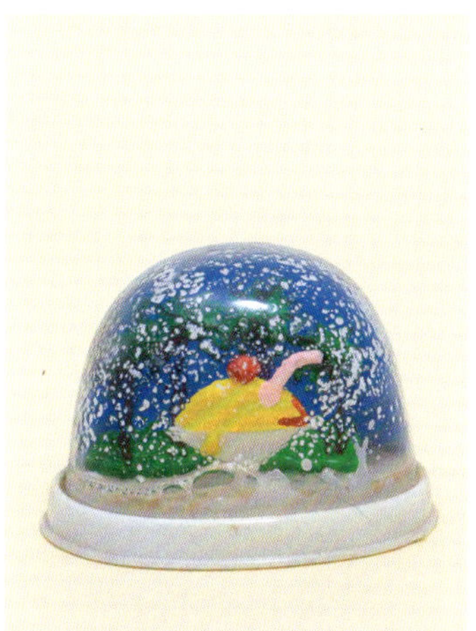

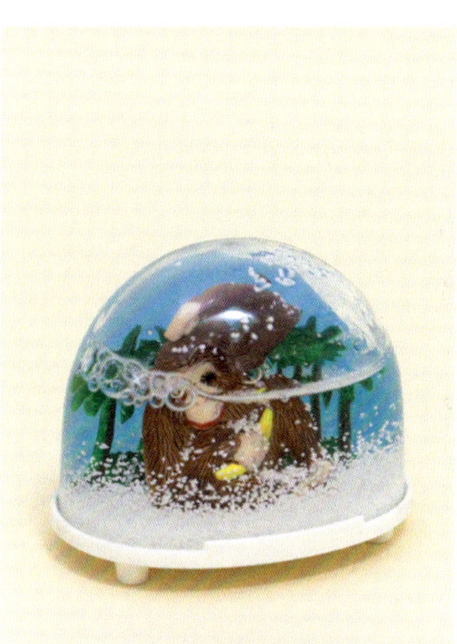

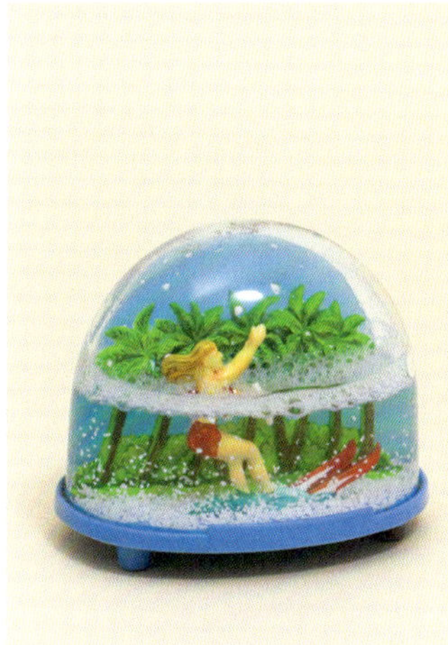

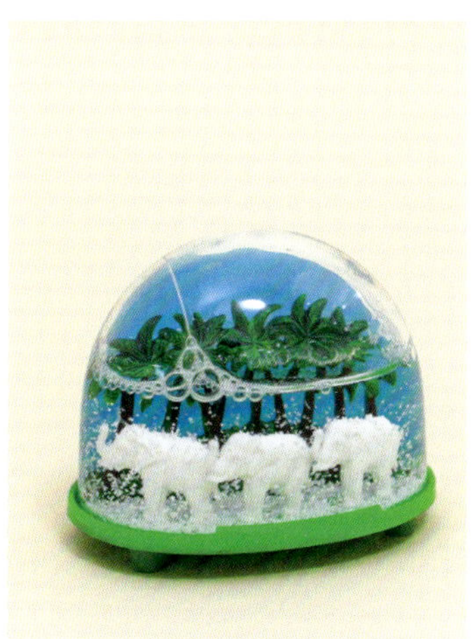

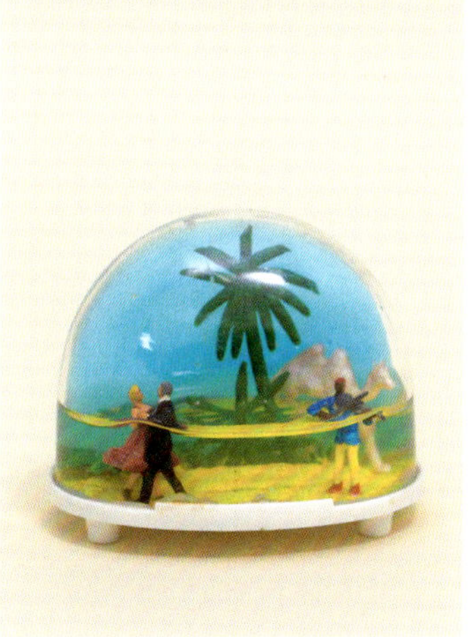

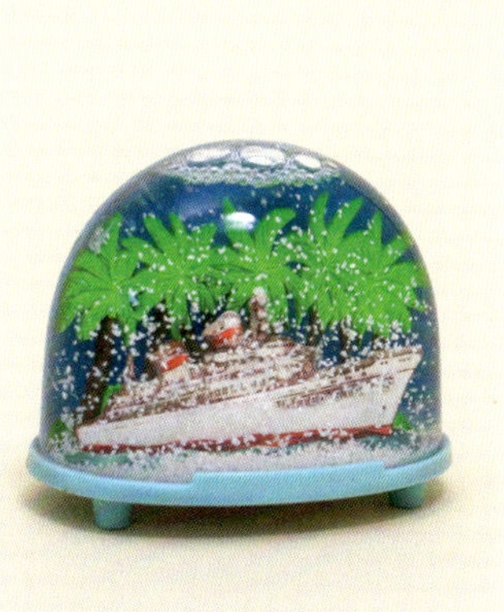

201
Schneekugel „Affe“
Kunststoff, Plexiglas, Wasser, Kunstschnee, 5,5 × 7 × 5 cm, 2013/Südafrika; leichte Gebrauchsspuren, etwas Wasser fehlt
Snow globe “Monkey”
plastic, plexiglass, water, artificial snow, 2.16 × 2.75 × 1.96 in, 2013/South Africa; slight signs of wear, some water missing

202
Schneekugel „Wasserski“
Kunststoff, Plexiglas, Wasser, Kunstschnee, 5,5 × 7 × 5 cm, 2002/Italien; etwas Wasser fehlt
Snow globe “Water ski”
plastic, plexiglass, water, artificial snow, 2.16 × 2.75 × 1.96 in, 2002/Italy; some water missing

203
Schneekugel „Elefanten“
Kunststoff, Plexiglas, Wasser, Kunstschnee, 5,5 × 7 × 5 cm, 2015/Flohmarkt; etwas Wasser fehlt
Snow globe “Elephants”
plastic, plexiglass, water, artificial snow, 2.16 × 2.75 × 1.96 in, 2015/fleamarket; some water missing

204
Schneekugel „Tanzendes Paar“
Kunststoff, Plexiglas, Wasser, Kunstschnee, 5,5 × 7 × 5 cm, 1991; von einem WG-Freund anlässlich der Hochzeit des Sammlers selbstgebastelt, eine Palme ist umgefallen, etwas Wasser fehlt, in Besitz von Alf Trojan
Snow globe “Dancing Couple”
plastic, plexiglass, water, artificial snow, 2.16 × 2.75 × 1.96 in, 1991; handmade by a flatmate at the occasion of the collector’s wedding, one palm tree collapsed, some water missing, property of Alf Trojan

205
Schneekugel „Kreuzfahrtschiff“
Kunststoff, Plexiglas, Wasser, Kunstschnee, 5,5 × 7 × 5 cm, undatiert; wie neu
Snow globe “Cruiseship” plastic, plexiglass, water, artificial snow, 2.16 × 2.75 × 1.96 in, undated; like new

206
Handbemalte Trinkflasche
(Füllmenge ca. 1,8 Liter), Wildleder, Kunststoff, 23,3 × 12 × 3,5 cm, 1988/Flohmarkt; leichte Gebrauchsspuren
Hand-painted drinking bottle
(volume ca 0.48 gallons), suede, plastic, 1.37 × 4.72 × 9.17 in, 1988/fleamarket; slight signs of wear

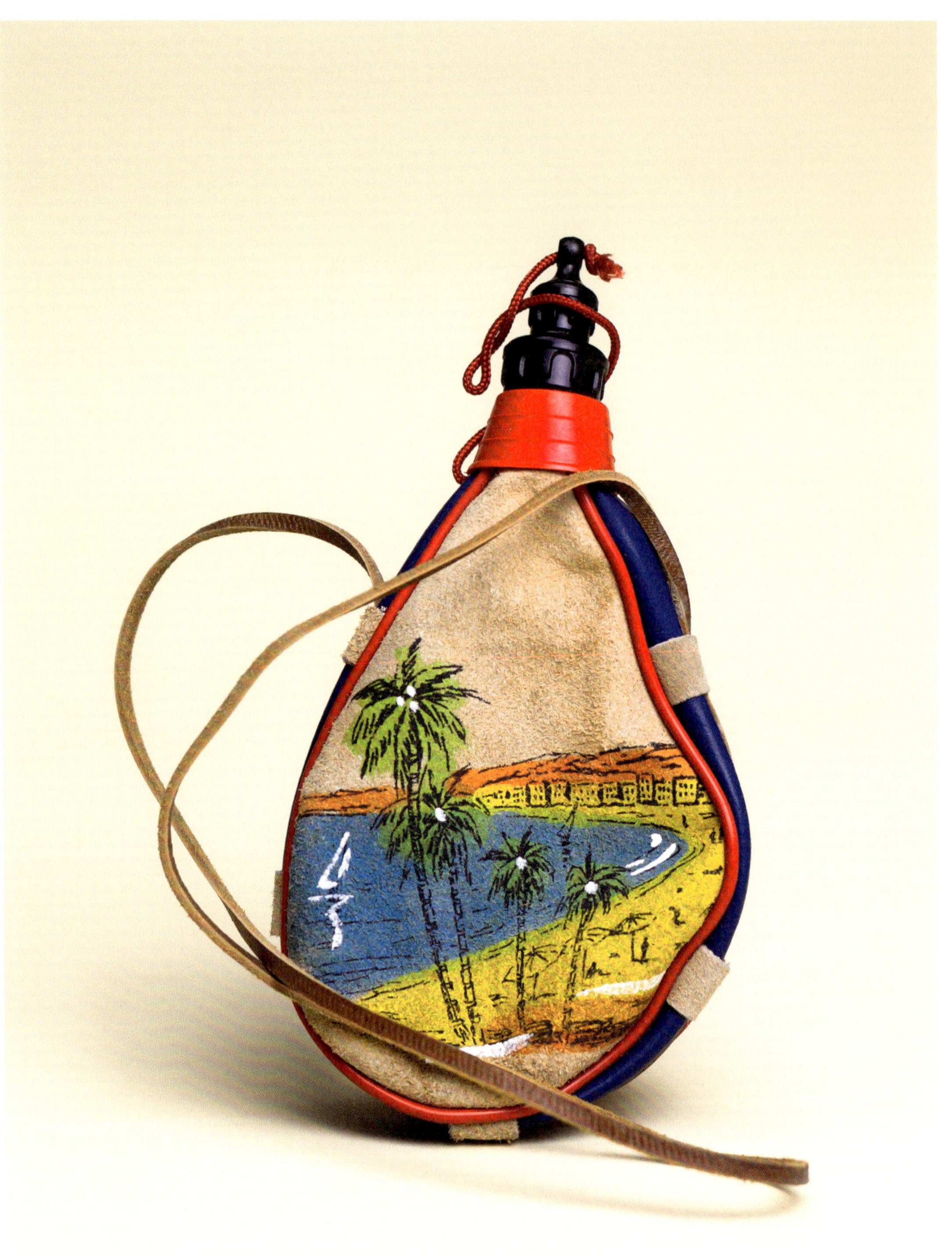

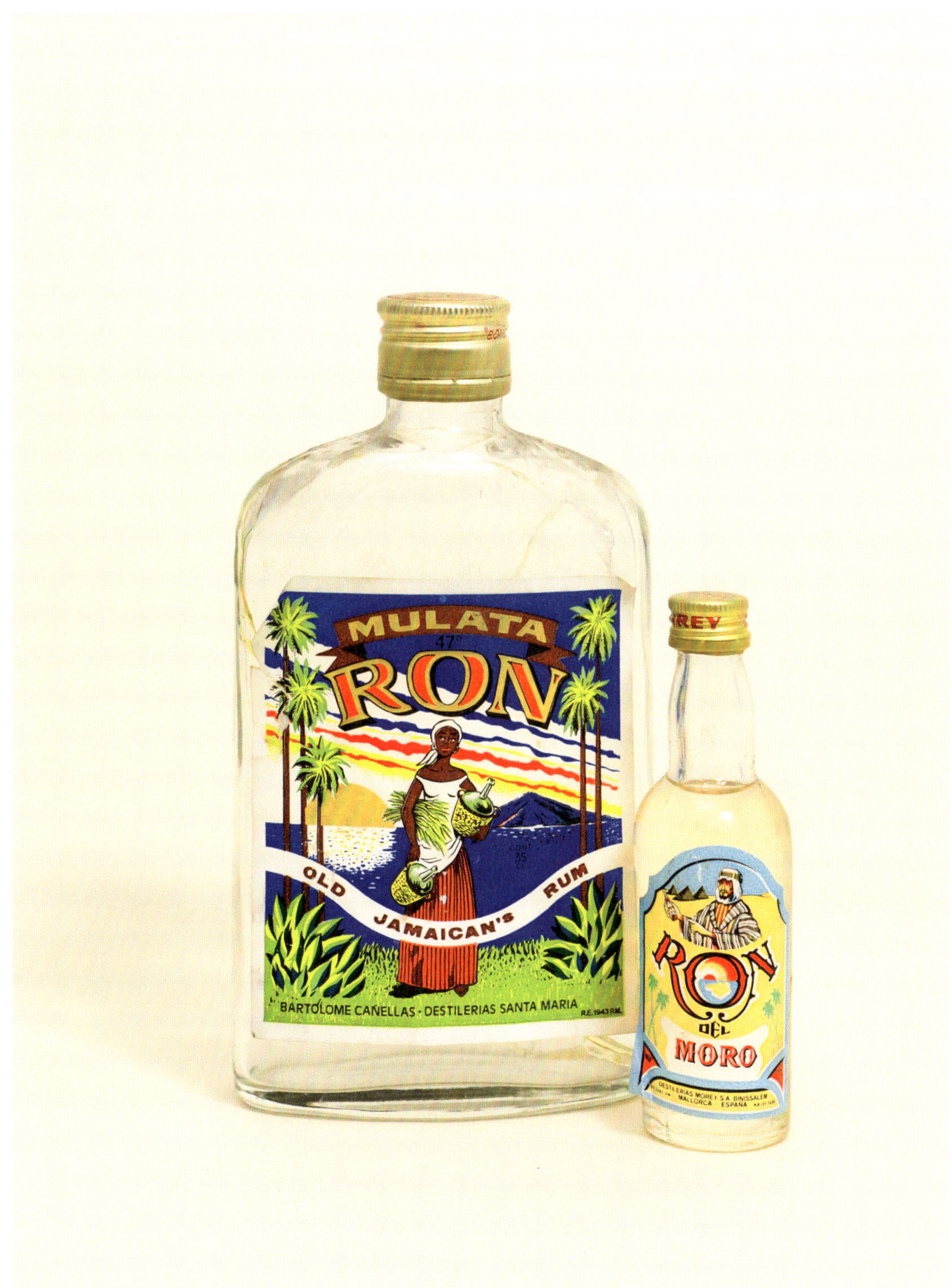

207–208
Schnapsflasche „Mulata Ron“
Glas, Papier, Aluminium, 18,7 × 10,3 × 4,1 cm, 2011/Souvenir, Jamaika; ohne Inhalt, Flecken, starke Gebrauchsspuren
Bottle of schnapps “Mulata Ron”
glass, paper, aluminum, 7.36 × 4.05 x 1.61 in, 2011/souvenir, Jamaica; without content, stains, heavy signs of wear

Schnapsflasche Rum „Ron del Moro“ Glas, Papier, Aluminium, 12 × 3,3 cm, 1997/Mallorca; ungeöffnet
Bottle of rum “Ron del Moro”
glass, paper, aluminum, 4.72 × 1.29 in, 1997/Mallorca; unopened

209
Cocktailmixer mit Zitronenpresse im Deckel Kunststoff, Plexiglas, 26,5 × 20 × 13,4 cm, 1985/ Taiwan; wie neu
Cocktail mixer with lemon squeezer lid plastic, plexiglass, 10.43 × 7.87 × 5.27 in, 1985/ Taiwan; like new

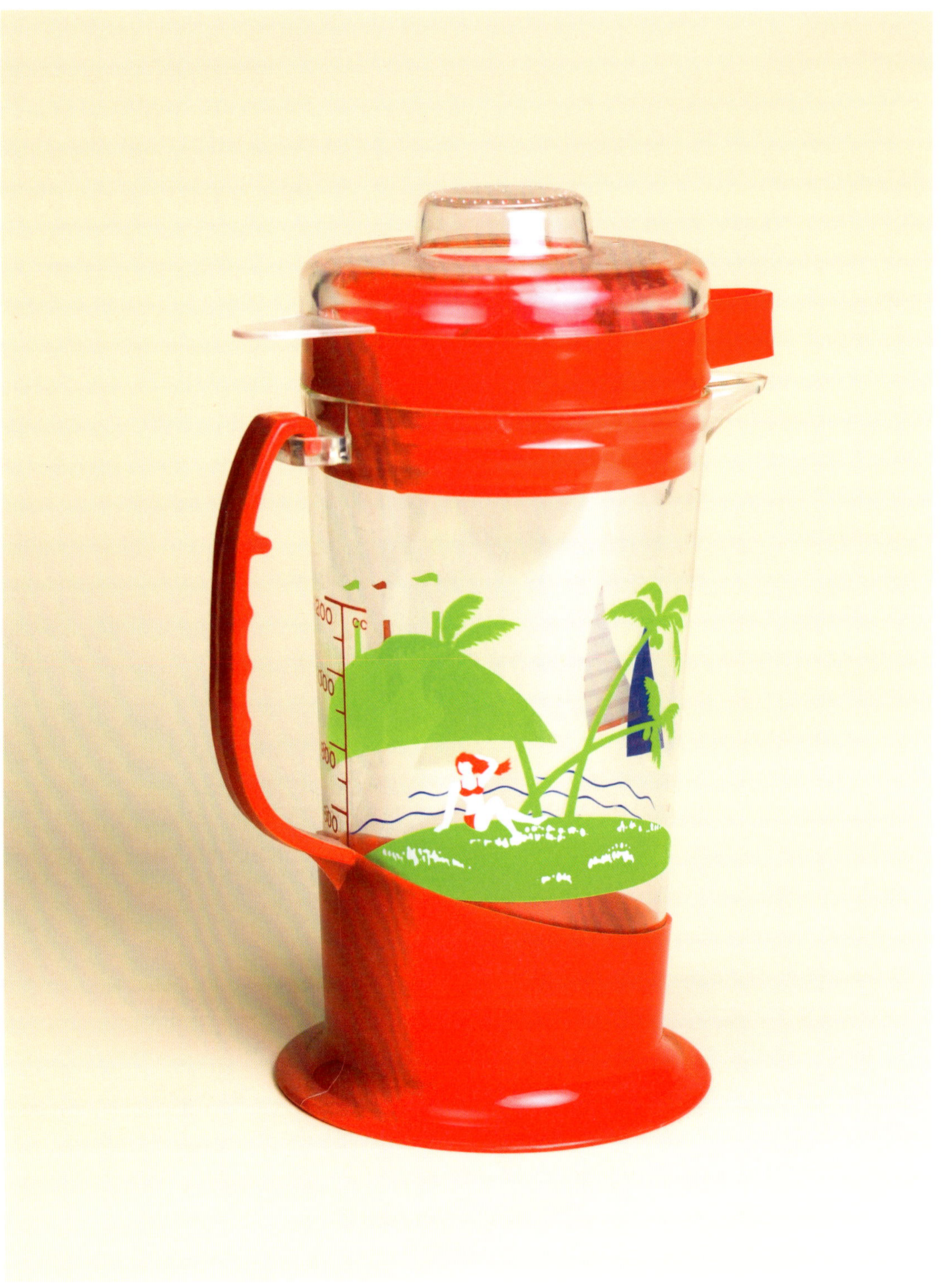

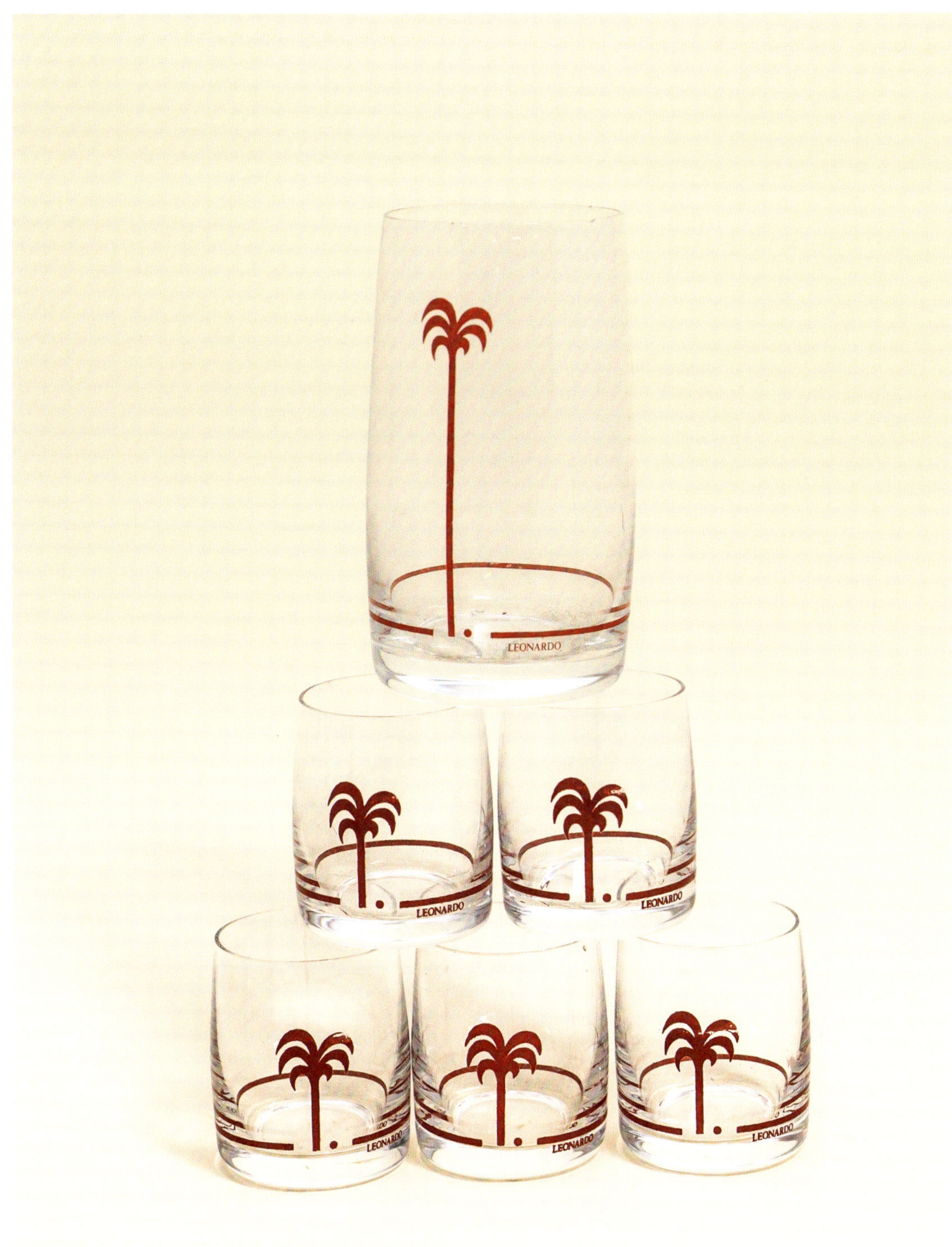

210–215
Leonardo-Glas Glas, 11,5 × 6 cm, 1994/Geschenkladen Hamburg-Eppendorf; Sprung im Glas
Leonardo-Glass glass, 4.52 × 2.36 in, 1994/giftshop Hamburg-Eppendorf; cracked

Fünf Leonardo-Gläser Glas, 6 × 4,5 cm, 1994/Geschenkladen Hamburg Eppendorf
Five Leonardo-Glasses glass, 2.36 × 1.77 in, 1994/giftshop Hamburg-Eppendorf

216–217
Zwei Kerzenhalter mit zwei Stabkerzen, Messing, 14,1 × 15 × 15 cm, 2011; Geschenk der Ehefrau, eine Kerze leicht gekrümmt, in Besitz von Alf Trojan
Two candle holders with straight candles, brass, 5.55 × 5.9 × 5.9 in, 2011; gift from wife, one candle slightly bent, property of Alf Trojan

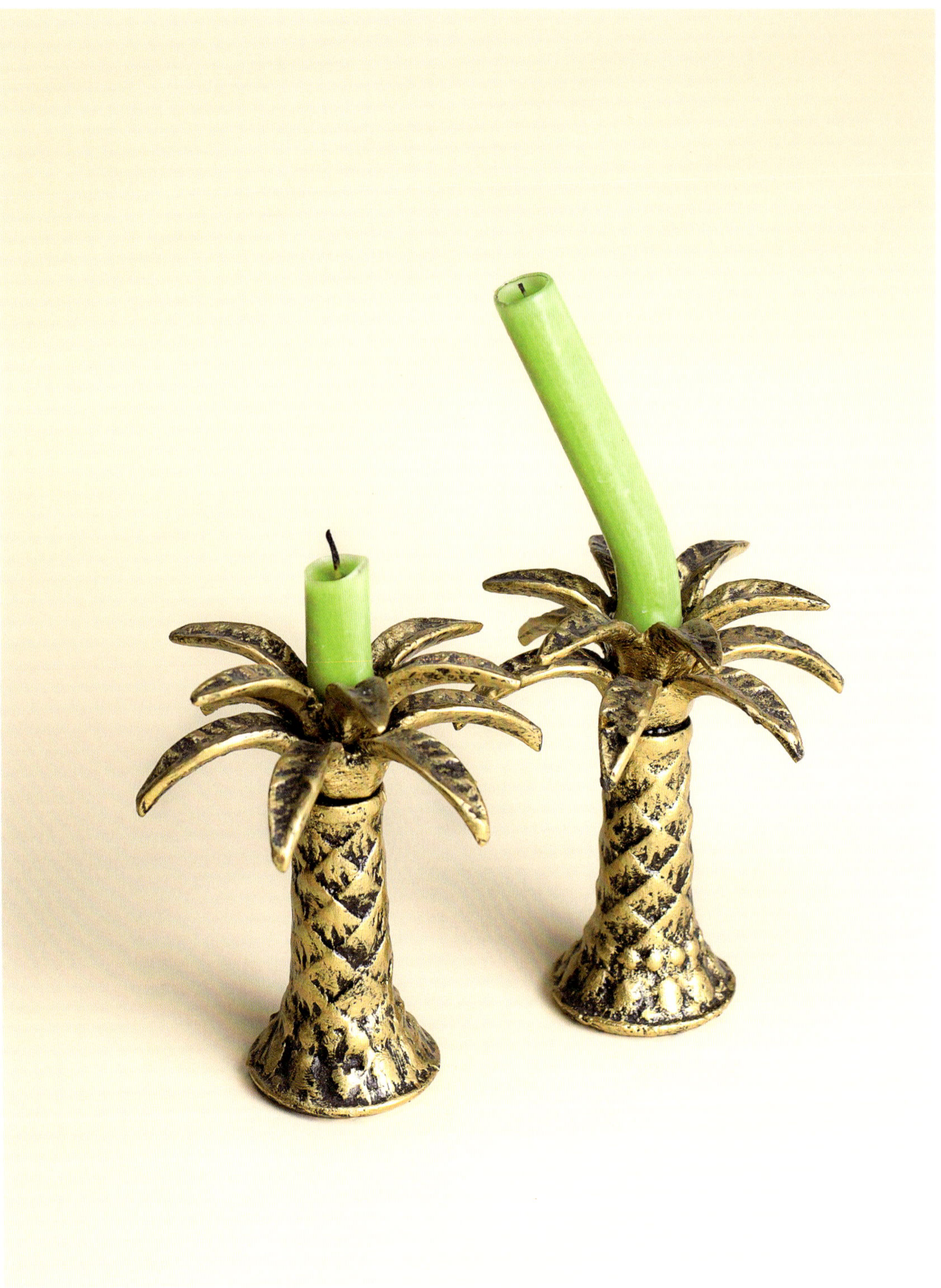

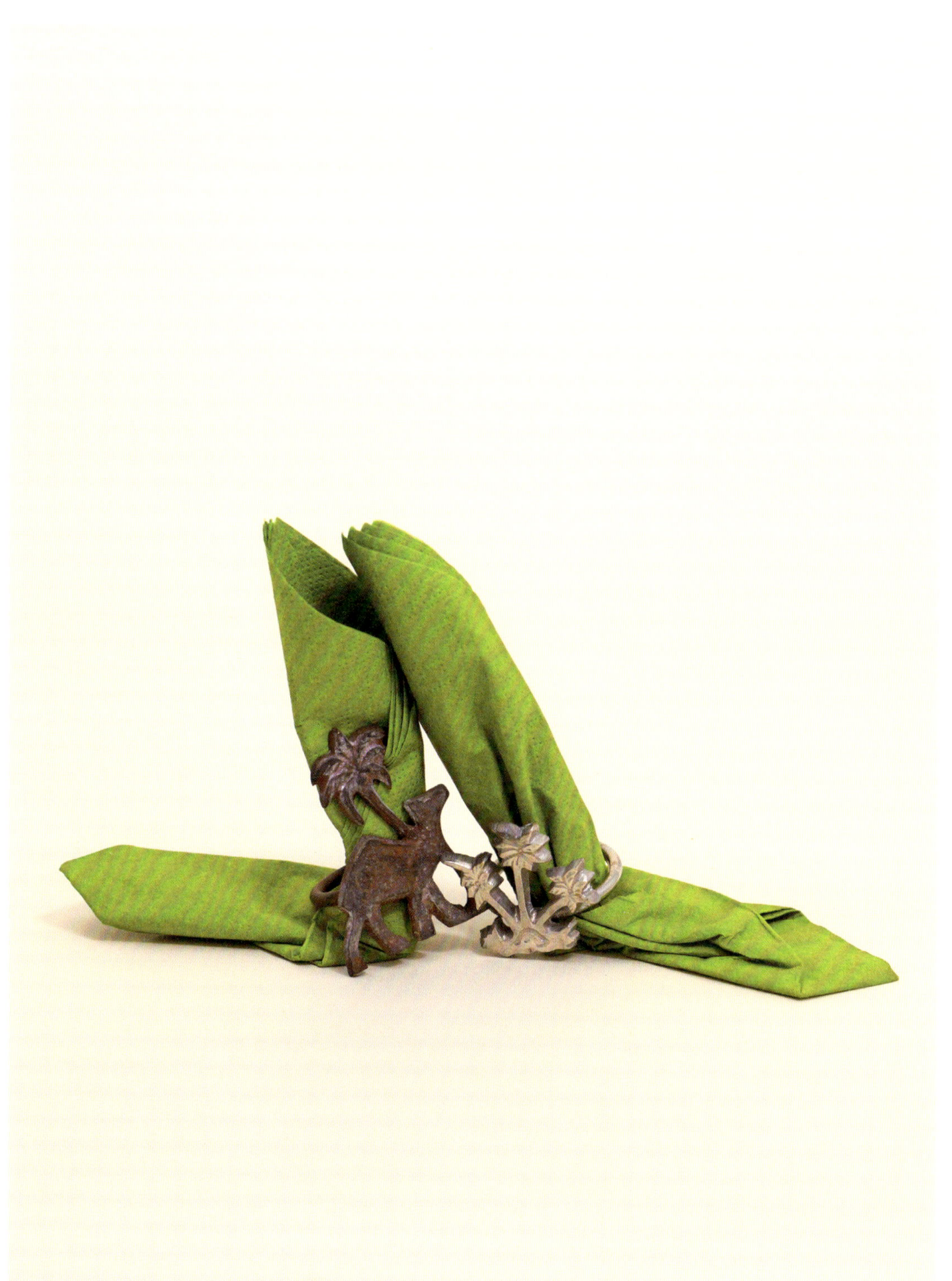

218–219
Serviettenring „Kamel mit Palme“
mit Papierserviette, Metall, 6,4 × 4,5 × 4 cm, 1993/Antikladen in der Eifel; starker Rost, in Besitz von Alf Trojan
Napkin ring “Camel with palm tree”
with paper napkin, metal, 2.51 × 1.77 × 1.57 in, 1993/antique shop in the Eifel region; heavy rust, property of Alf Trojan

Serviettenring „Drei Palmen“
mit Papierserviette, Eisen, 3,6 × 4,6 × 4 cm, undatiert; in Besitz von Alf Trojan
Napkin ring “Three palm trees”
with paper napkin, iron, 1.41 × 1.81 × 1.57 in, undated; property of Alf Trojan

220–221
Zwei handbemalte Vasen
mit getrockneter Rose, Glas,
10,7 × 7 cm und 17,5 × 5 cm,
undatiert; Farbe blättert leicht ab,
in Besitz von Alf Trojan
Two hand-painted vases
with dried rose, glass,
4.21 × 2.76 in and 6.89 × 1.96 in,
undated; lightly flaking paint,
property of Alf Trojan

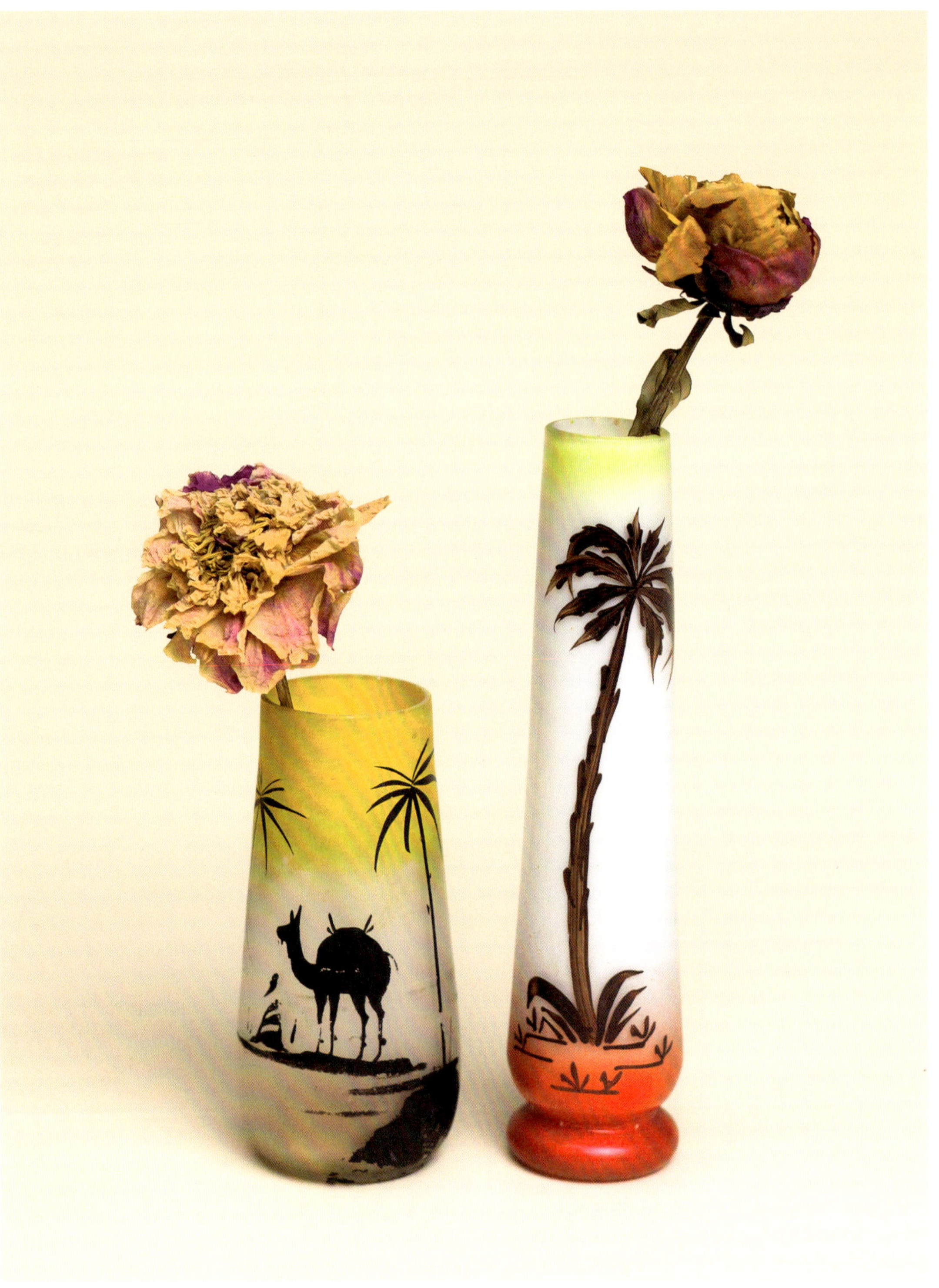

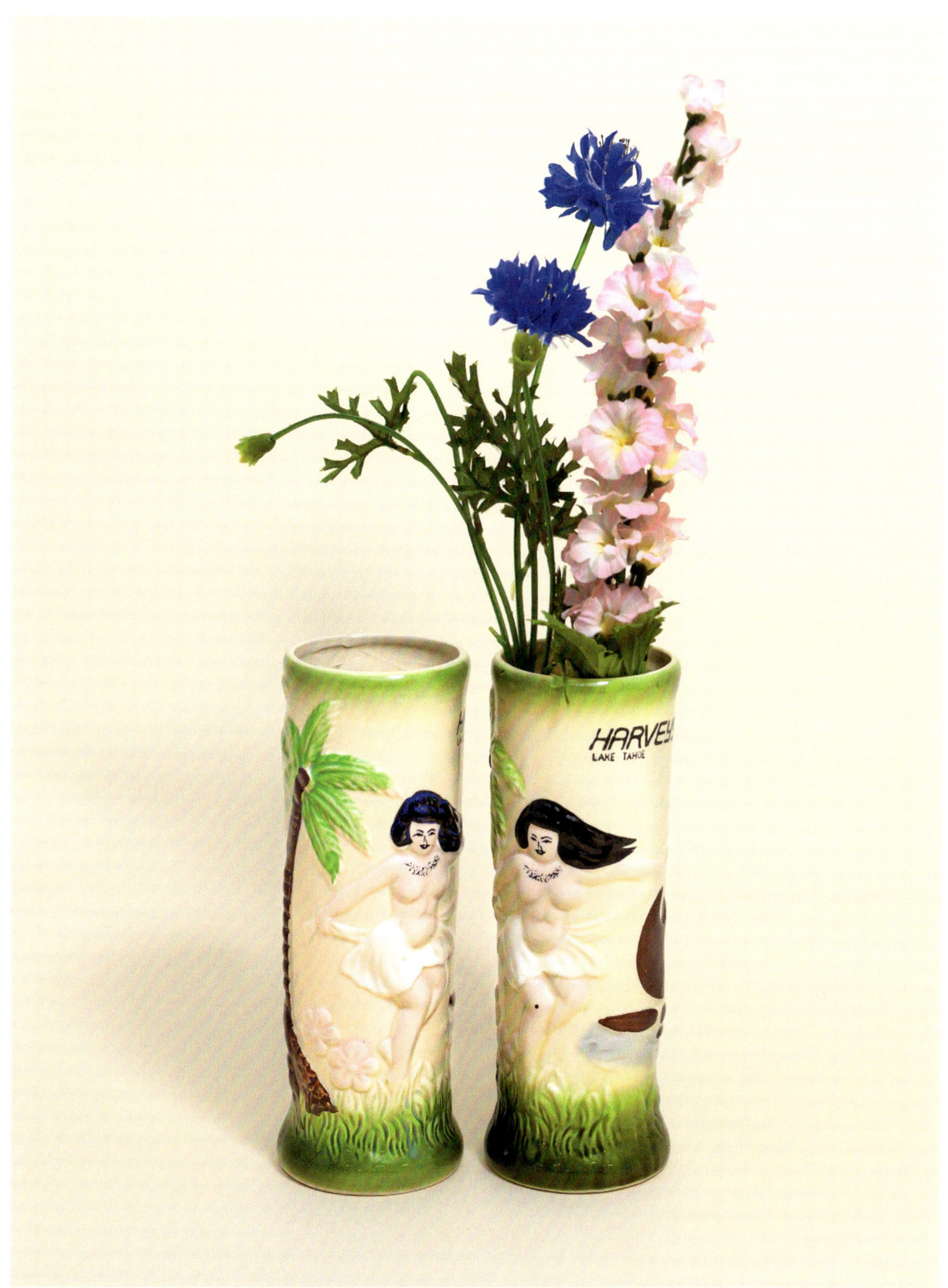

222–223
Zwei Tiki-Mugs mit Kunstblumen, Keramik, 20,9 × 7,5 cm, 2007/ Souvenir Lake Tahoe; Kratzspuren, wird als Blumenvase genutzt, in Besitz von Alf Trojan
Two Tiki-Mugs with artificial flowers, ceramic, 8.22 × 2.95 in, 2007/ tourist shop LakeTahoe; scratch marks, used as flower vase, property of Alf Trojan

224–225
Thermoskanne mit Deckel
Edelstahl, 23,8 × 7,6 cm, 1971/ Souvenir Jemen; noch vor Beginn der Sammelleidenschaft erworben, leichte Gebrauchsspuren
Thermos flask with lid
stainless steel, 9.37 × 2.99 in, 1971/ souvenir Yemen; purchased before collector's passion began, slight signs of wear

Thermoskanne mit Henkel
(made in China), Aluminium, Kork, 25,7 × 15,1 × 2,3 cm, 1976/Hinterhofflohmarkt Hamburg; verbeult
Thermos flask with handle
(made in China), aluminum, cork, 10.11 × 5.94 × 4.84 in, 1976/yard sale Hamburg; dented

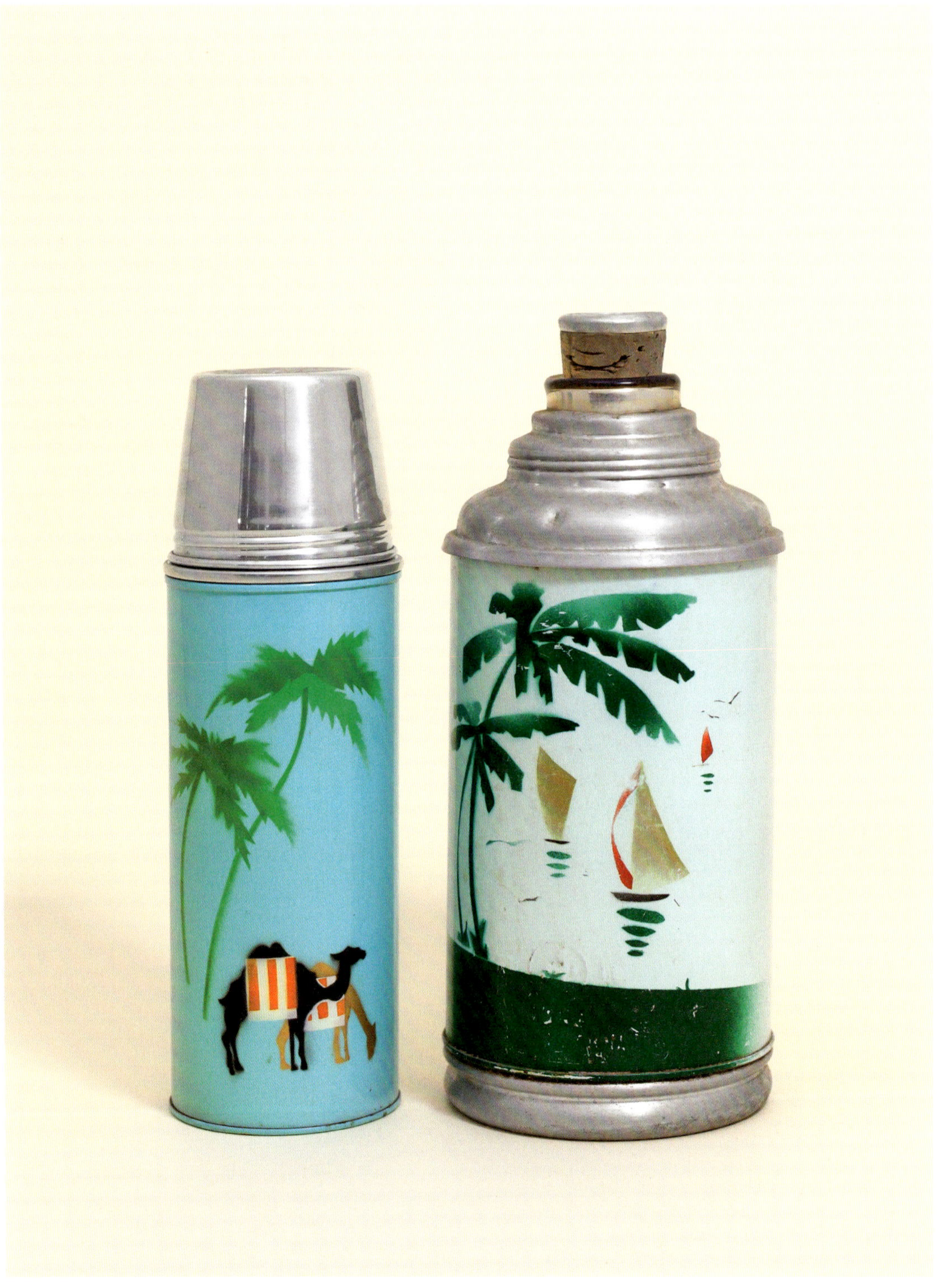

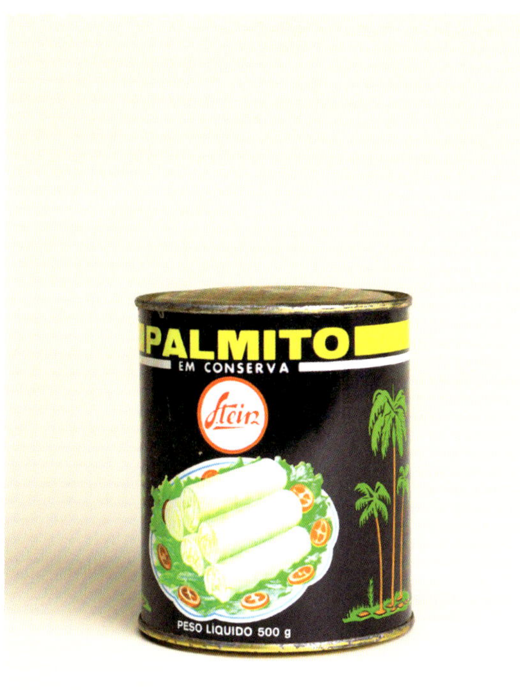

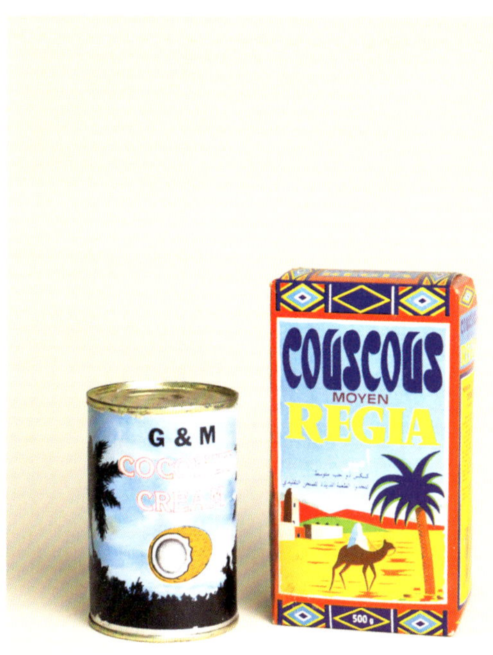

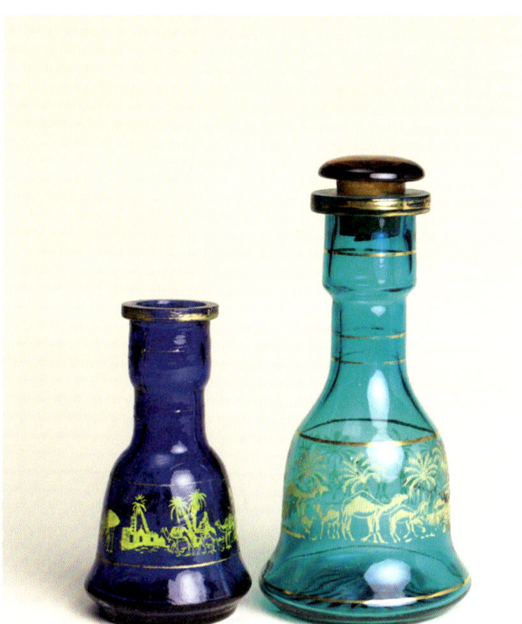

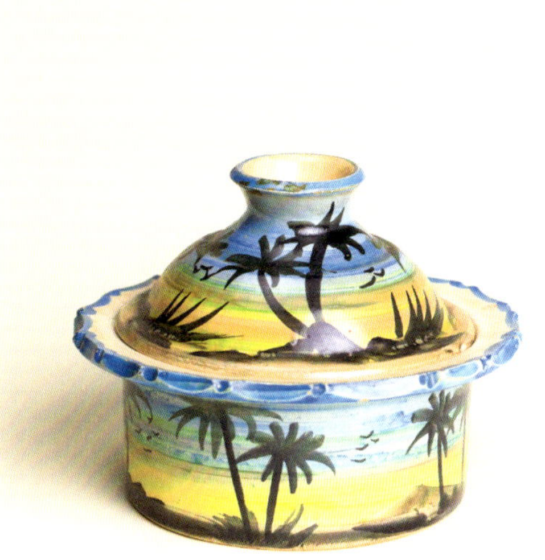

226
Konservendose mit Palmenherzen Metall, Wasser, Palmenherzen, 12,1 × 10,2 cm, 1980/Brasilien; starke Gebrauchsspuren, starker Rost, ungeöffnet
Tin with hearts of palm metal, water, hearts of palm, 4.76 × 4.01 in, 1980/Brasil; heavy signs of wear, heavy rust, unopened

227–228
Konservendose Kokosnussmilch Metall, 10,2 × 6,8 cm, 1988/ Jamaika; starke Gebrauchsspuren, ohne Inhalt
Tin with coconut milk metal, 4.01 × 2.67 in, 1988/Jamaica; heavy signs of wear, without content

Lebensmittelverpackung Couscous Karton, 15,2 × 8,4 × 5,5 cm, 1996/Frankreich; starke Gebrauchsspuren, Neupreis 4,90 Franc
Grocery packaging couscous cardboard, 5.98 × 3.3 × 2.16 in, 1996/ France; heavy signs of wear, original price 4,90 francs

229–230
Flasche mit Malerei Glas, 16,4 × 10,5 cm, undatiert; Deckel fehlt, Farbe blättert ab
Bottle with painting glass 6.45 × 4.13 in, undated; lid missing, flaking paint

Flasche mit Malerei Glas, 22 × 11,4 cm, undatiert
Bottle with painting glass, 8.66 × 4.48 in, undated

231
Tajine Steingut, 6,8 × 16,7 cm, 2002/ Marokko; Deckel geklebt
Tajine earthenwear, 2.67 × 6.57 in 2002/Morocco; lid repaired

232
Pappkarton Karton, 7,2 × 20 × 16 cm, undatiert; starke Flecken
Cardboard box cardboard, 2.83 × 7.87 × 6.29 in, undated; heavy stains

233
Schachtel Karton, 10,4 × 18,3 × 24,9 cm, 2010; Geschenk der Ehefrau, Flecken
Box cardboard, 4.09 × 7.2 × 9.8 in, 2010; gift from wife, stains

234
Bemalte Büchse mit Henkel Gusseisen, 17,2 × 11,3 cm, undatiert; Rost, Kratzer
Painted can with handle cast iron, 6.77 × 4.44 in, undated; rust, scratches

235
Teekiste Holz, Nägel, 8,9 × 12,5 × 23 cm, 1984/ Indien; jahrelang in der Küche genutzt, starke Gebrauchsspuren
Tea box wood, nails, 3.5 × 4.92 × 9.05 in, 1984/ India; for years in kitchen use, heavy signs of wear

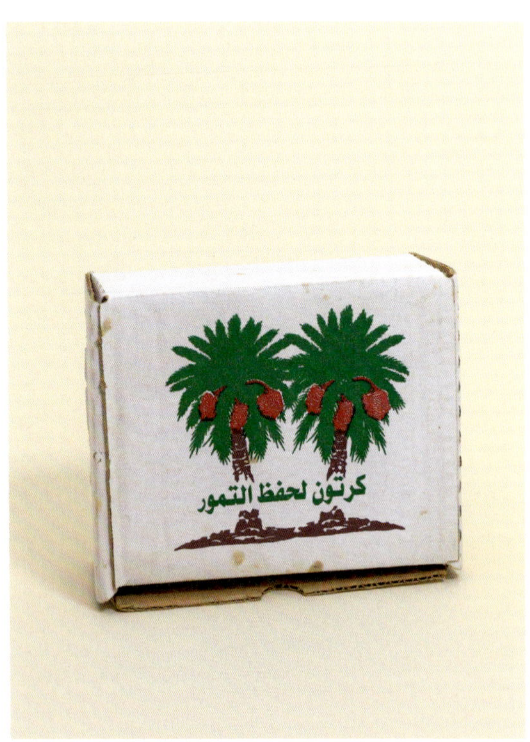

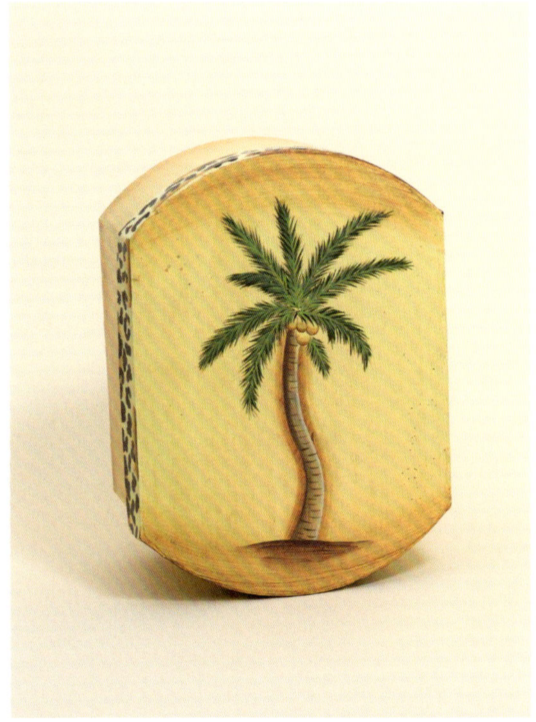

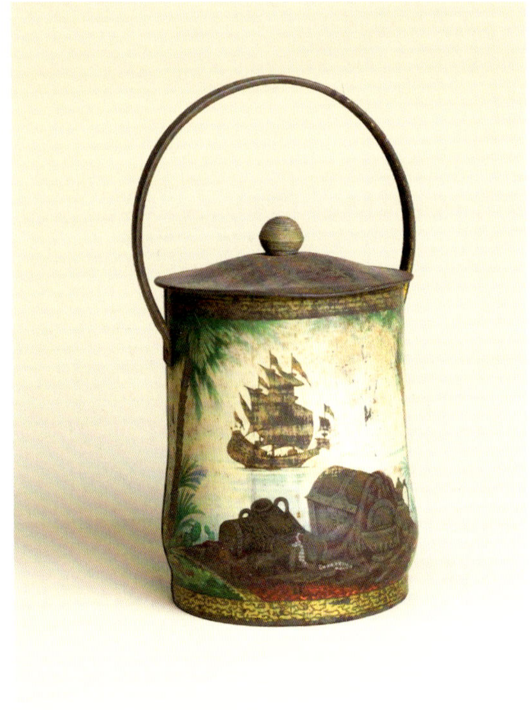

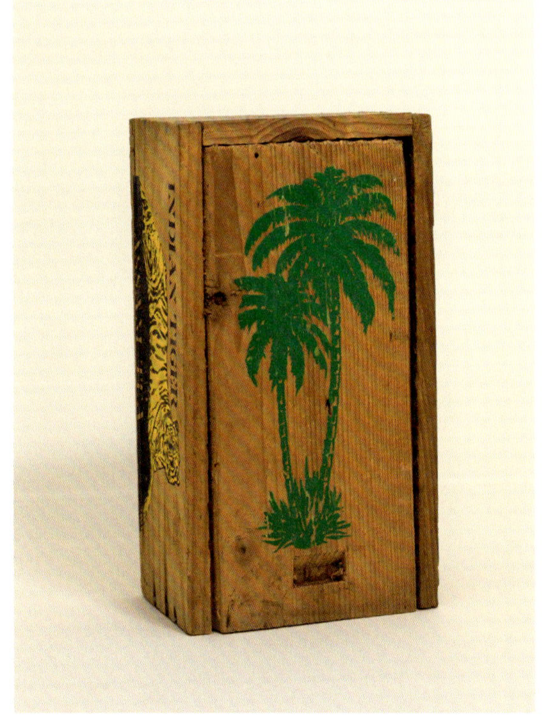

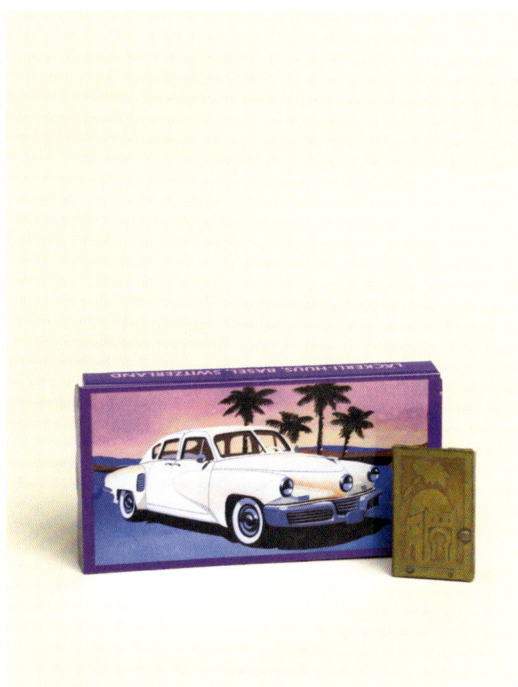

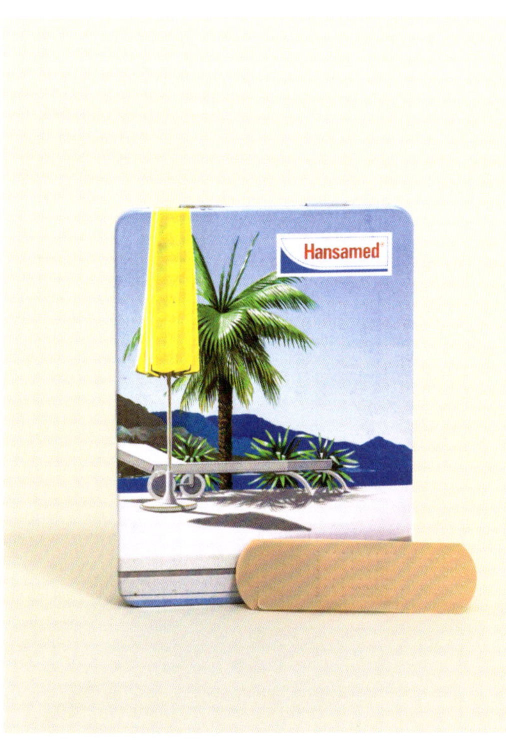

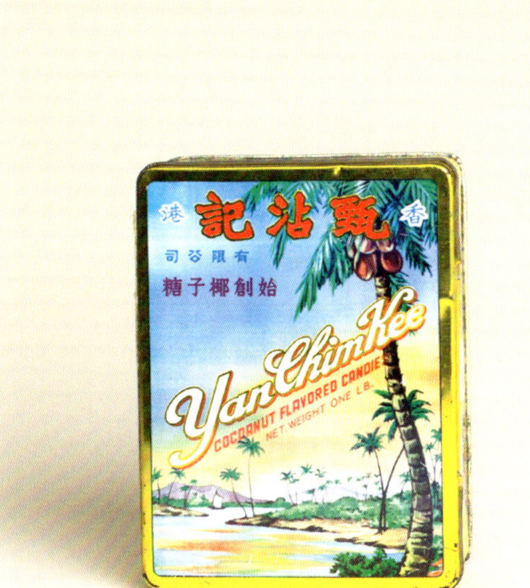

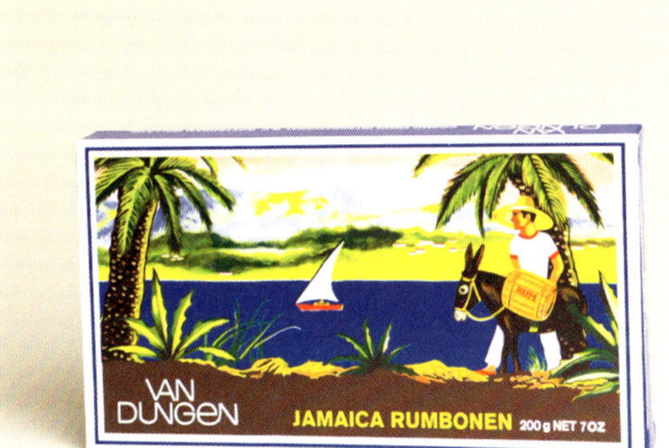

236–237
Bonbondose Metall, 1,2 × 8,4 × 4,2 cm, Läckerli-Huus Basel; Schiebedeckel, leichte Kratzer
Candy box metal, 0.47 × 3.3 × 1.65 in, Läckerli-Huus Basel; sliding lid, light scratches

Miniaturdose Metall, 3 × 1,7 cm, undatiert; leichte Kratzer
Miniature tin metal, 1.18 × 0.37 in, undated, light scratches

238
„Hansamed“ Pflasterbox mit 13 Pflastern, Metall, Kunststoff, 11,3 × 8,6 × 1,5 cm, 2004/ Hamburg; leichte Kratzer
Band-aid box “Hansamed” with 13 band-aids, metal, plastic, 4.44 × 3.38 × 0.59 in, 2004/ Hamburg; light scratches

239
Kokosnuss-Bonbondose (made in Hongkong) mit 46 Postkarten, Metall, 7 × 25 × 17,3 cm, undatiert; Aufbewahrungsbox für zugesandte Palmenpostkarten, in Besitz von Alf Trojan
Coconut candy box (made in Hongkong) with 46 postcards, metal, 2.76 × 9.84 × 6.81 in, undated; container for sent palm tree postcards, property of Alf Trojan

240
Rumbohnen-Verpackung Karton, Kunststoff, 2,7 × 26,8 × 14,5 cm, 2004/Rotterdam; Löcher
Rum bean packaging cardboard, plastic, 1.06 × 10.55 × 5.7 in, 2004/ Rotterdam; holes

241–242
Teller Emaille,
2,3 × 15,2 cm, undatiert; als Aschenbecher genutzt, Rost, Kratzer
Plate enamel,
0.9 × 5.98 in, undated; used as ashtray, rust, scratches

Löffel Silber,
1,2 × 10,3 × 2 cm, 1979/Japan; leicht angelaufen
Spoon silver,
0.47 × 4.05 × 0.78 in, 1979/Japan; slightly tarnished

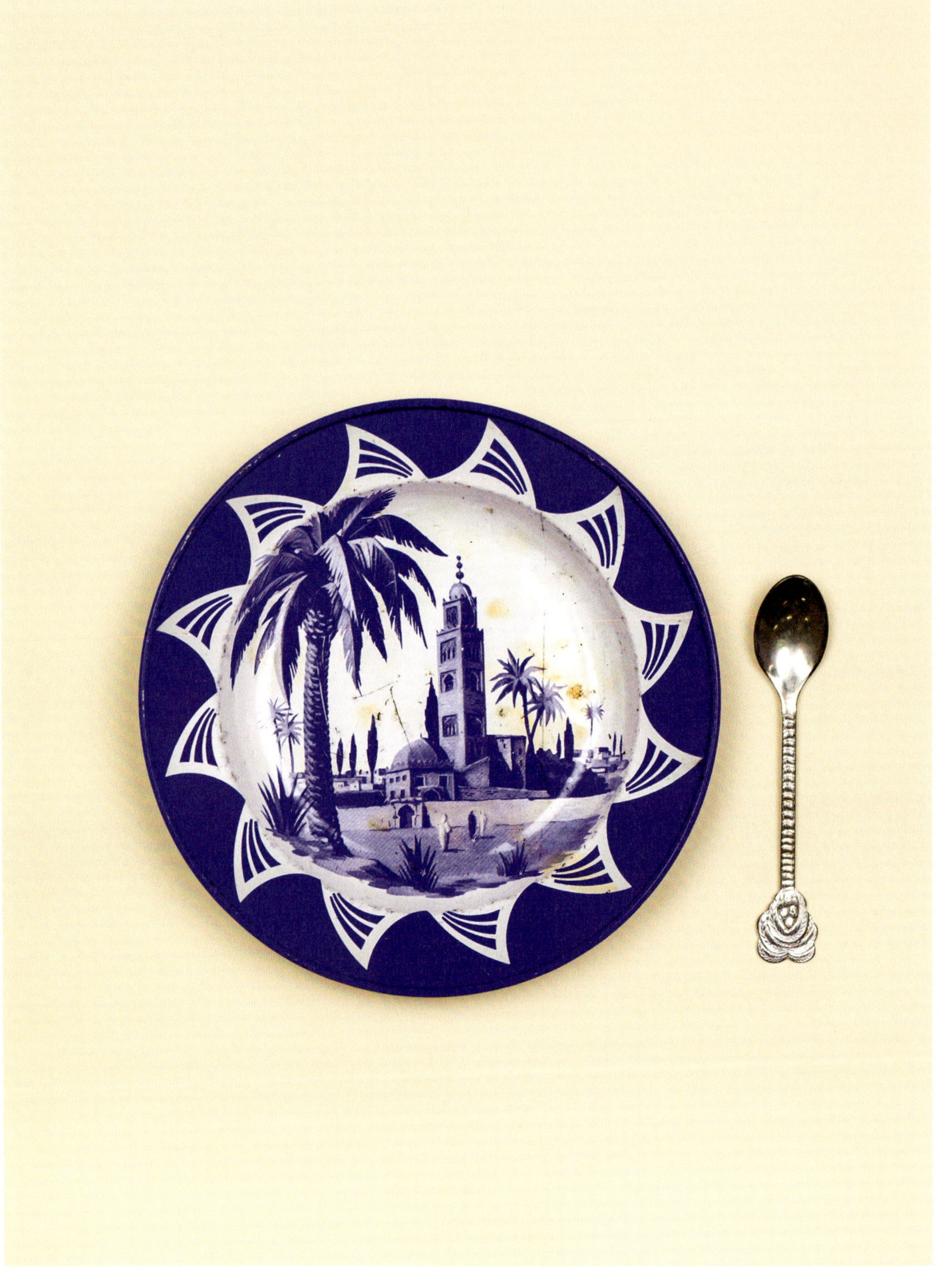

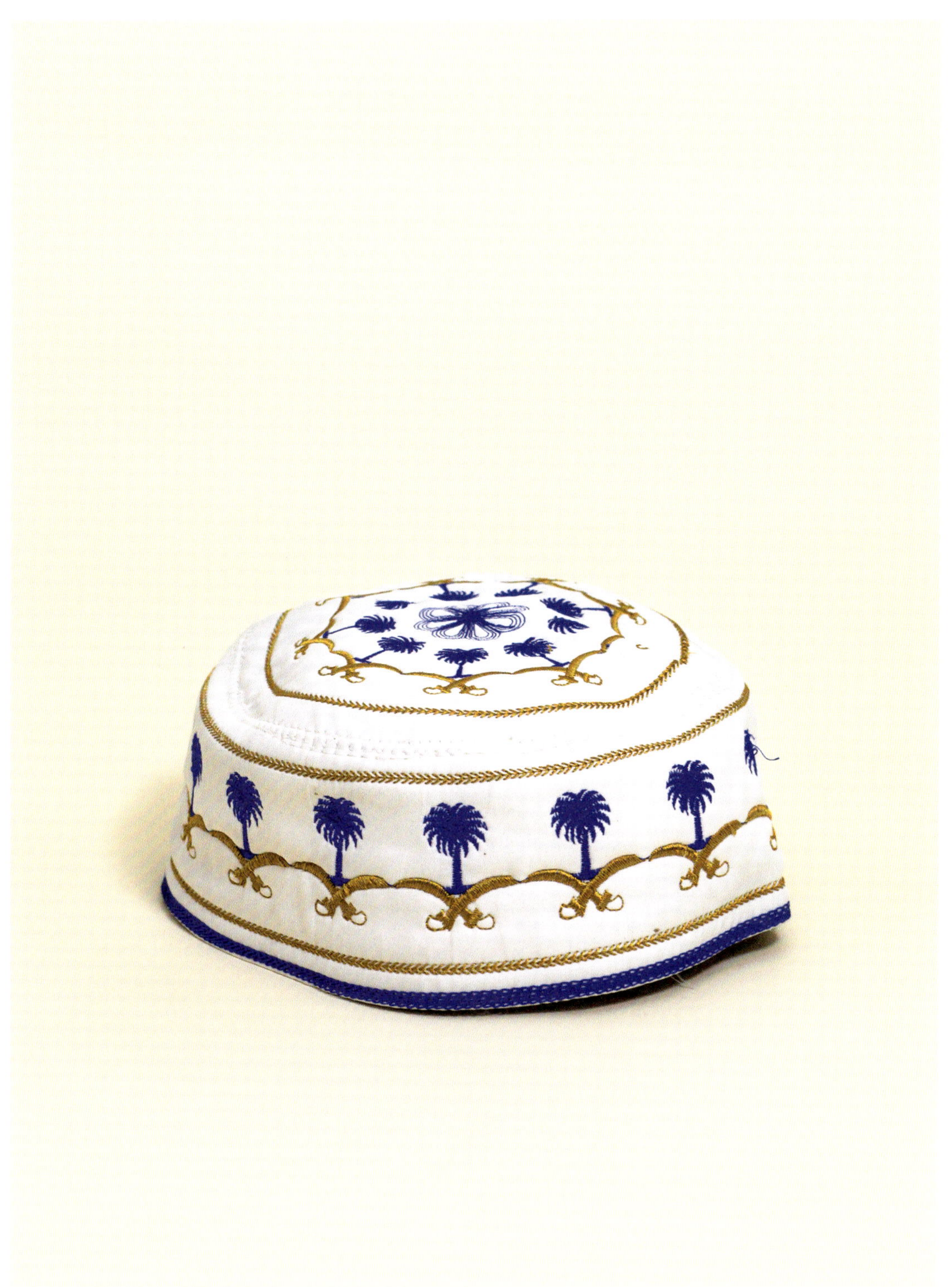

243
Hut Gr. 58 (made in China), Baumwolle, Polyester, 6,5 × 18 cm, 2007/Wochenmarkt in Had Draa, Marokko; Geschenk der Ehefrau, wie neu
Hat size 58 (made in China), cotton, polyester, 2.56 × 7.09 in, 2007/market Had Draa, Morocco; gift from wife, like new

244
Modellbaupalme Kunststoff, 13,9 × 5,5 cm, undatiert; wie neu
Model kit palm tree plastic, 5.47 × 2.16 in, undated; like new

245
Dekopalme Kunststoff, 5,9 × 4,6 cm, undatiert; leicht verstaubt
Decorative palm tree plastic, 2.32 × 1.81 in, undated; slightly dusty

246
Dekopalme Holz, 12,2 × 7,3 × 1,8 cm, undatiert; leichte Gebrauchsspuren
Decorative palm tree wood, 4.8 × 2.87 × 0.7 in, undated; slight signs of wear

247
Dekopalmenlandschaft (Handarbeit), Ton, 8,2 × 14,9 × 7,4 cm, undatiert; Palmenwedel fehlen, leichte Gebrauchsspuren
Decorative palm tree landscape (handmade), clay, 3.22 × 5.86 × 2.91 in, undated; palm fronds missing, slight signs of wear

248
Dekopalme, Kunststoff 13,8 × 9 × 2,2 cm, undatiert; in Besitz von Alf Trojan
Decorative palm tree plastic, 5.43 × 3.54 × 0.86 in, undated; property of Alf Trojan

249
Biegsame Dekopalme Aluminiumdraht, 22,1 x 16 cm, undatiert
Bendable decorative palm tree aluminum wire, 8.7 × 6.29 in, undated

250
Modellbaupalme Kunststoff, 18,5 × 12,5 × 8,1 cm, undatiert
Model kit palm tree plastic, 7.28 × 4.92 × 3.18 in, undated

251
Dekopalme bemalt, Zinn, 13,8 × 9,2 × 2,5 cm, undatiert; Geschenk der Ehefrau, Farbe leicht abgeblättert, ein Palmenwedel geknickt
Decorative palm tree painted, tin, 5.43 × 3.62 × 0.98 in, undated; gift from wife, slightly flaking paint

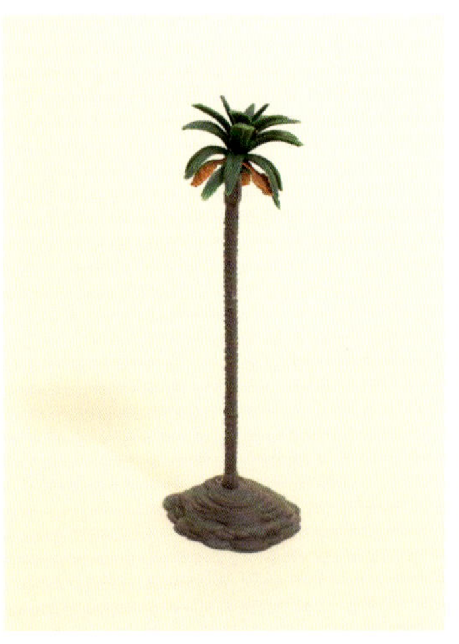
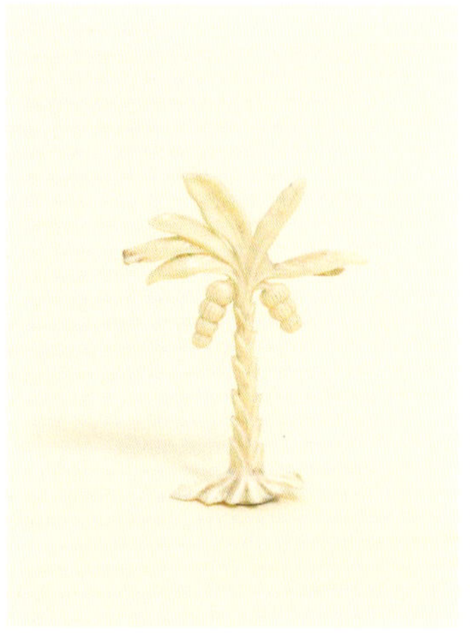
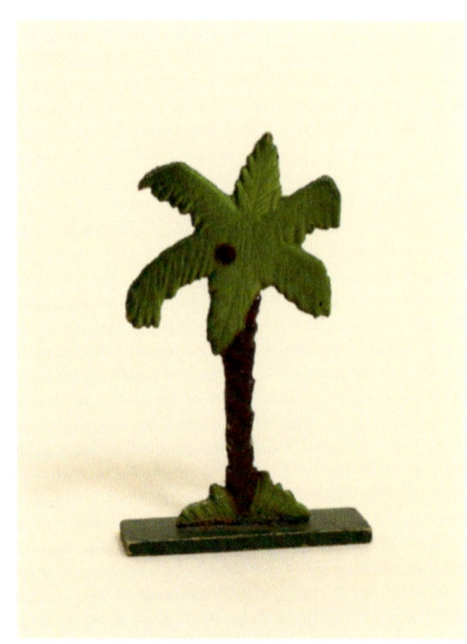
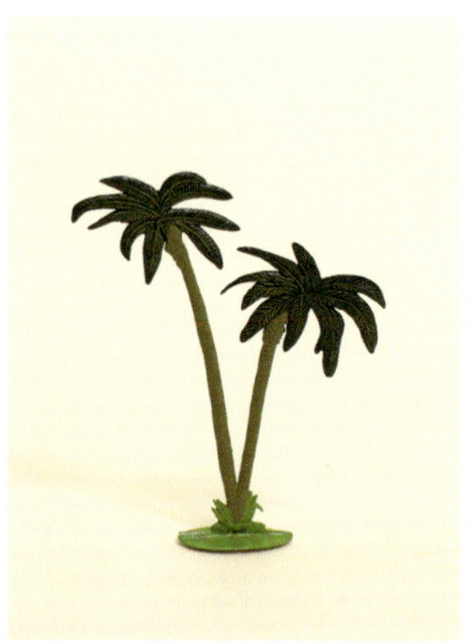
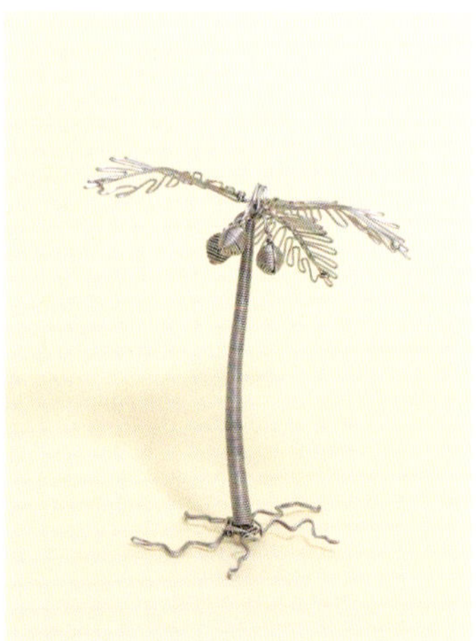
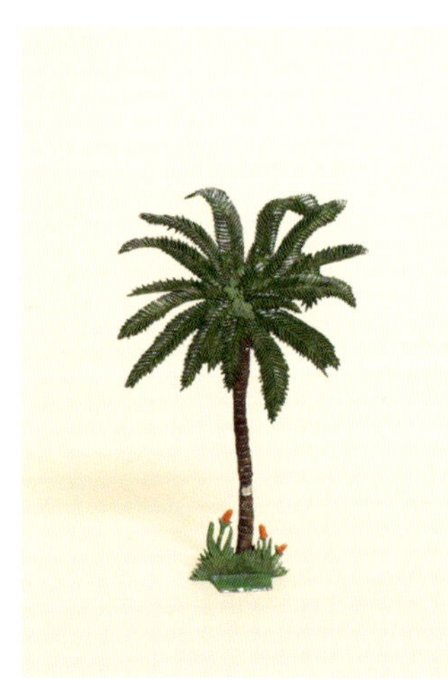
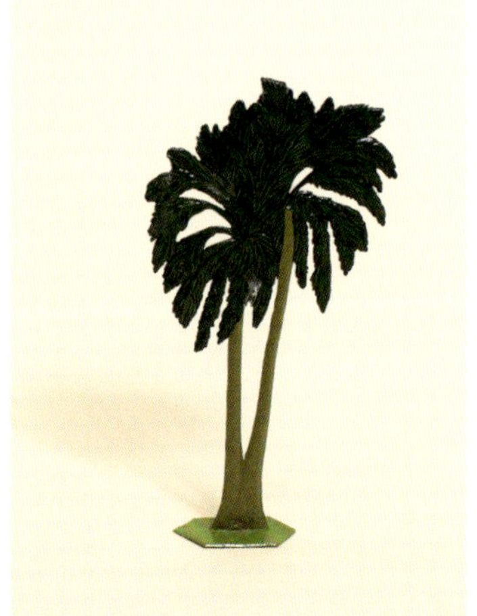

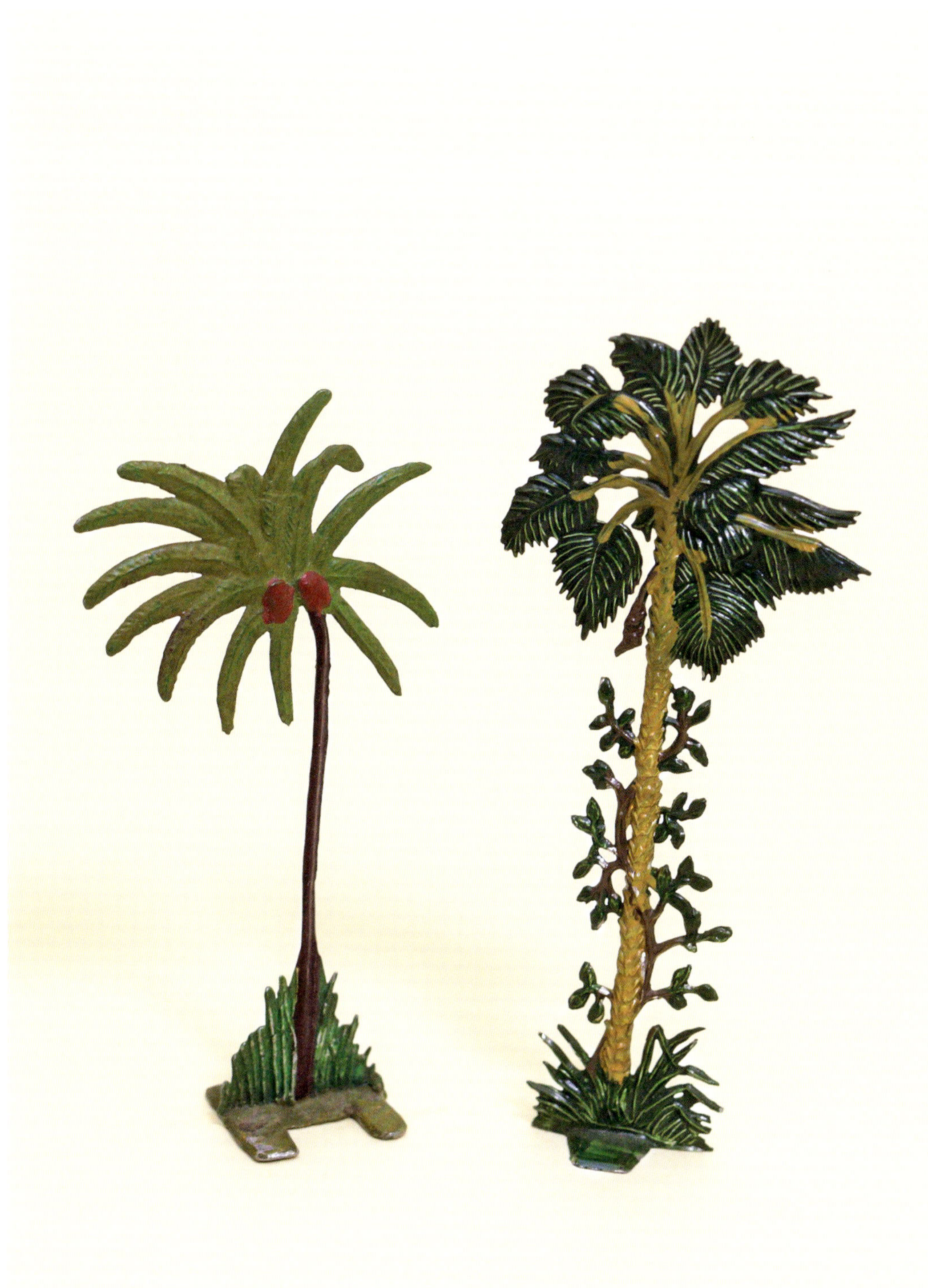

252
Dekopalme handbemalt, Zinn, 14,1 × 7,4 × 2,1 cm, undatiert
Decorative palm tree hand-painted, tin, 5.55 × 2.91 × 0.82 in, undated

253–254
Dekopalme handbemalt, Zinn, 9,9 × 5,3 × 2,3 cm, undatiert; leicht gebogen
Decorative palm tree hand-painted, tin, 3.89 × 2.08 × 0.9 in, undated, slightly bent

Handbemalte Dekopalme Zinn, 11,4 × 5 × 2,1 cm, undatiert;
Decorative palm tree hand-painted, tin, 4.48 × 1.96 × 0.82 in, undated;

255
Halskette mit drei Palmen-anhängern Koralle, Chrysokoll, Messing, 43,5 cm/4 × 2 cm, undatiert; Geschenk der Ehefrau, leichte Gebrauchsspuren
Necklace with three palm tree pendants coral, chrysocolla, brass, 17.12 in/1.57 × 0.78 in, undated; gift from wife, slight signs of wear

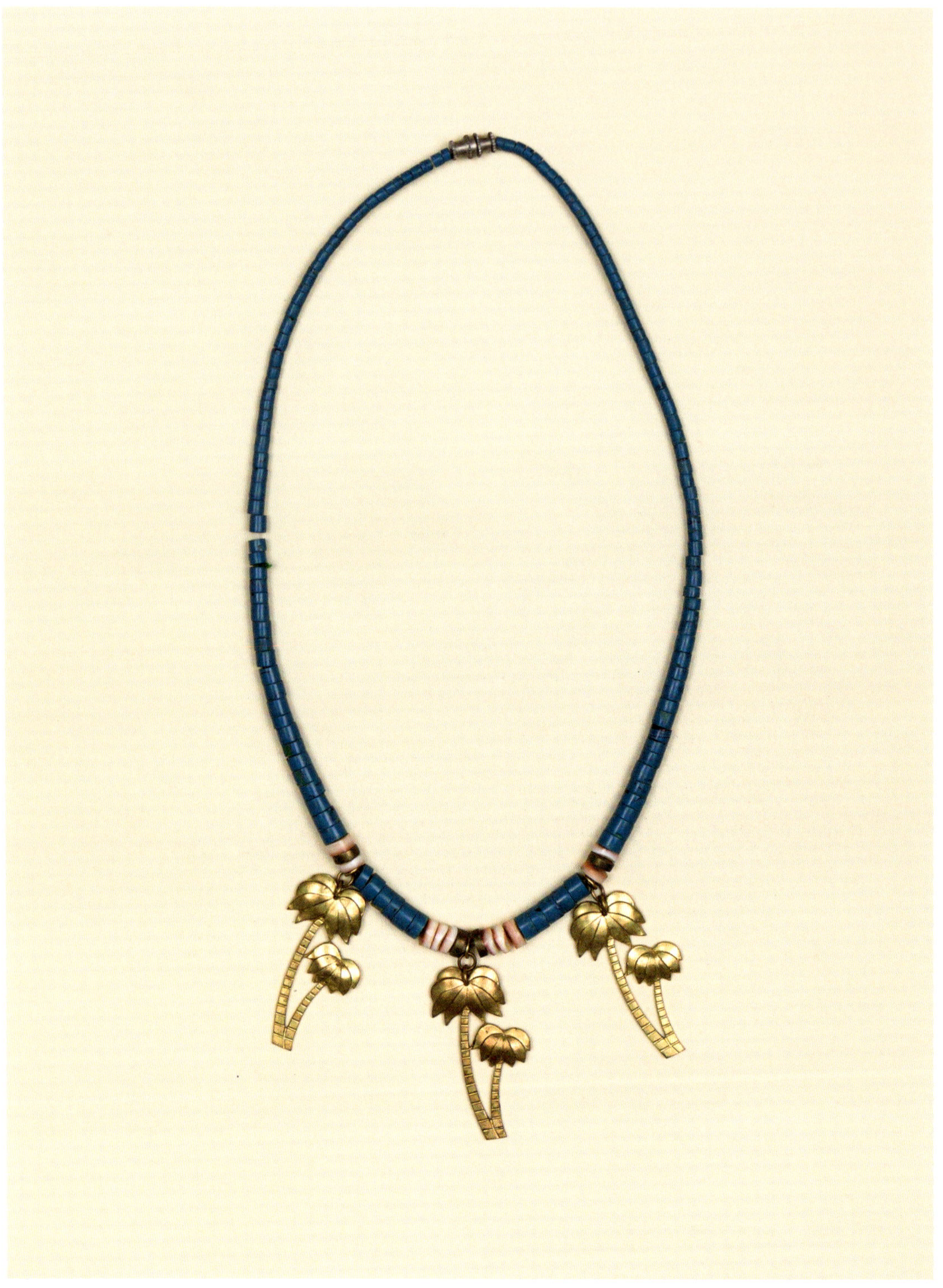

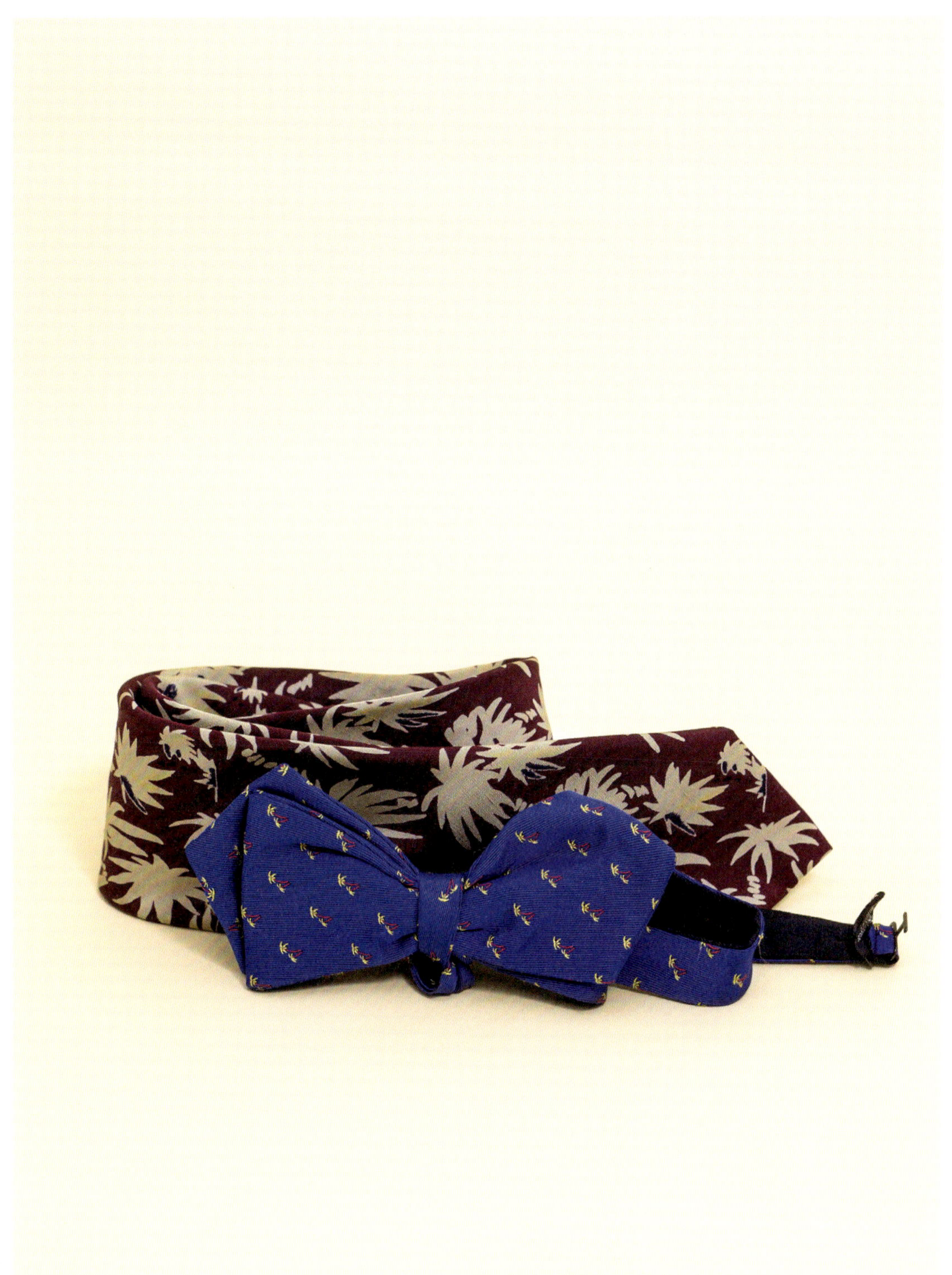

256–257
Fliege Seide, 7 × 5 cm, 2015/ Schweiz; wie neu
Bow tie silk, 2.75 × 5.9 in, 2015/ Switzerland; like new

Krawatte handgenäht, Seide, 143 × 7,6 cm, 2013/ Deutschland; Geschenk der Ehefrau, wie neu
Tie hand-sewn, silk, 56.29 × 2.99 in, 2013/ Germany; gift from wife, like new

258–259
Ohranhänger Perlmutt, Metall, 8 × 3,5 cm, undatiert; in Besitz von Alf Trojan
Ear pendant nacre, metal, 3.14 × 1.37 in, undated; property of Alf Trojan

Ohranhänger Perlmutt, 7 x 5 cm, undatiert; in Besitz von Alf Trojan
Ear pendant, nacre, 2.75 × 1.96 in, undated; property of Alf Trojan

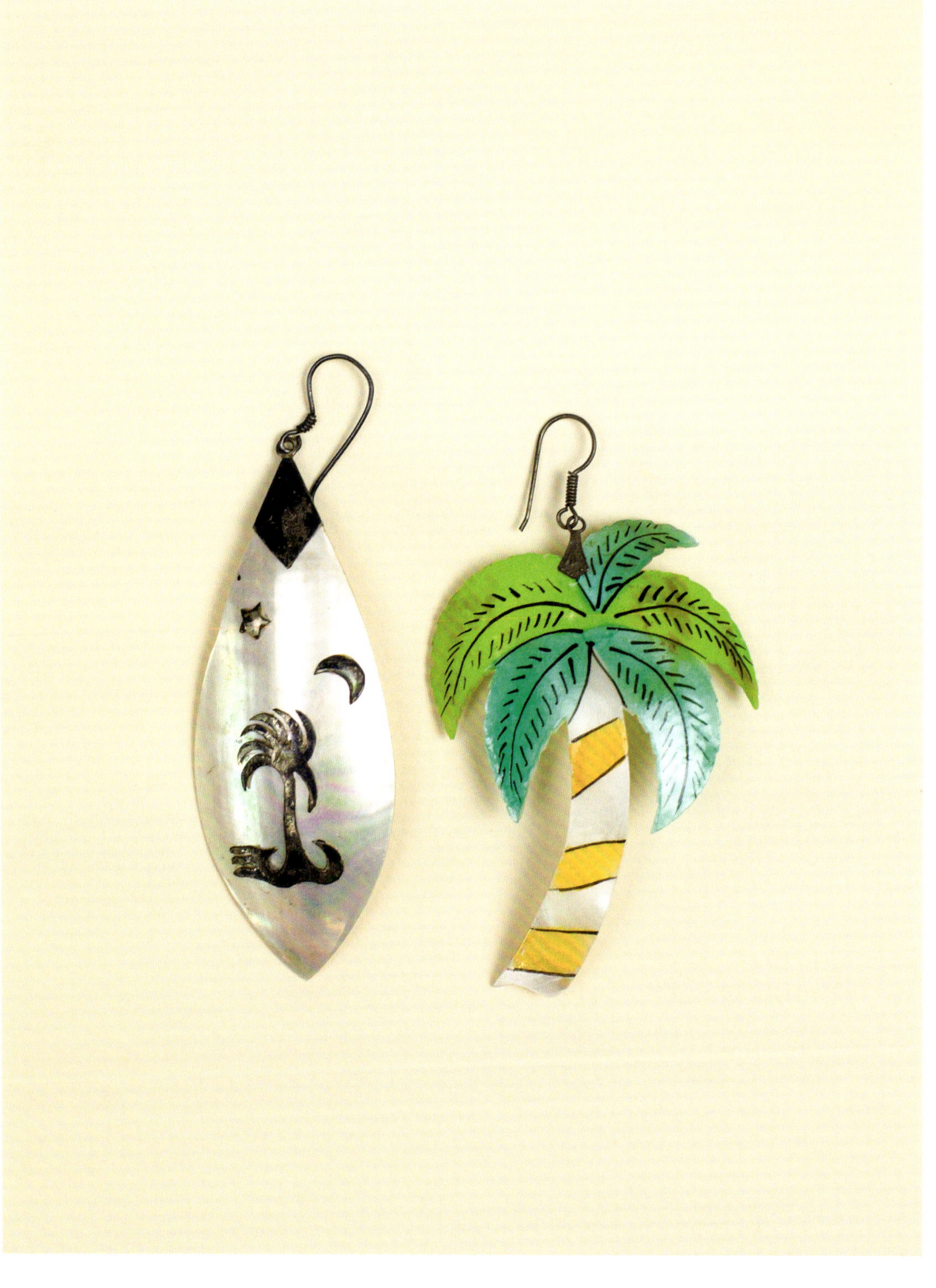

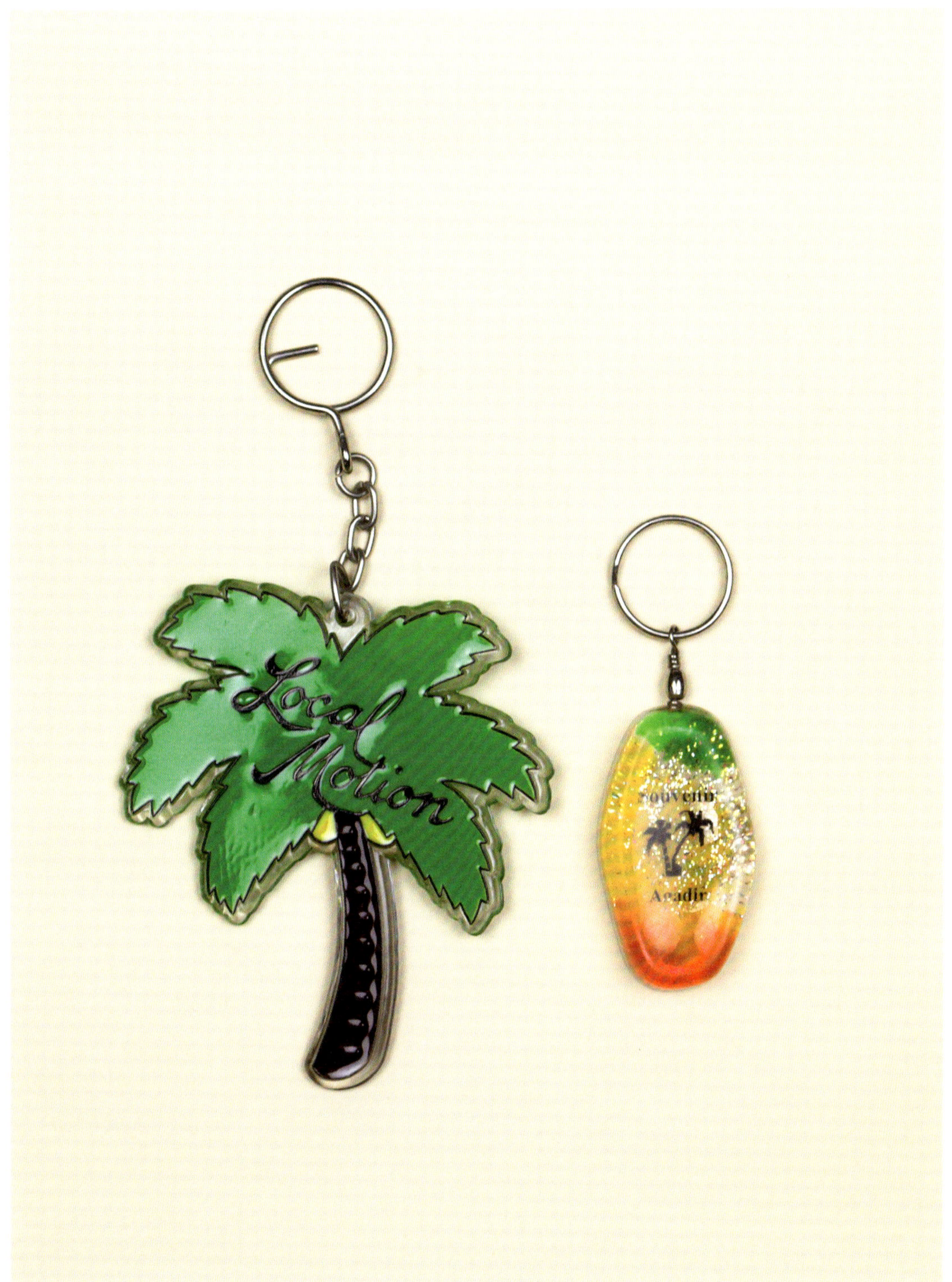

260–261
Schlüsselanhänger „Local Motion“ Acrylglas, Metall, 10 × 8,4 cm, 1999/ Jamaika; wie neu
Keyring pendant “Local Motion” acrylic glass, metal, 3.93 × 3.3 in, 1999/Jamaica; like new

Schlüsselanhänger Kunststoff, Metall, 0,9 × 5,3 × 3,4 cm, 2005/ Agadir; wie neu
Keyring pendant plastic, metal, 0.35 × 2.08 × 1.33 in, 2005/ Agadir; like new

262–292
Kunststoffbox mit einunddreißig Palmenansteckern
Kunststoff, 30,5 × 16,5 × 1,8 cm, undatiert; täglich in Gebrauch, in Besitz von Alf Trojan
Plastic box with thirty-one palm tree pins
plastic, 12 × 6.49 × 0.7 in, undated; in everyday use, property of Alf Trojan

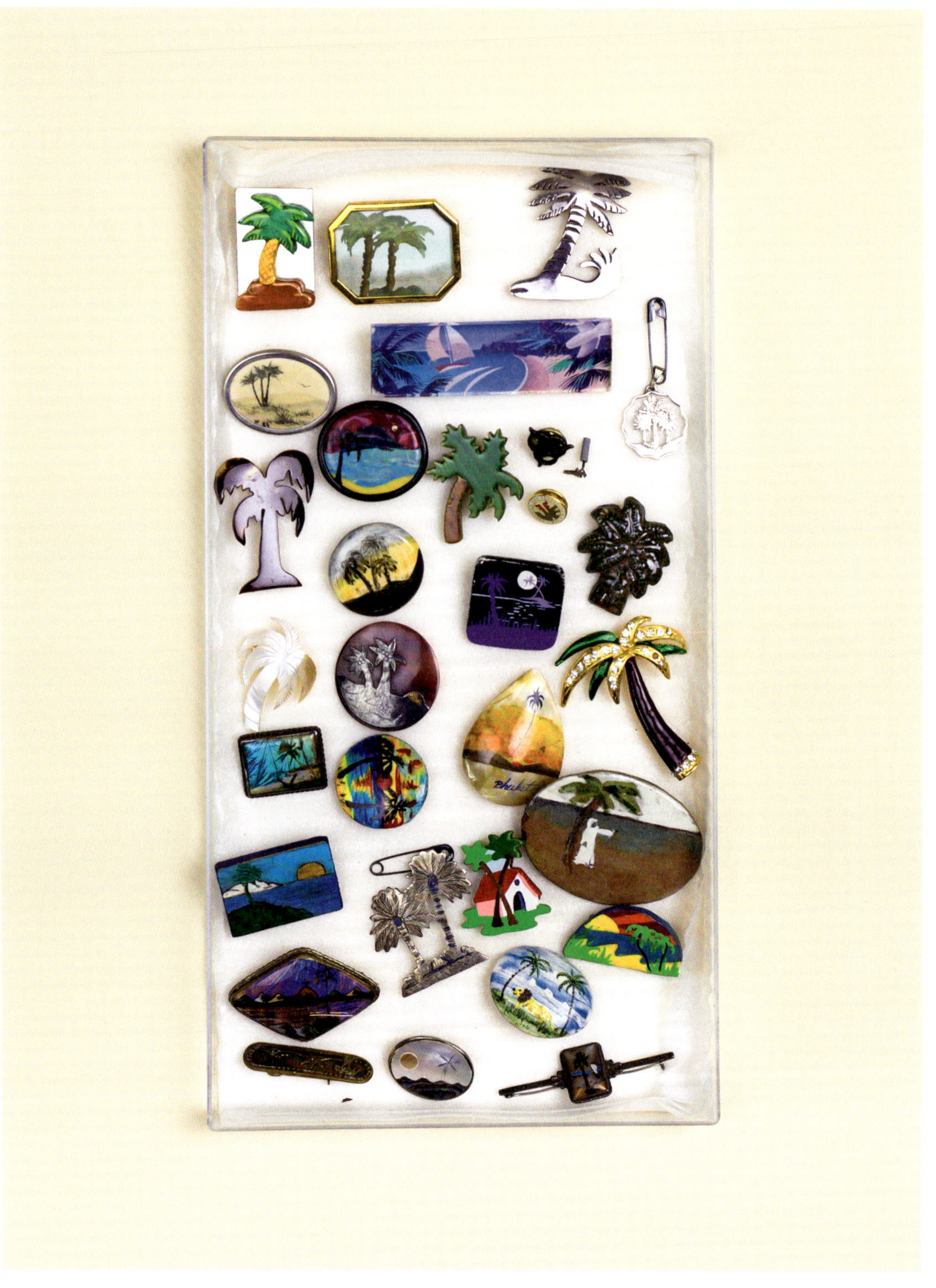

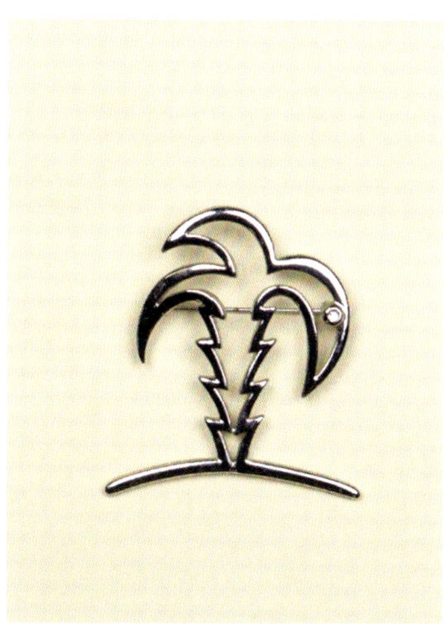
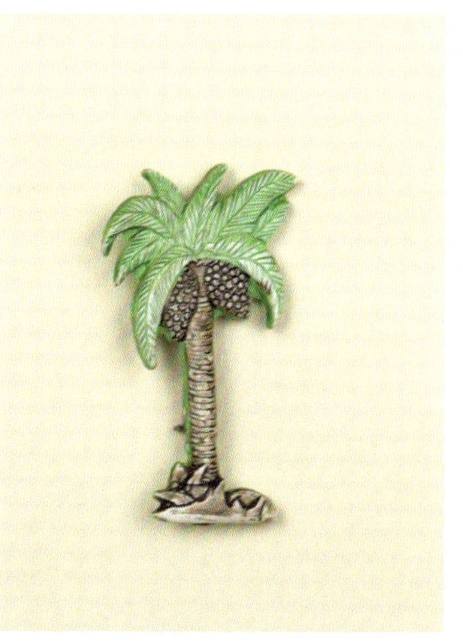
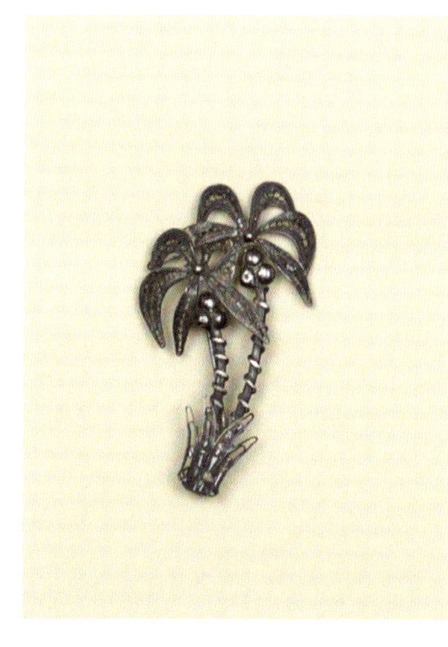
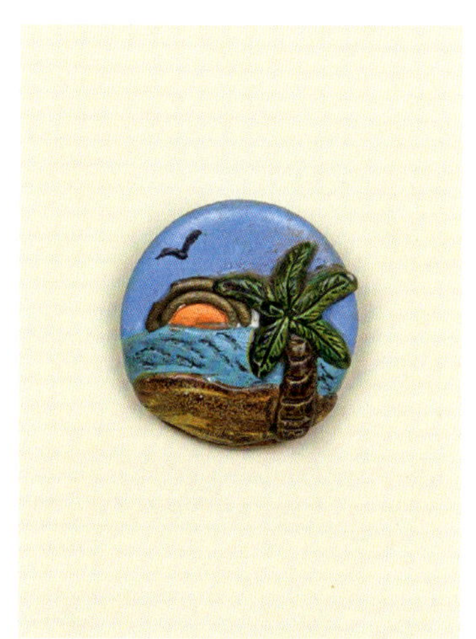
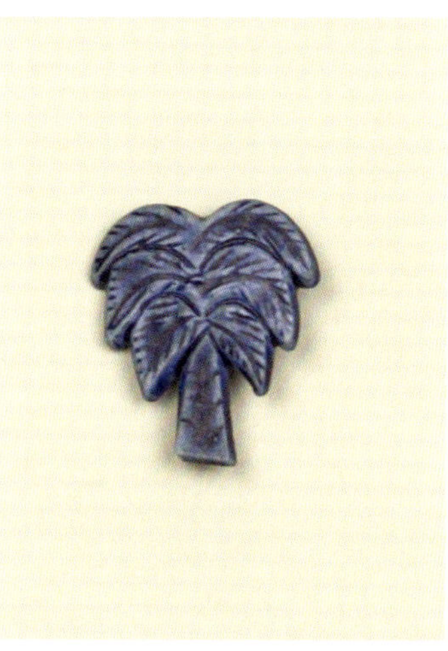
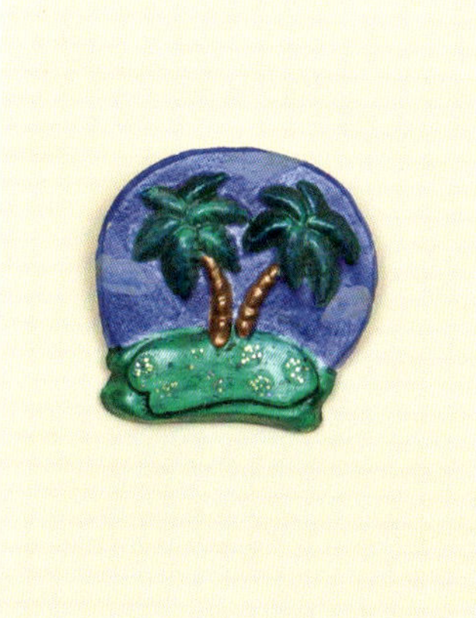
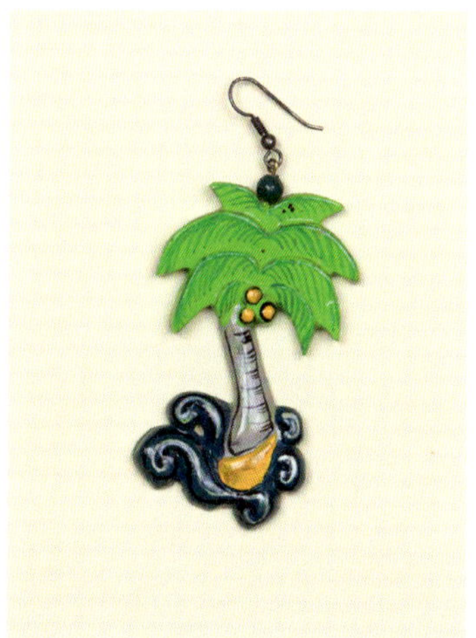
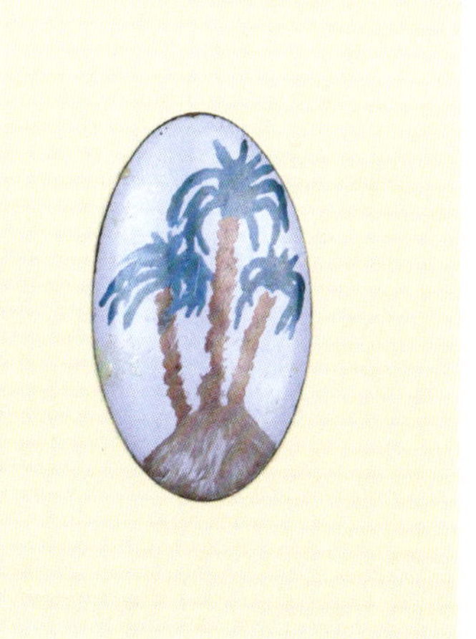
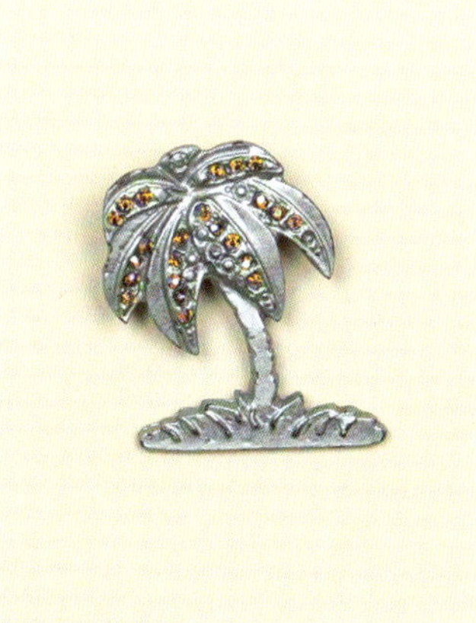

293
Anstecker Metall, 5,7 × 5,3 cm, undatiert; wie neu
Pin metal, 2.24 × 2.08 in, undated; like new

294
Anstecker Kunststoff, 5,4 × 3,1 cm, undatiert; Farbe leicht ausgeblichen
Pin plastic, 2.12 × 1.22 in, undated; slightly faded colors

295
Anstecker Metall, 4,3 x 2,4 cm, undatiert; wie neu
Pin metal, 1.69 x 0.94 in, undated; like new

296
Anstecker handgemacht, Fimo-Knetmasse, 3,4 × 4,4 cm, undatiert
Pin handmade, Fimo-polymer clay, 1.33 × 1,73 in, undated

297
Anstecker Kunststoff, 3,2 × 2,6 cm, undatiert; leicht ausgeblichen
Pin plastic, 1.25 × 1.02 in, undated; slightly faded colors

298
Anstecker handgemacht, Ton, 6 × 6,2 cm, undatiert; leichte Gebrauchsspuren
Pin handmade, clay, 2.36 × 2.44 in, undated; slight signs of wear

299
Ohranhänger Holz, Metall, 7,1 × 4,2 cm, undatiert; leichte Gebrauchsspuren
Ear pendant wood, metal, 2.79 × 1.65 in, undated; slight signs of wear

300
Anstecker Metall, 5,8 × 3,4 cm, undatiert; Flecken
Pin metal, 2.28 × 1.33 in, undated; stains

301
Anstecker Metall, 3,8 × 3,3 × 0,8 cm, undatiert; leichte Gebrauchsspuren
Pin metal, 1.49 × 1.29 × 0.31 in, undated; slight signs of wear

302
Kunstwerk Gusseisen, Holz, Gummi, 28,5 × 6,3 × 6,3 cm, 2002; Geschenk an den Sammler, angefertigt von einem Künstlerfreund, der vorrangig mit Materialien aus Müll arbeitet, in Besitz von Alf Trojan
Artwork cast iron, wood, rubber, 11.22 × 2.48 × 2.48 in, 2002; gift to the collector, handmade by an artist friend, who primarily recycles garbage materials in his work, property of Alf Trojan

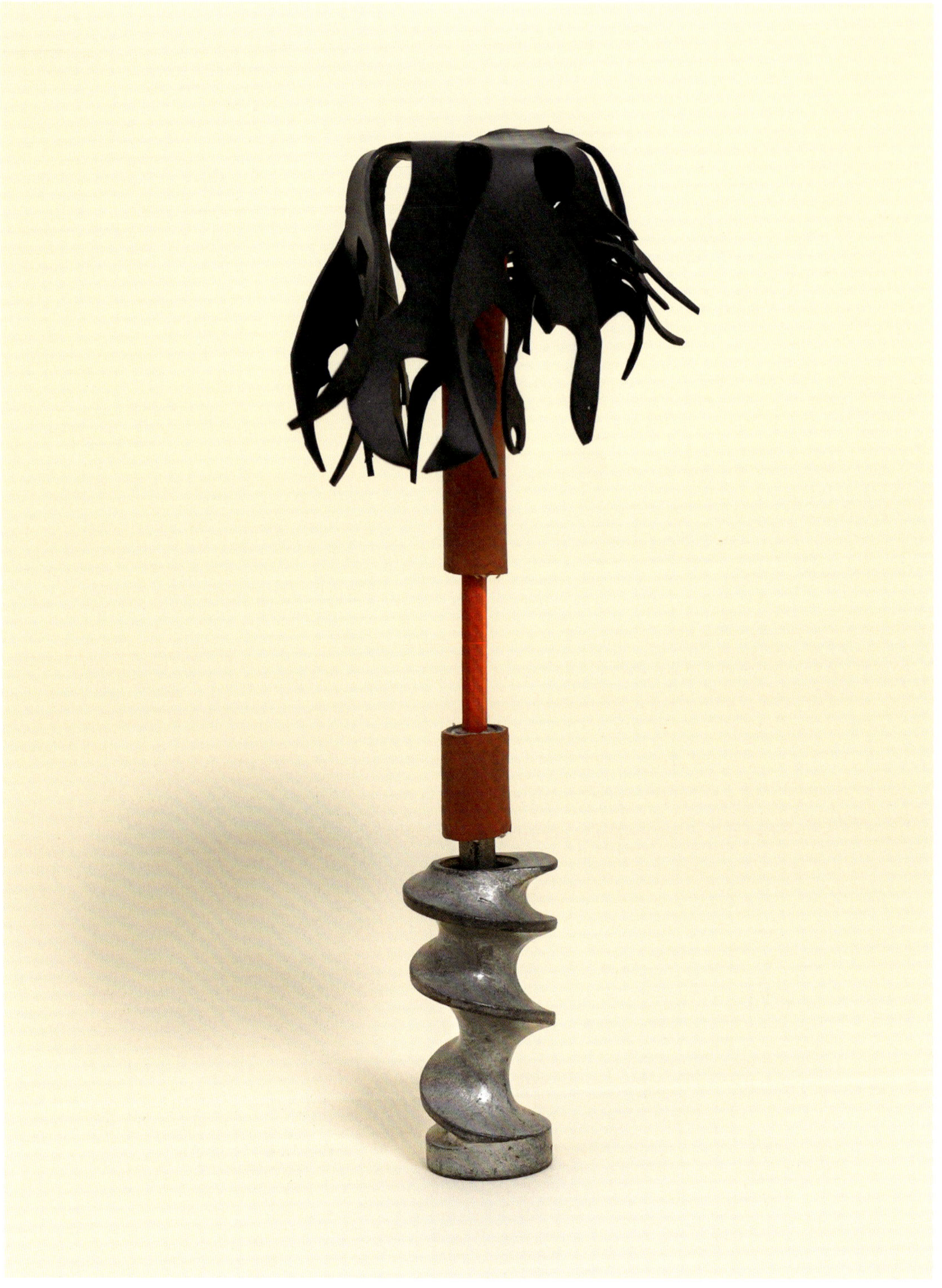

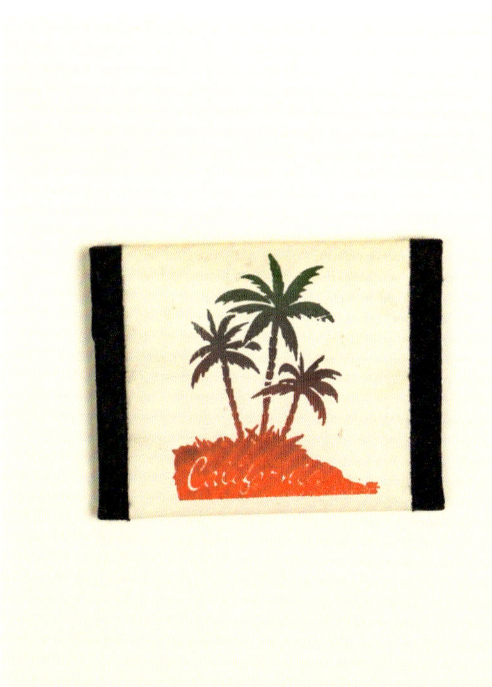

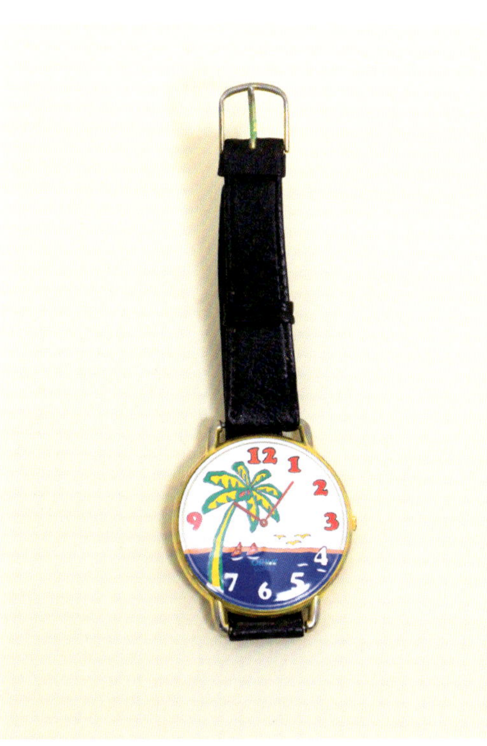

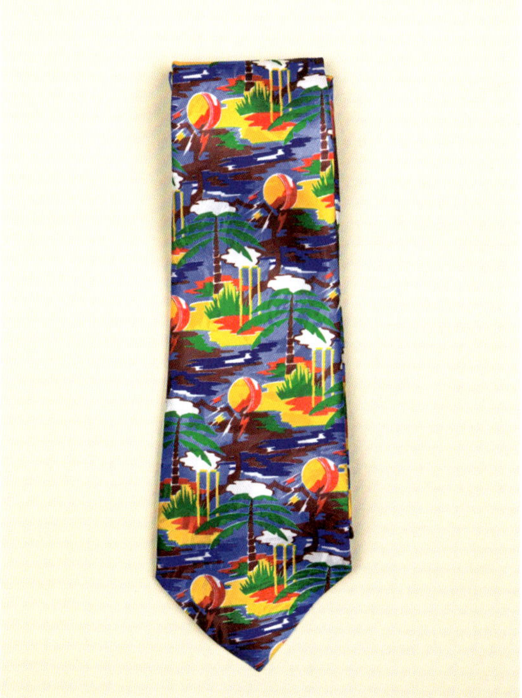

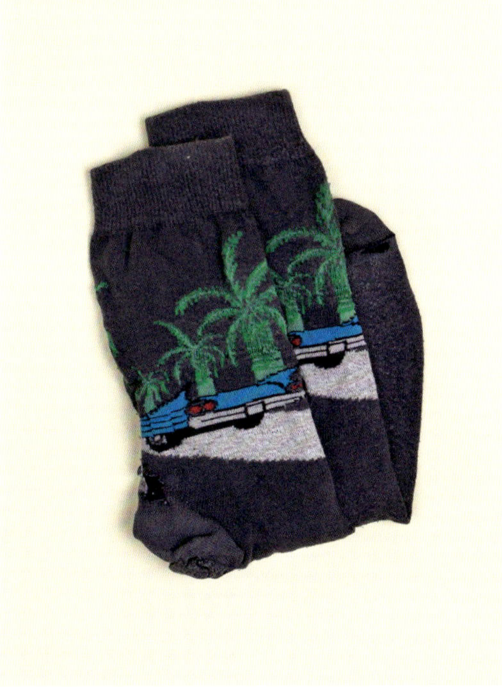

303
Geldbörse mit Klettverschluss
Polyester, 11,8 × 8,9 cm, undatiert; leichte Flecken
Wallet with velcro fastener
polyester, 4.64 × 3.5 in, undated; light stains

304
Armbanduhr Metall, Kunststoff, Leder, 15 × 4 × 4 cm, bemaltes Ziffernblatt; wird nur zu besonderen Anlässen getragen, in Besitz von Alf Trojan
Wristwatch metal, plastic, leather, 5.90 × 1.57 × 1.57 in, painted clock face; only used at special occasions, property of Alf Trojan

305
Krawatte Polyester, 143 × 9 cm, 1990/London; Geschenk der Ehefrau, wie neu
Tie polyester, 56.29 × 3.54 in, 1990/London; gift from wife

306
Ein Paar Socken Baumwolle, 34,5 × 8,3 cm, undatiert; stark durchgelaufen, in Besitz von Alf Trojan
Pair of socks cotton, 13.58 × 3.26 in, undated; well worn, property of Alf Trojan

307–308
Flasche „Florida Water“
Glas, Papier, Parfum, 11,7 × 5 cm, 2003/Jamaika; ¾ gefüllt
Bottle of “Florida Water”
glass, paper, perfume, 4.6 × 1.96 in, 2003/Jamaica; ¾ filled

Flasche Glas, Papier, 6,5 × 2,7 × 1,7 cm, undatiert; ohne Inhalt
Bottle glass, paper, 2.55 × 1.06 × 0.66 in, undated; without content

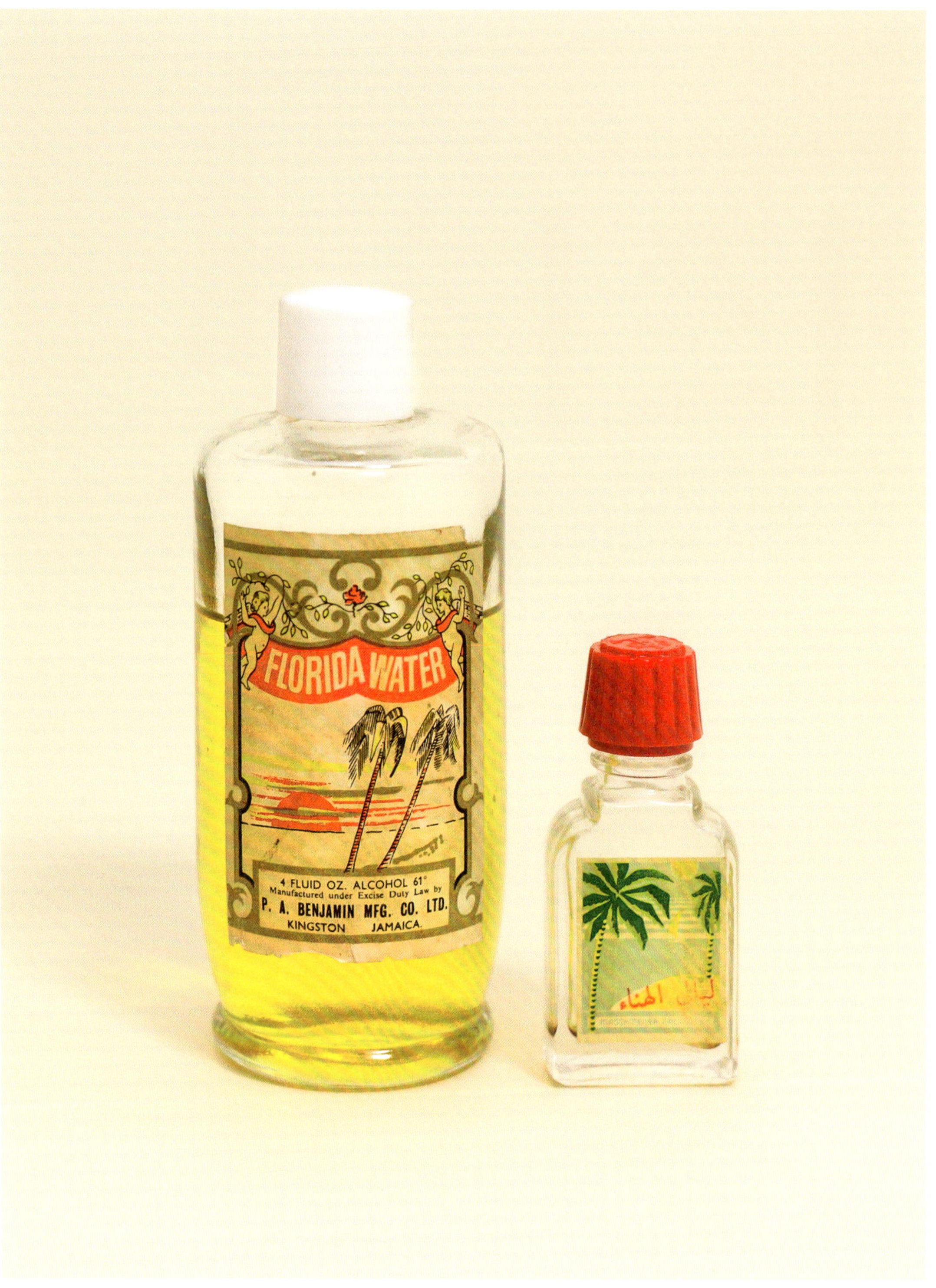

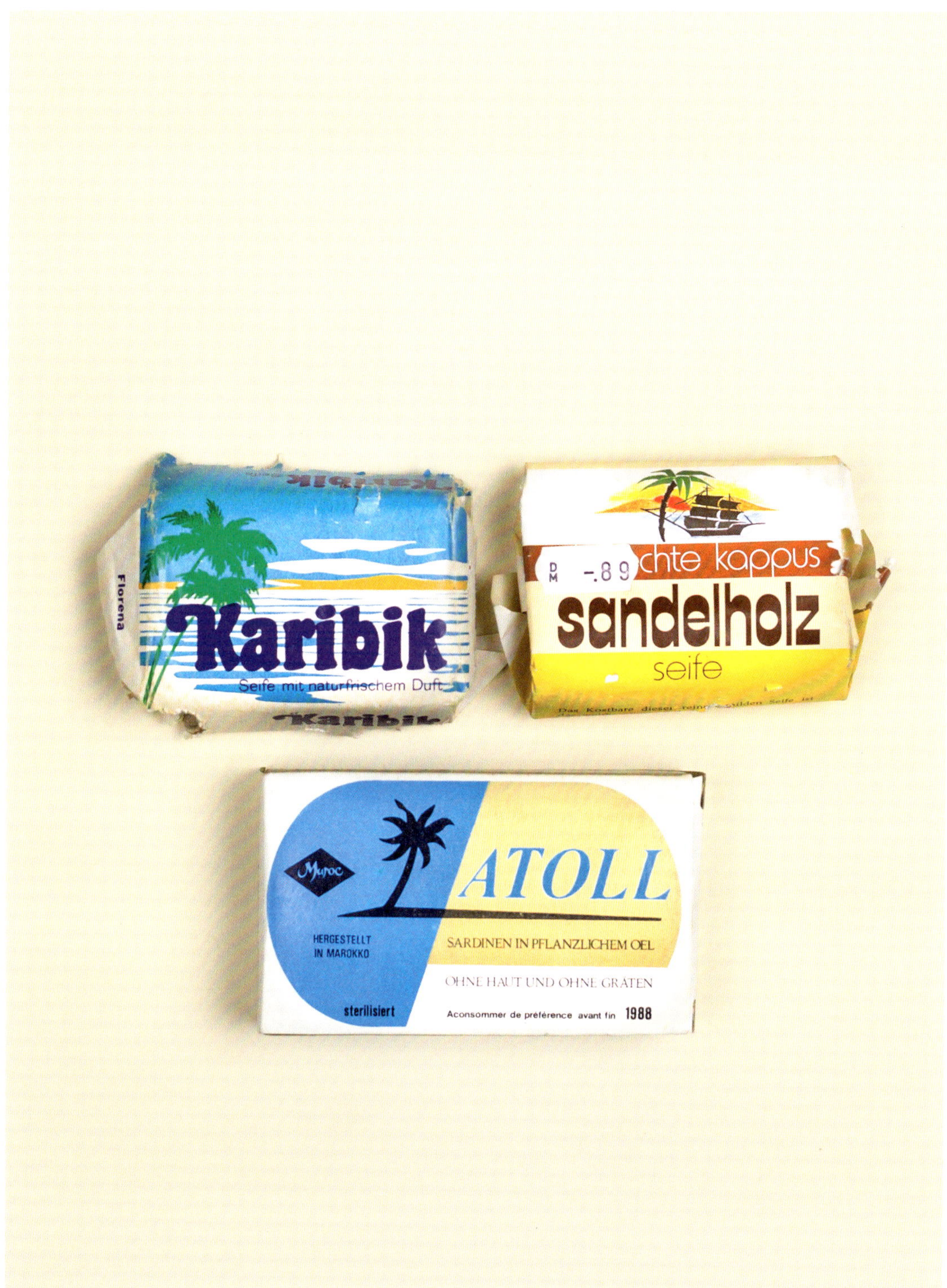

309–311
Seife „Karibik“ Papier, Seife, 3 × 8 × 6,2 cm, undatiert; starke Gebrauchsspuren
Soap “Caribbean” paper, soap, 1.18 × 3.14 × 2.44 in, undated; heavy signs of wear

Sandelholzseife Papier, Seife, 2,8 × 8,4 × 6,2 cm, 1998/Deutschland; starke Gebrauchsspuren, Neupreis 0,98 DM
Sandelwood soap paper, soap, 1.1 × 3.3 × 2.44 in, 1998/Germany; heavy signs of wear, original price 0,98 DM

Sardinenbüchse „Atoll“ Metall, Karton, Sardinen, 3,2 × 10,6 × 6,3 cm, 1998/Souvenir Marokko; ungeöffnet
Tin of sardines “Atoll” metal, cardboard, sardines, 1.25 × 4.17 × 2.48 in, 1998/souvenir Morocco; unopened

312
Tüte Papier, Polyester, 24,2 × 14 × 5,5 cm, 1978/ Ladengeschäft „Babylonia“ Rom; Gebrauchsspuren
Bag paper, polyester, 9.52 × 5.51 × 2.16 in, 1978/ retail store “Babylonia” Rome; signs of wear

313
Laptophülle von „Woouf“ Polyester, Metall, 22,5 × 33 × 1,5 cm, 2017; Geschenk (kurz vor Aufgabe der Sammlung)
Laptop case by “Woouf” polyester, metal, 8.85 × 12.99 × 0.59 in, 2017; gift (shortly before collection was dissolved)

314
Snoopy-Tragetasche „Born to be in the sun“ Polyester, Baumwolle, 36 × 45 cm, 2006/Dubrovnik; in Besitz von Alf Trojan
Snoopy – carrier bag “Born to be in the sun” polyester, cotton, 14.17 × 17.71 in, 2006/Dubvronik; property of Alf Trojan

315
Faltordner mit Briefen Papier, Karton, Baumwolle, 17,2 × 25,4 × 7 cm, 2002; Geschenk der Ehefrau, in Besitz von Alf Trojan
Foldable file with letters paper, cardboard, cotton, 6.77 × 10 × 2.75 in, 2002; gift from wife, property of Alf Trojan

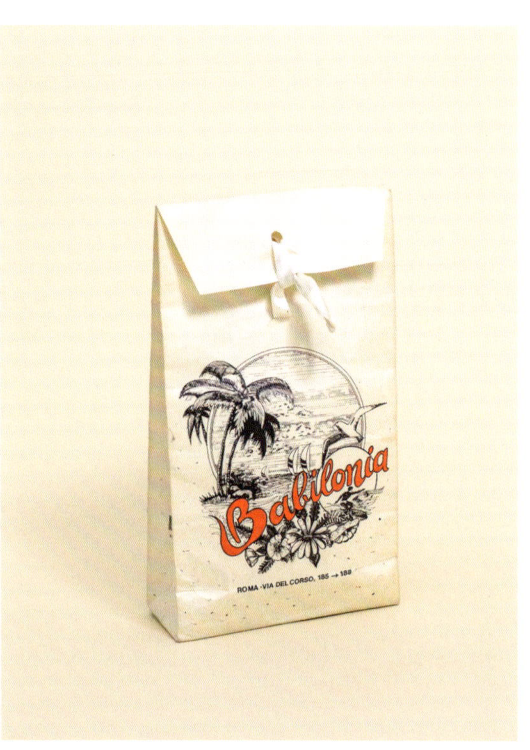

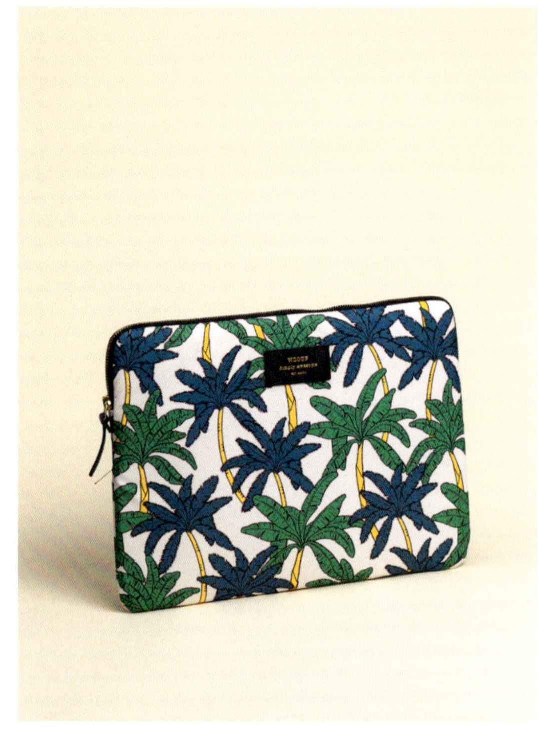

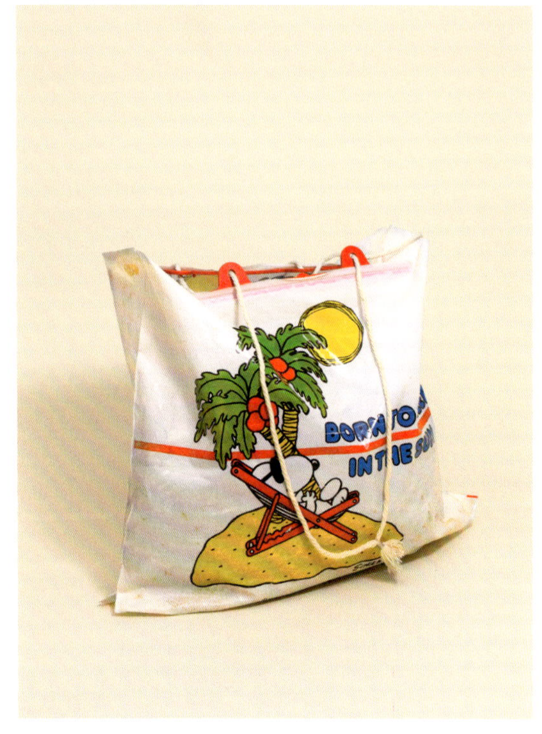

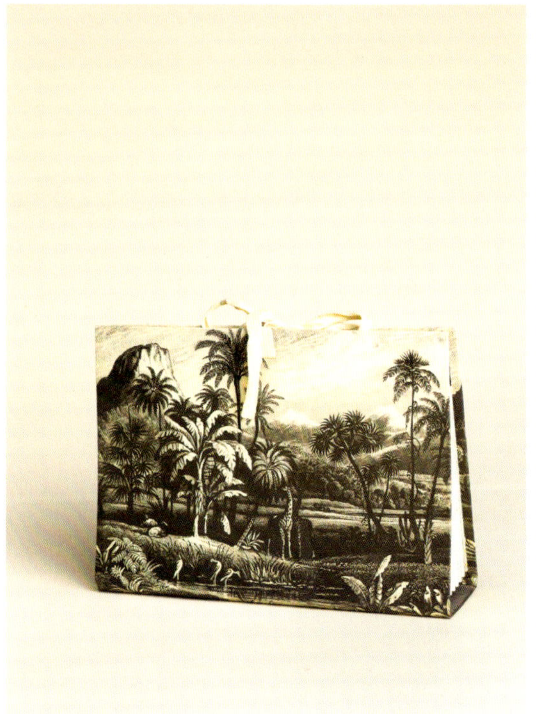

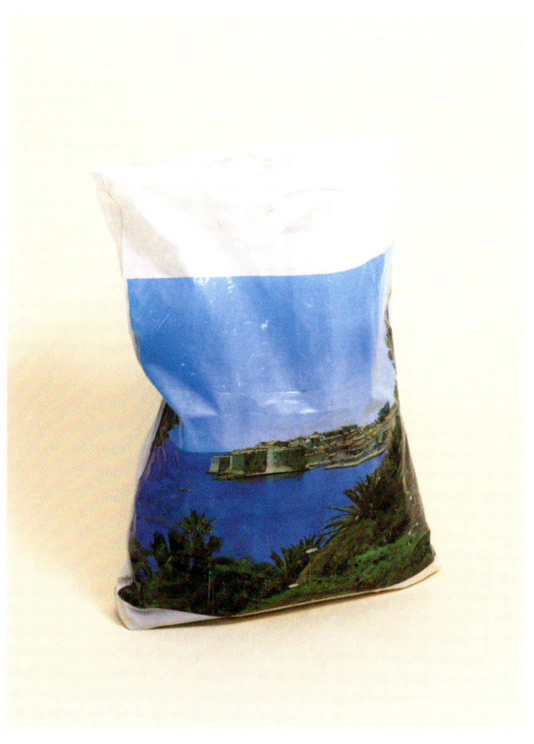

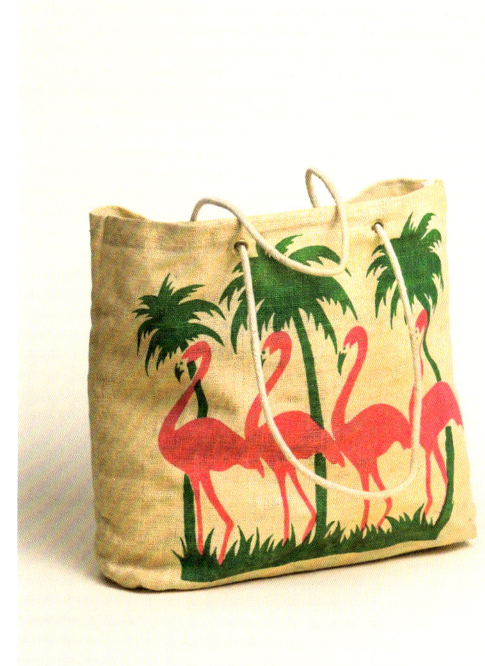

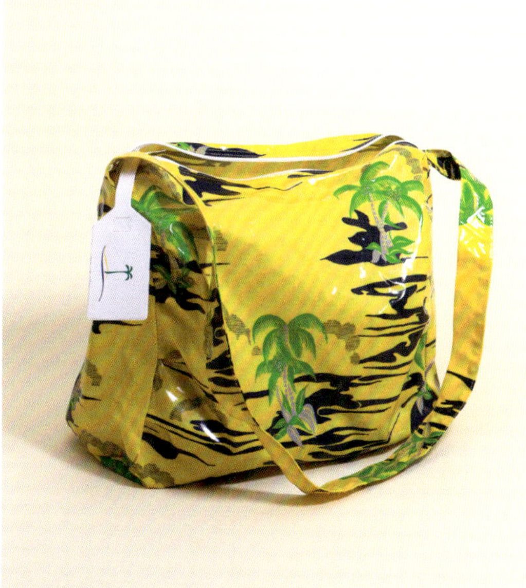

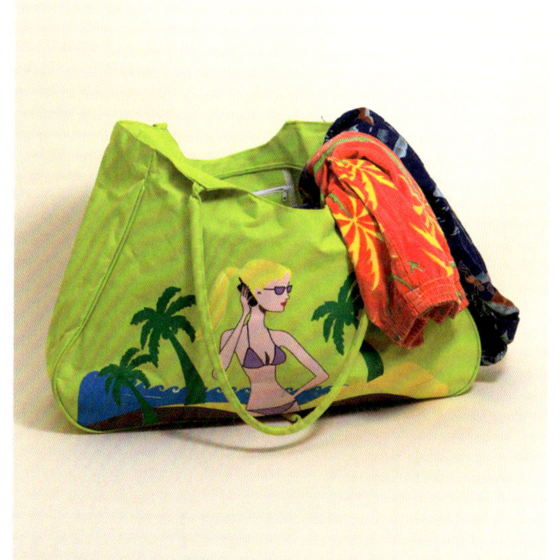

316
Tragetüte Kunststoff, 37 × 44 cm, 2010/Dubrovnik; starke Gebrauchsspuren, Löcher
Carrier bag plastic, 14.56 × 17.32 in, 2010/Dubrovnik; heavy signs of wear, holes

317
Einkaufstasche Bast mit Kunststofffutter, 36 × 39 × 13 cm, undatiert; leichte Gebrauchsspuren
Shopping bag raffia with plastic lining, 14.17 × 15.35 × 5.11 in, undated; slight signs of wear

318
Umhängetasche mit Adressanhänger Polyester, 27,5 × 34,7 × 15,6 cm, undatiert; leichte Flecken
Shoulder bag with address tag polyester, 10.82 × 13.66 × 6.14 in, undated; slight stains

319–321
Strandtasche Stoff, 37,5 × 54,5 × 14,5 cm, undatiert; gut erhalten
Beach bag fabric, 14.76 × 21.45 × 5.7 in, undated; in good condition

Bermuda-Hose Baumwolle (Gr. M), 45 × 33 cm, undatiert; ausgeblichen
Bermuda shorts cotton (size M), 17.71 × 12.99 in, undated; faded colors

Hawaii-Shirt Viskose, 82 × 49, 5 cm, undatiert; in Besitz von Alf Trojan
Hawaiian shirt viscose, 32.28 × 19.49 in, undated; property of Alf Trojan

322–323
Partypalme Selbstgebastelt, Pappe, Krepppapier, 27 × 8,5 × 4,5 cm, undatiert; Wasserschaden
Party palm tree handmade, cardboard, crepe paper, 10.62 × 3.35 × 1.77 in, undated; water damage

Luftschlange Papier, 20 m, undatiert; benutzt
Party streamer paper, 65.61 ft, undated; used

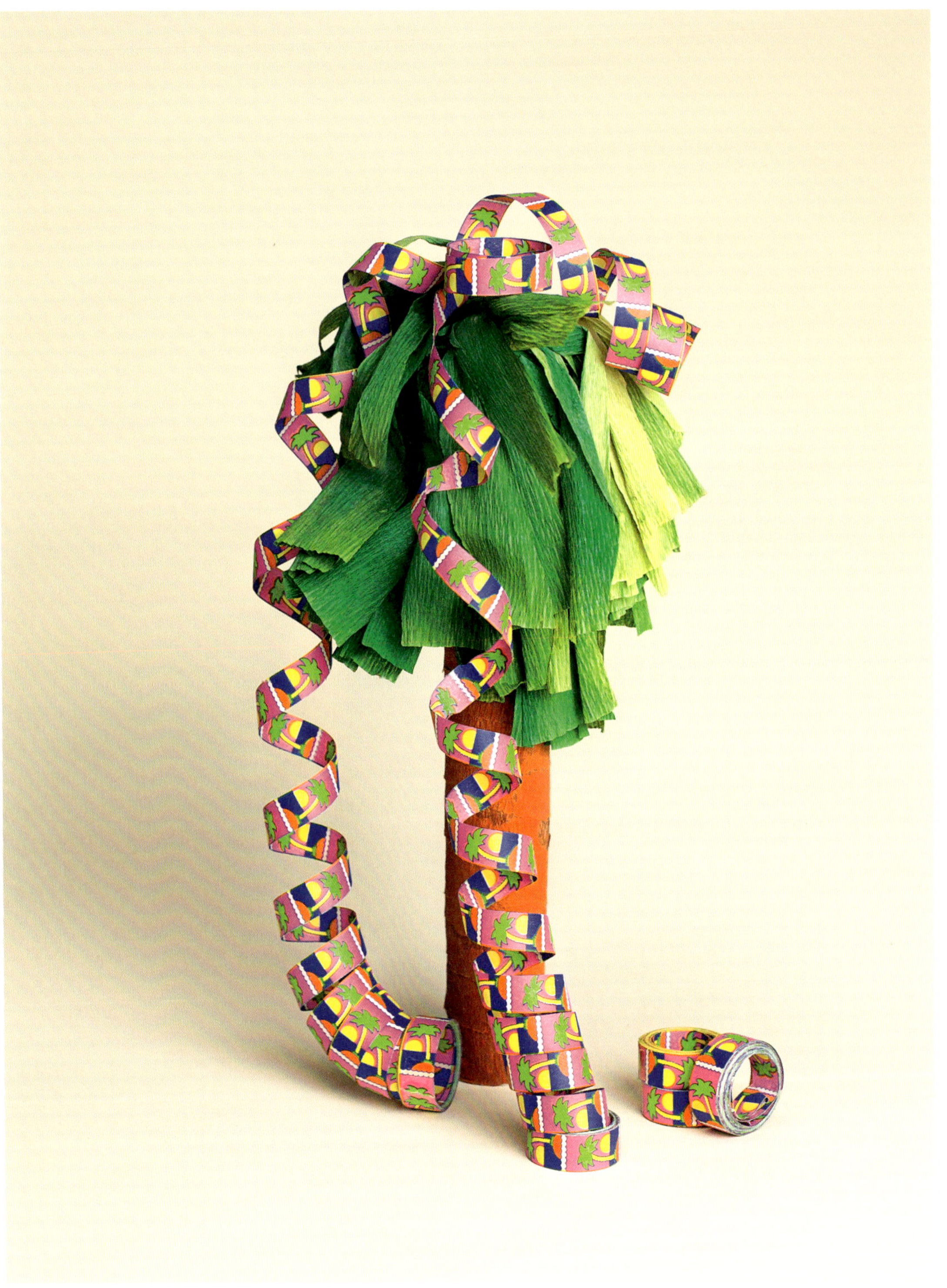

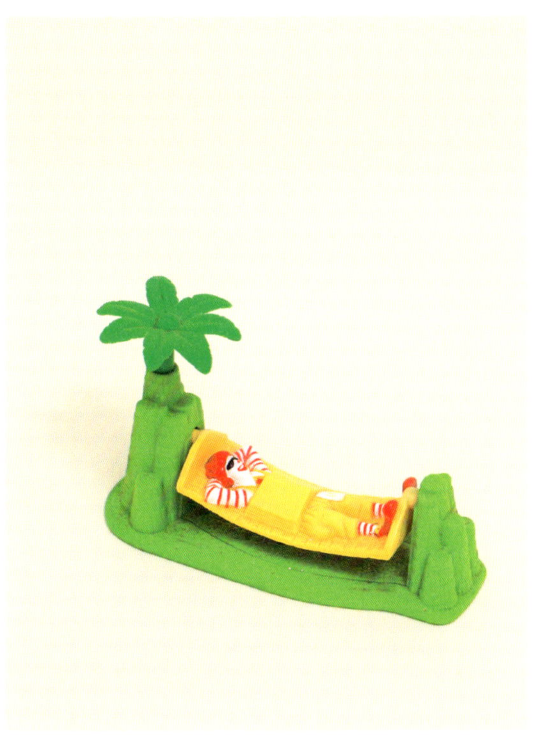

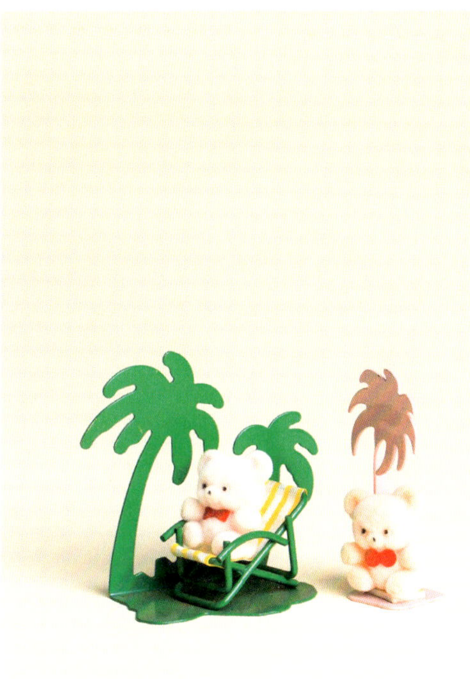

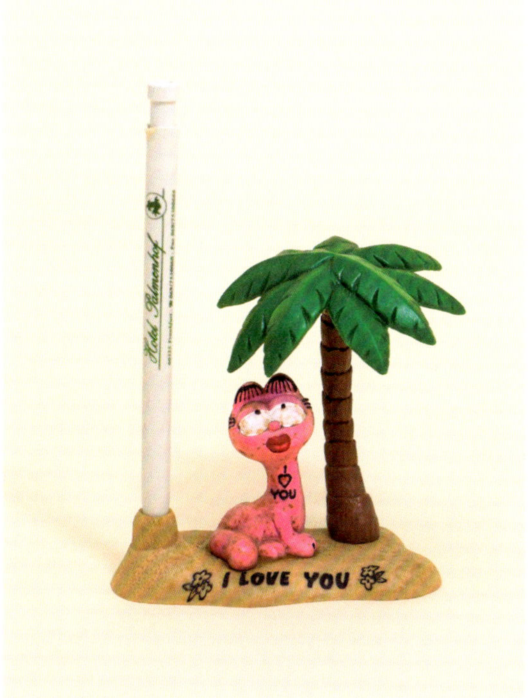

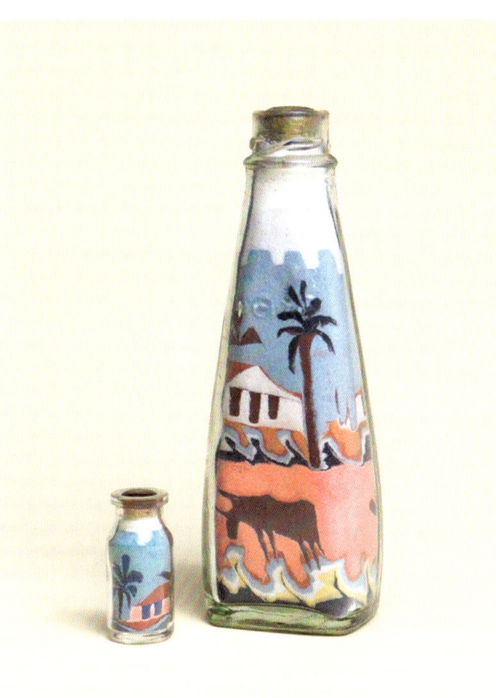

324
Sammelfigur „Ronald McDonald“ (made in China), Kunststoff, 6,7 x 11,4 x 5,2 cm, 1996; Beilage im Happy Meal bei McDonald's, leichte Gebrauchsspuren
Collectable figure “Ronald McDonald” (made in China), plastic, 2.63 x 4.48 x 2.04 in, 1996; supplement of a McDonald's Happy Meal deal, slight signs of wear

325–326
Zwei Dekofiguren „Bärli“ Metall, Stoff, 6,5 x 7,7 x 3,8 cm/6,2 x 3,3 x 2,4 cm, 1989; Geschenk eines Kollegen, leichte Gebrauchsspuren
Two decorative figures “Bärli” metal, fabric, 2,55 x 3,03 x 1,49 in/ 2.44 x 1.29 x 0.94 in, 1989; gift from a colleague, slight signs of wear

327–328
Garfield-Stiftehalter Kunststoff, 8,9 x 9,9 x 4,9 cm, 1985; Geschenk einer ehemaligen Mitbewohnerin, diente jahrzehntelang als Schreibtischdeko, starke Flecken
Garfield pen holder plastic, 3.5 x 3.89 x 1.92 in, 1985; gift from a former flatmate, as desk decoration in use for decades, heavy stains

Kugelschreiber vom Hotel Palmenhof Kunststoff, Mine, 13,7 cm, 1989; Diebesgut aus dem Hotel Palmenhof, Frankfurt am Main
Ball pen from Hotel Palmenhof plastic, pen refill, 5.39 in, 1989; stolen good from Hotel Palmenhof, Frankfurt am Main

329–330
Zwei Sandmalereien Glas, farbiger Sand, 4,9 x 2,1 cm/17,2 x 6 x 4,3 cm, undatiert; wie neu
Two sand paintings glass, colored sand, 1.92 x 0.82 in/6.77 x 2.36 x 1.69 in, undated; like new

331–333
Zwei Joy-Gläser Milchglas, 9 × 7,2 cm, undatiert; leicht verstaubt
Two joy-glasses frosted glass, 3.54 × 2.83 in, undated; slightly dusty

Strohhalm mit Palmendeko Kunststoff, Papier, 20 × 6 cm, undatiert; benutzt
Straw with palm tree decoration plastic, paper, 7.87 × 2.36 in, undated; used

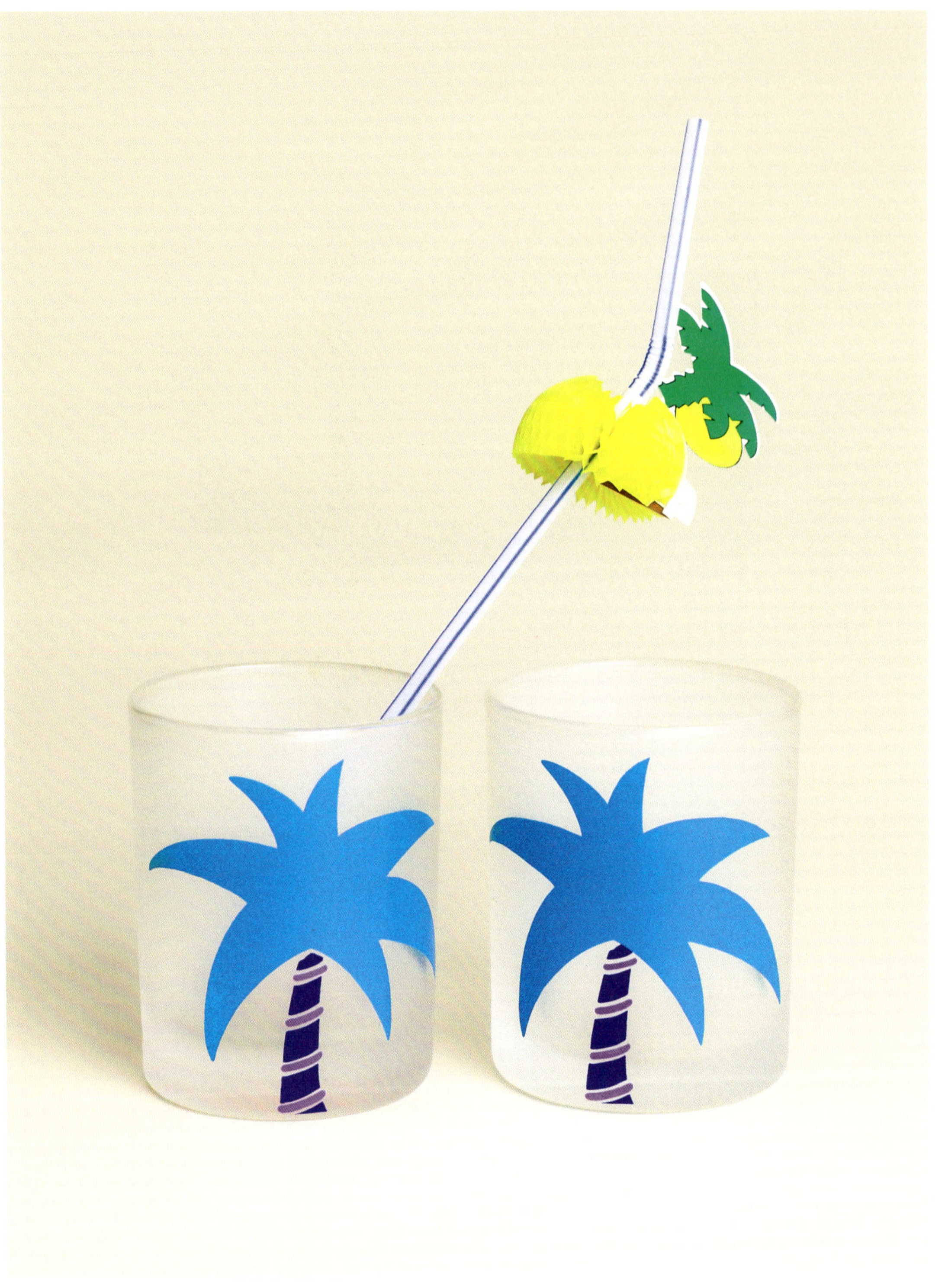

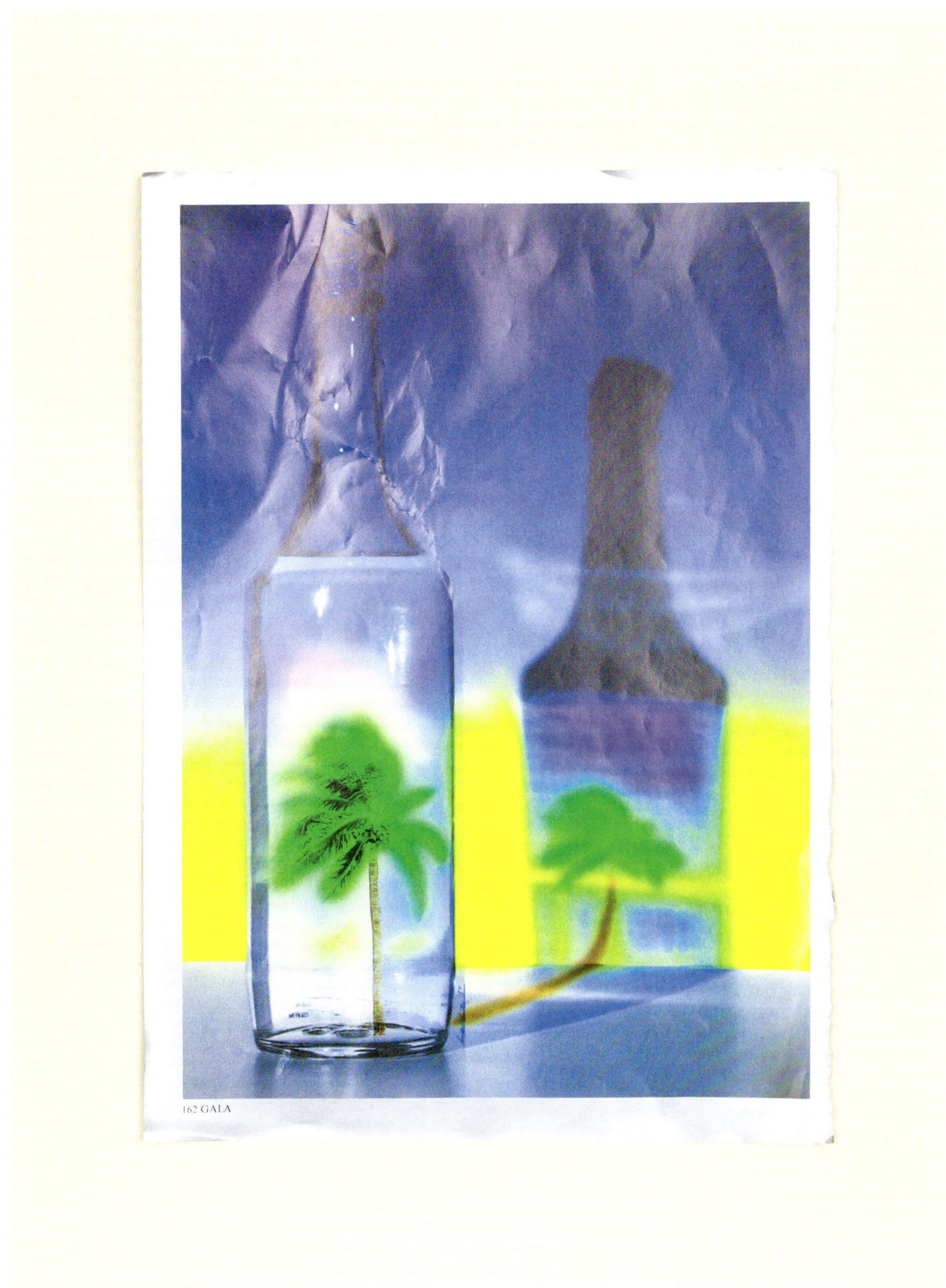

334
Ausriss aus der Zeitschrift Gala
Papier, 30 × 21 cm, 1997; Geschenk eines Nachbarn, leicht zerknittert, in Besitz von Alf Trojan
Page pulled out from magazine Gala paper, 11.81 × 8.26 in, 1997; gift from a neighbor, slightly crumpled, property of Alf Trojan

335–338
Zwei Serviettenringe Holz, 9,8 × 5,4 × 2,3 cm, undatiert; leicht verdreckt
Two napkin rings wood, 3.85 × 2.12 × 0.9 in, undated; slightly dirty

Zwei Papierservietten 3-lagig, Papier, 30 × 30 cm, undatiert; verwendet als Tischdekoration bei geselligen Abendessen, leicht zerknittert
Two paper napkins three-layered, paper, 11.81 × 11.81 in, undated; used as table decoration at convivial dinners, slightly crumpled

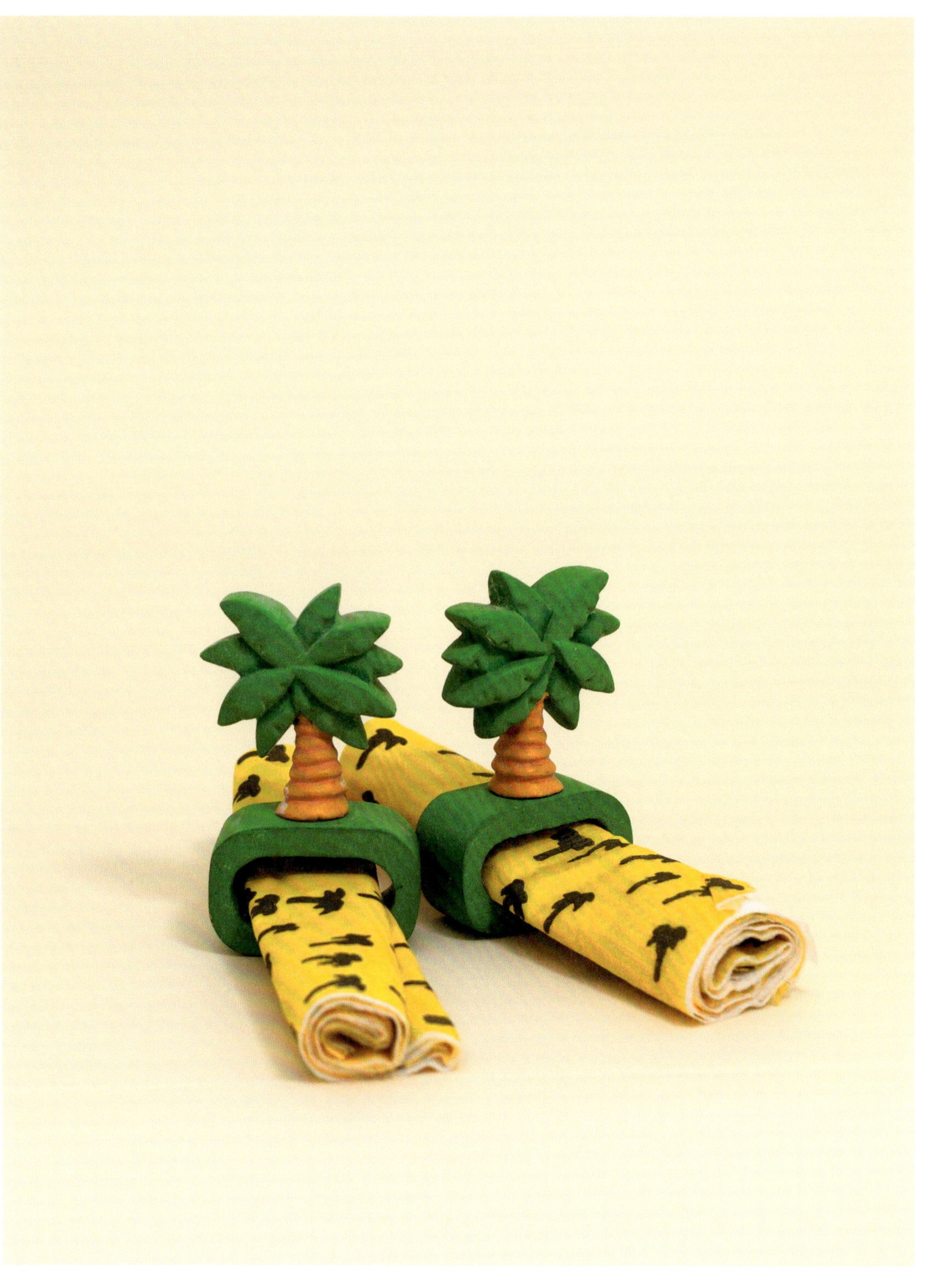

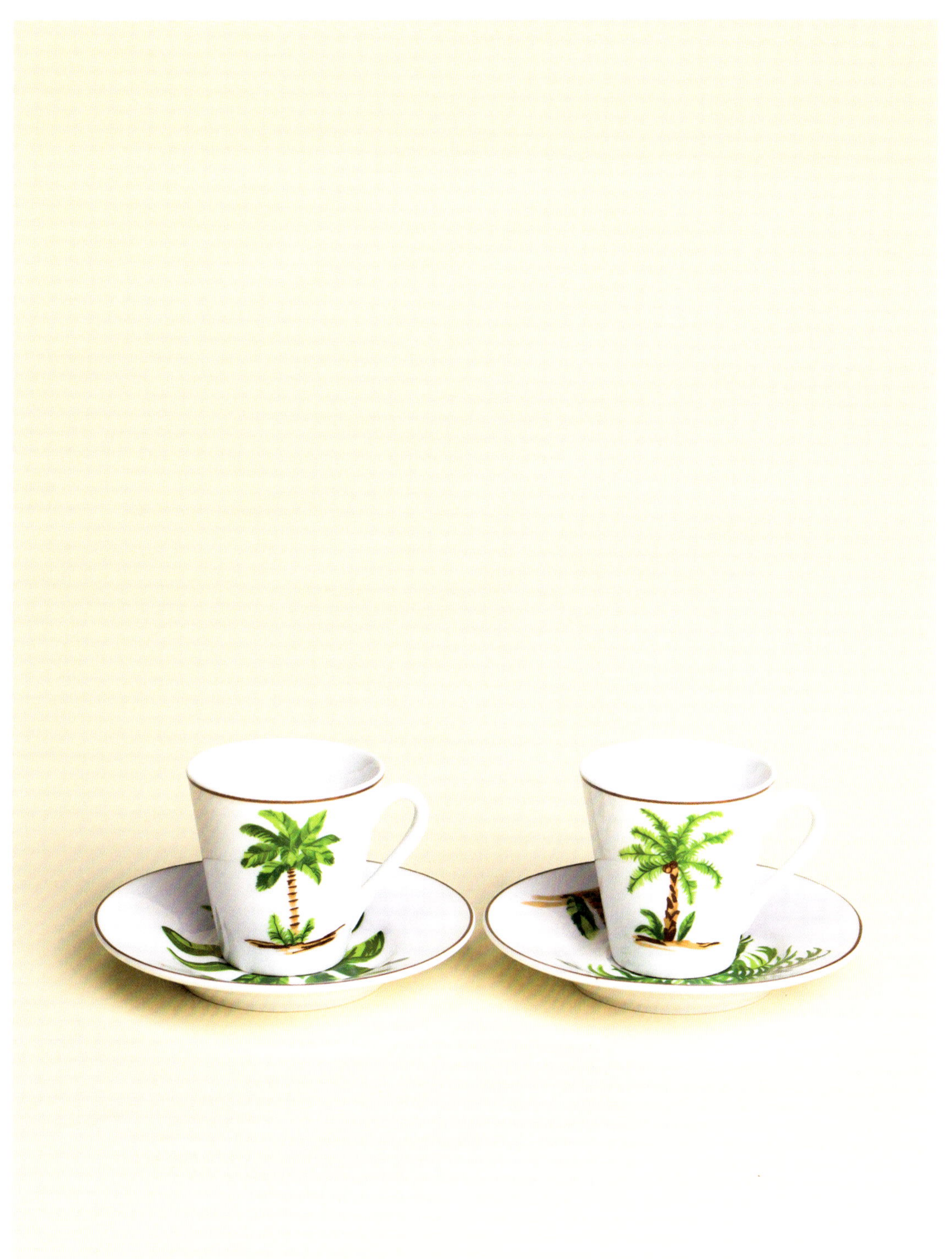

339–340
Zwei bemalte Espressotassen mit Untertassen Porzellan, 6 × 8 × 6 cm/12 × 12 cm, undatiert; wie neu
Two painted espresso cups with saucers porcelain, 2.36 × 3.14 × 2.36 in/4.72 × 4.72 in, undated; like new

341–343
Feuerzeug „Tokai“ Kunststoff, 8,1 × 2,5 × 1 cm, undatiert; leichte Gebrauchsspuren
Lighter "Tokai" plastic, 3.18 × 0.98 × 0.39 in, undated; slight signs of wear

Feuerzeug „Crown“ Kunststoff, Metall, 7,6 x 2,4 x 1,7 cm, undatiert; starke Gebrauchsspuren
Lighter "Crown" plastic, metal, 2.99 × 0.94 × 0.66 in, undated; heavy signs of wear

Feuerzeug „Tokai“ Kunststoff, 8,1 × 2,5 × 1 cm, undatiert
Lighter "Tokai" plastic, 3.18 × 0.98 × 0.39 in, undated

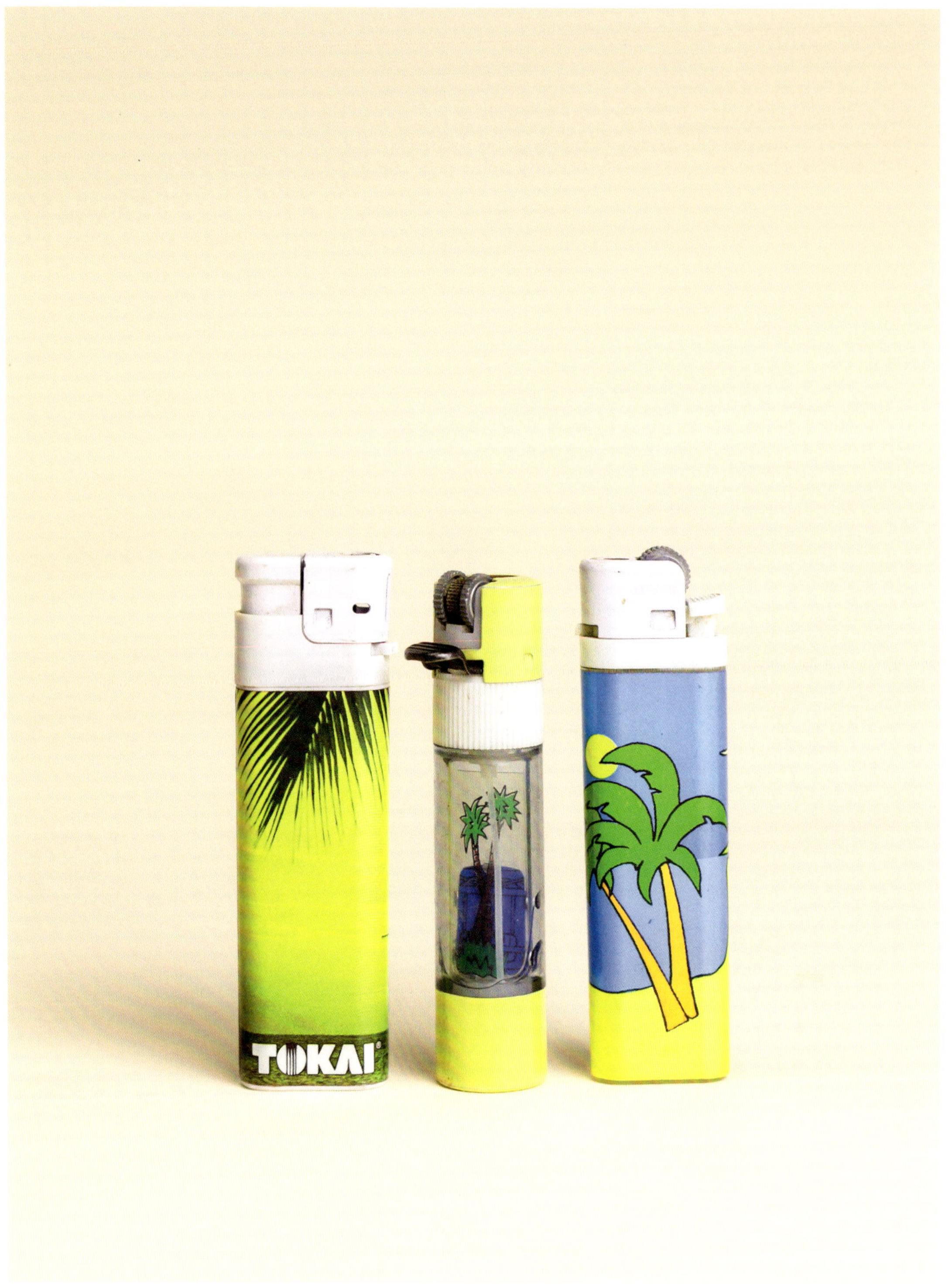

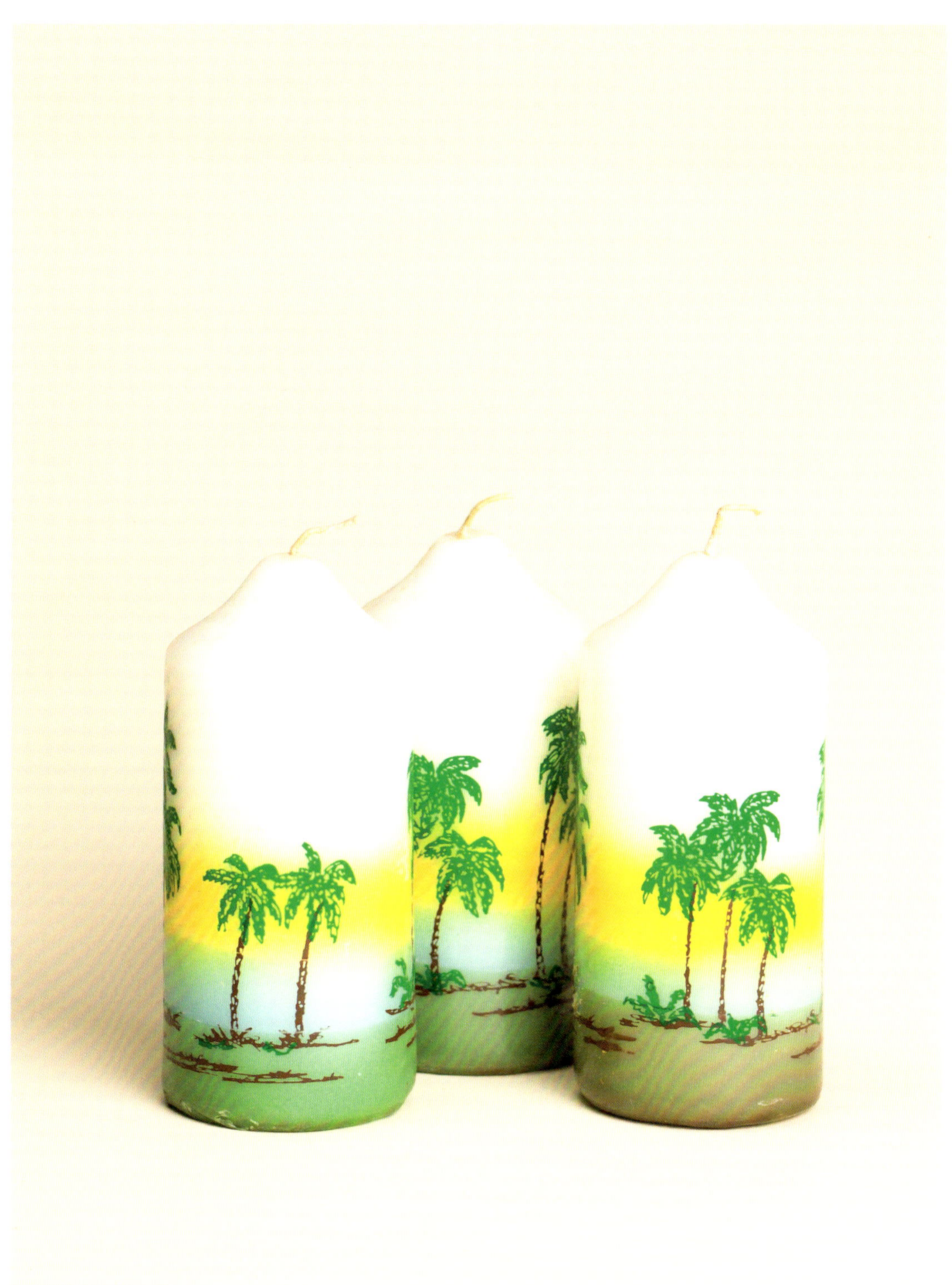

344–346
Drei Stumpfkerzen Wachs, 13 × 6 cm, undatiert; leicht verfärbt
Three stump candles wax, 5.11 × 2.36 in; slighty discolored

347–348
Streichholzschachtel mit Zündhölzern 5 × 3,5 × 2,1 cm, 2010; Handarbeit eines Freundes
Matchbox with matches
1.96 × 1.37 × 0.82 in, 2010; handmade by a friend

Zigarettenschachtel mit Inhalt
Pappe, Tabak, 8,8 × 4,5 × 1,9 cm, 1998/Seychellen
Cigarette box with content
cardboard, tobacco, 3.46 × 1.77 × 0.74 in, 1998/Seychelles

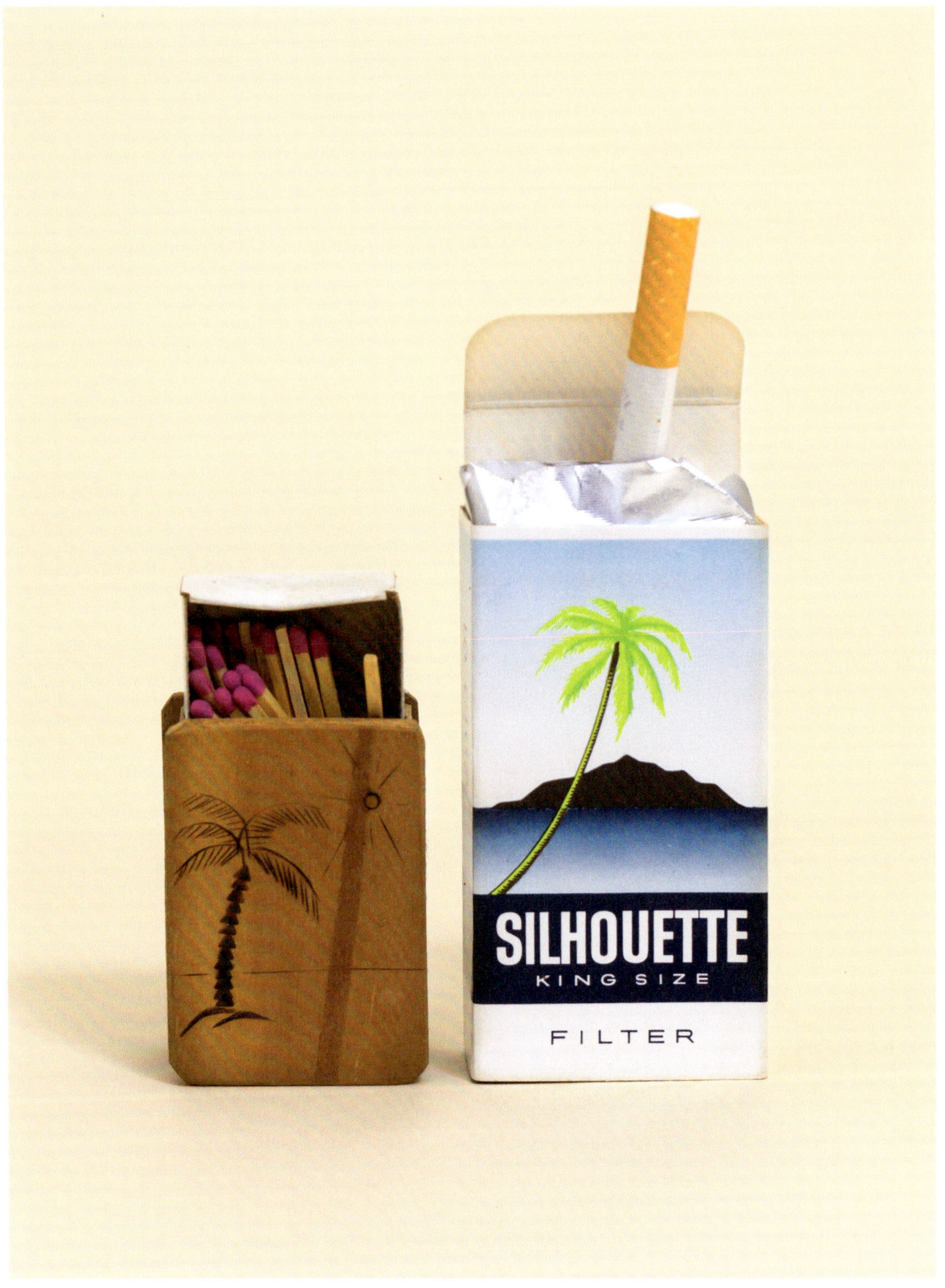

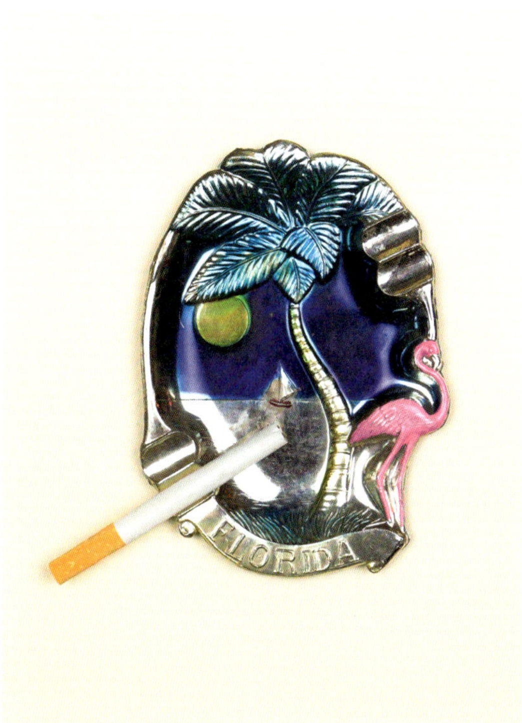

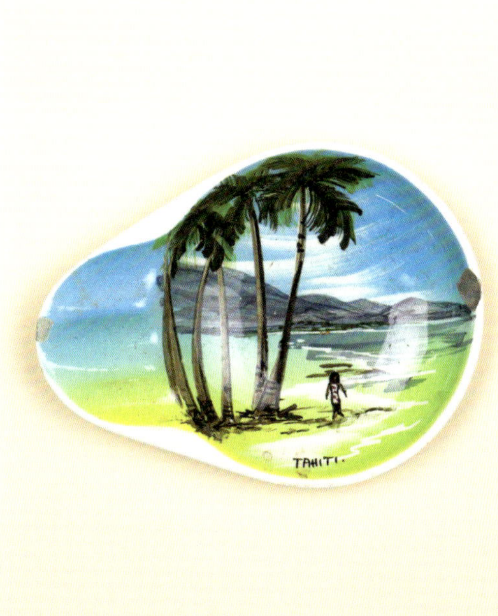

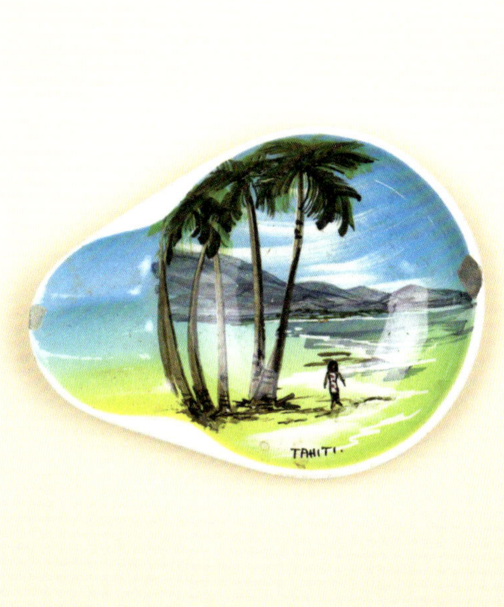

349
Aschenbecher mit Zigarette
Aluminium, 13,4 × 10 cm, 2000/Florida; leichte Gebrauchsspuren
Ashtray with cigarette
aluminum, 5.27 × 3.93 in, 2000/Florida; slight signs of wear

350
Aschenbecher Ton, 9,6 × 12,7 cm, 1995/Tahiti; Teile abgesplittert
Ashtray clay, 3.77 × 5 in, 1995/Tahiti; partly chipped

351
Aschenbecher Intarsienarbeit, Holz, 13,4 × 13,4 cm, 1997/Rio de Janeiro; Sprung im Holz
Ashtray, inlay work, wood, 5.27 × 5.27 in, 1997/Rio de Janeiro; crack in wood

352
Aschenbecher Kunststoff, 7,5 × 12,2 cm, 1982/Hawaii; in Besitz von Alf Trojan
Ashtray plastic, 2.95 × 4.8 in, 1982/Hawaii; property of Alf Trojan

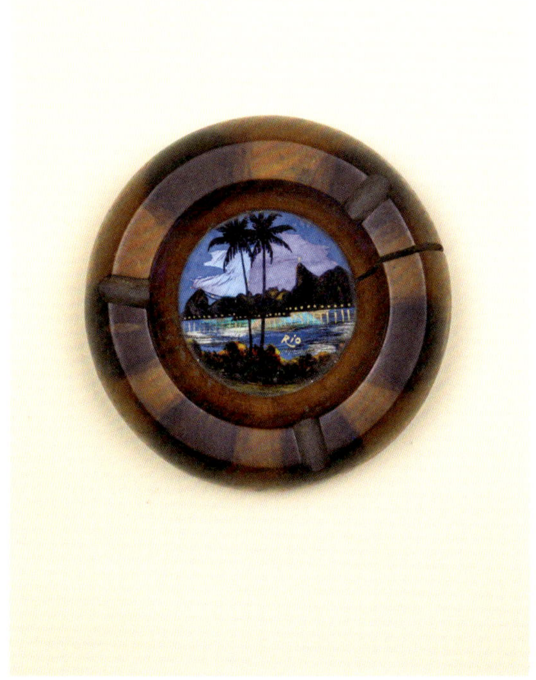

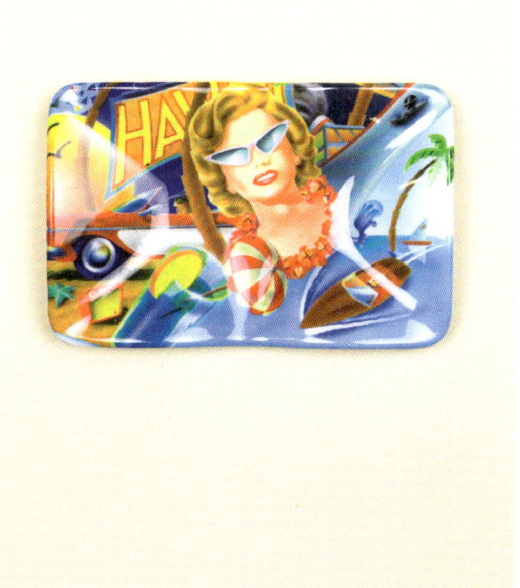

353–357
Partyteller 6er-Pack, Pappe, 23 cm, 2002/England; wie neu
Party plate 6-pack, cardboard, 9.05 in, 2002/England; like new

Partybecher 8er-Pack, Pappe, 12,2 × 7,1 cm, 2002/England; wie neu
Party cups 8-pack, cardboard, 4.8 × 2.79 in, 2002/England; like new

Vier Glitzerpalmen Holz, Aluminium, 15 cm, undatiert; gebraucht
Four decorative glitter palm trees wood, aluminum, 5.9 in, undated; used

Acht Cocktailschirmchen „Happy Party" Holz, Papier, 9,9 × 8,8 cm, undatiert; originalverpackt
Eight cocktail parasols "Happy Party" wood, paper, 3.89 × 3.46 in, undated; original packaging

Einundzwanzig Tischdeko Konfettipalmen Aluminium, 1 × 0,3 cm, undatiert
Twenty-one table decoration confetti palm trees aluminum, 0.39 × 0.19 in, undated

358–359
Zwei Flaschen Kokosnusslikör „Malibu" Glas, Aluminium, 27,3 × 7,6 cm/11,8 × 3,6 cm, 2000/Spanien; ohne Inhalt
Two bottles of coconut liqueur "Malibu" glass, aluminum, 10.74 × 2.99 in/4.56 × 1.41 in, 2000/Spain; without contents

360–365
Likör „L'Hermitage" Glas, Alkohol, 12,2 × 3,4 cm, 2004/Flohmarkt
Liqueur "L'Hermitage" glass, alcohol, 4.8 × 1.33 in, 2004/fleamarket

Kiwi-Likör „Bols" Glas, Alkohol, 11,7 × 3,3 × 3,3 cm, 2004/Flohmarkt
Kiwi-liqueur "Bols" glass, alcohol, 4.6 × 1.29 × 1.29 in, 2004/fleamarket

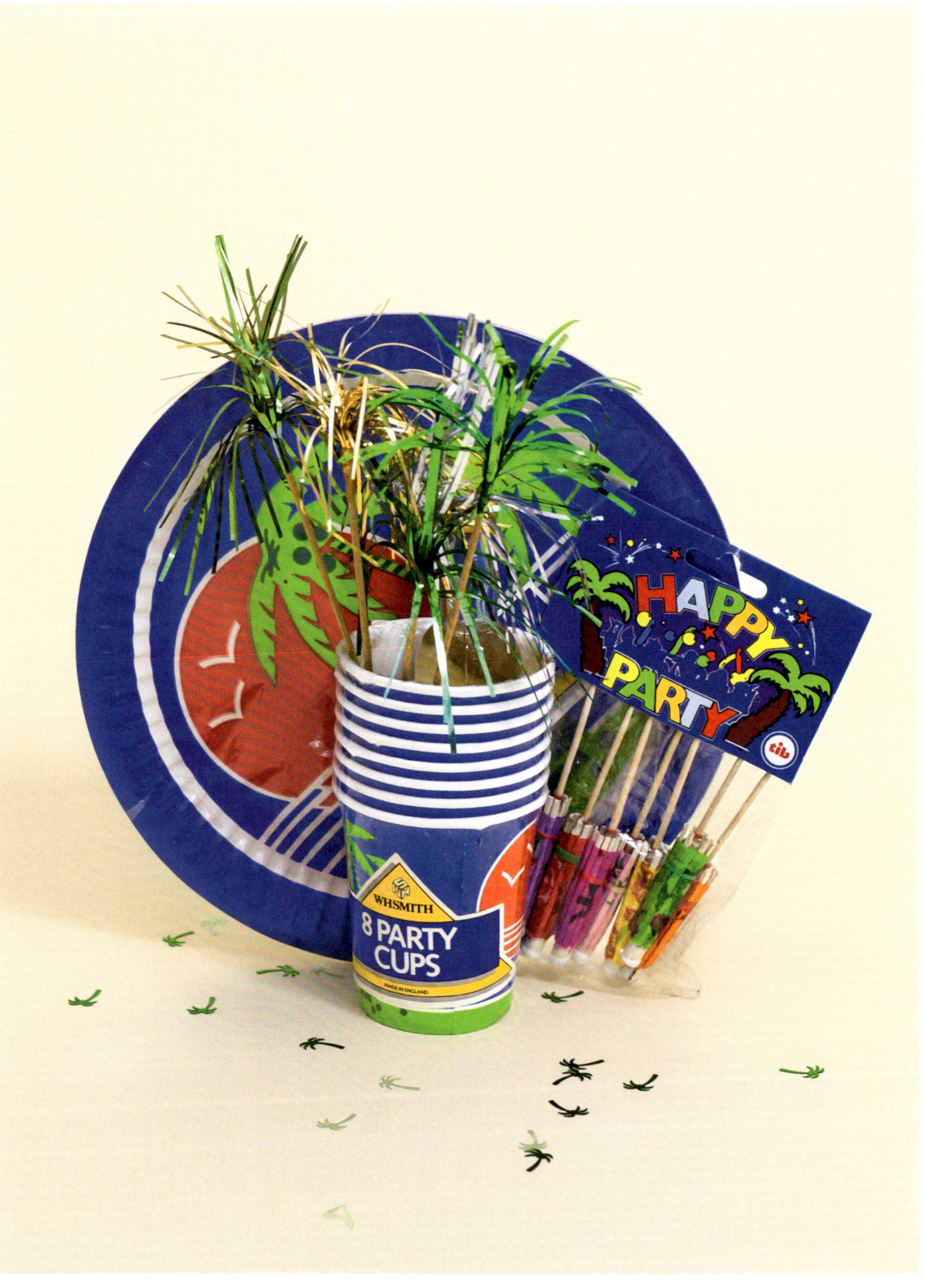

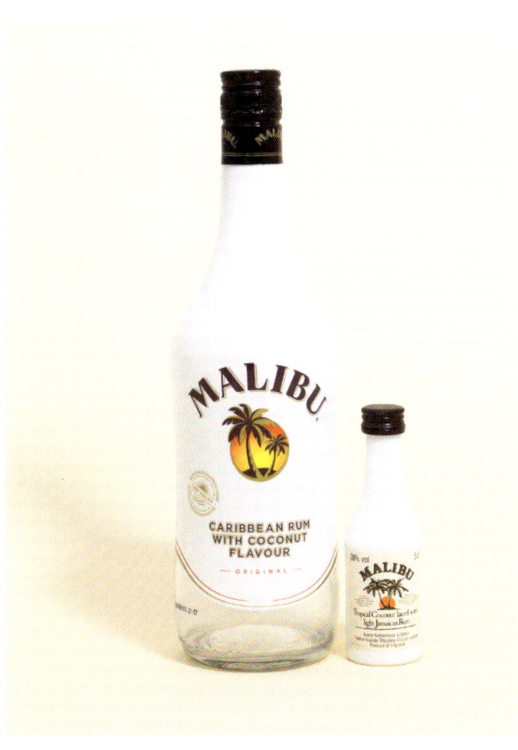

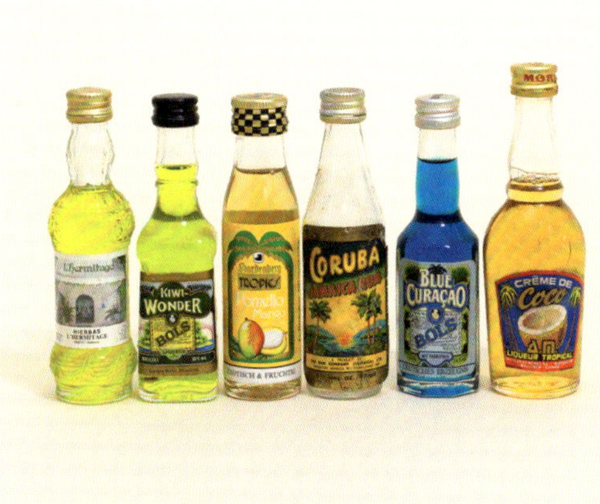

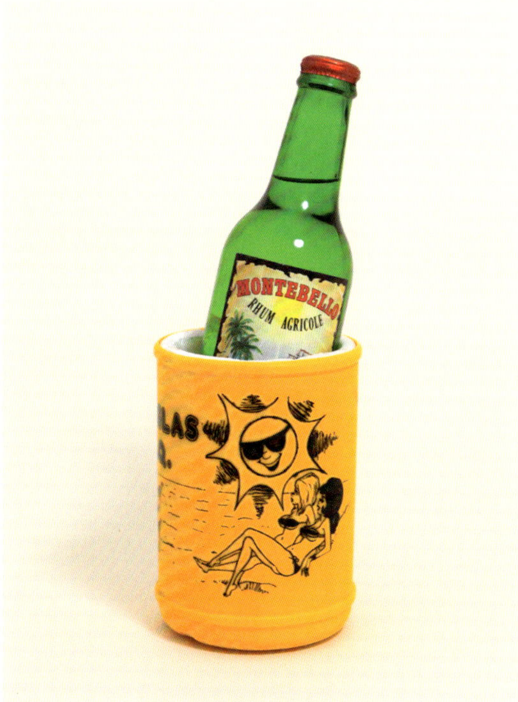

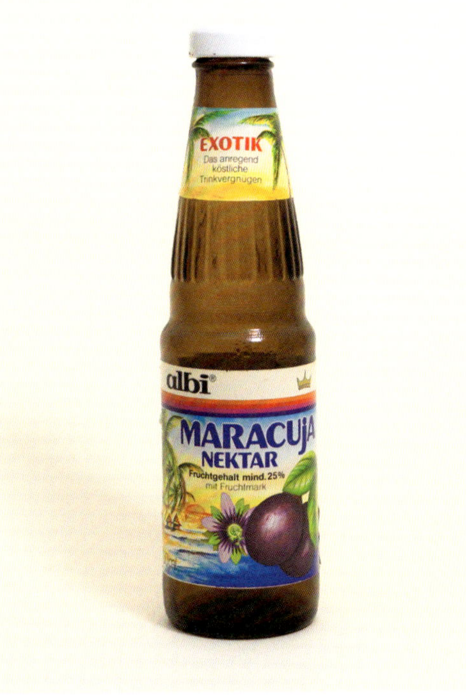

Pomello-Mango-Likör
Glas, Alkohol, 11,7 × 3 cm, 2004/Flohmarkt
Pomelo-mango-liqueur
glass, alcohol, 4.6 × 1.18 in, 2004/fleamarket

Flasche Jamaica Rum „Coruba“
Glas, 11,7 × 3,2 cm, undatiert; starke Gebrauchsspuren, ohne Inhalt
Bottle of Jamaica rum “Coruba”
glass, 4.6 × 1.25 in, undated; heavy signs of wear, without content

Blue Curaçao „Bols“
Glas, Alkohol, 11,5 × 3,4 cm, 2004/Flohmarkt
Blue Curaçao “Bols”
glass, alcohol, 4.52 × 1.33 in, 2004/fleamarket

Kokosnusslikör „Morey“ Glas, Alkohol, 13 × 3,7 cm, 2004/Flohmarkt
Coconut-liqueur “Morey”
glass, alcohol, 5.11 × 1.45 in, 2004/fleamarket

366–367
Flaschenkühler Kunststoff, Styropor, 12,3 × 8,7 cm, 1988; Mitbringsel von einem Kongress in Port Douglas, Australien, Styropor beschädigt
Bottle cooler plastic, styrofoam, 4.84 × 3.42 in, 1988; souvenir from a congress in Port Douglas, Australia, styrofoam damaged

Rum „Guadeloupe“
Glas, Alkohol, 18,7 × 5,6 cm, undatiert
Rum “Guadeloupe”
glass, alcohol, 7.36 × 2.2 in, undated

368
„Albi“ Maracujanektar Glas, Papier, 27,8 × 7,2 cm, undatiert; ohne Inhalt, klebrig
Bottle of “Albi” passionfruit juice drink glass, paper, 10.94 × 2.83 in, undated; without content, sticky

369
Kissen Satin, Federn, 45 × 46 cm, 2012; Geschenk der Ehefrau, dient als Schlafzimmer-dekoration, in Besitz von Alf Trojan
Cushion satin, feathers, 17.71 × 18.11 in, 2012; gift from wife, serves as bedroom decoration, property of Alf Trojan

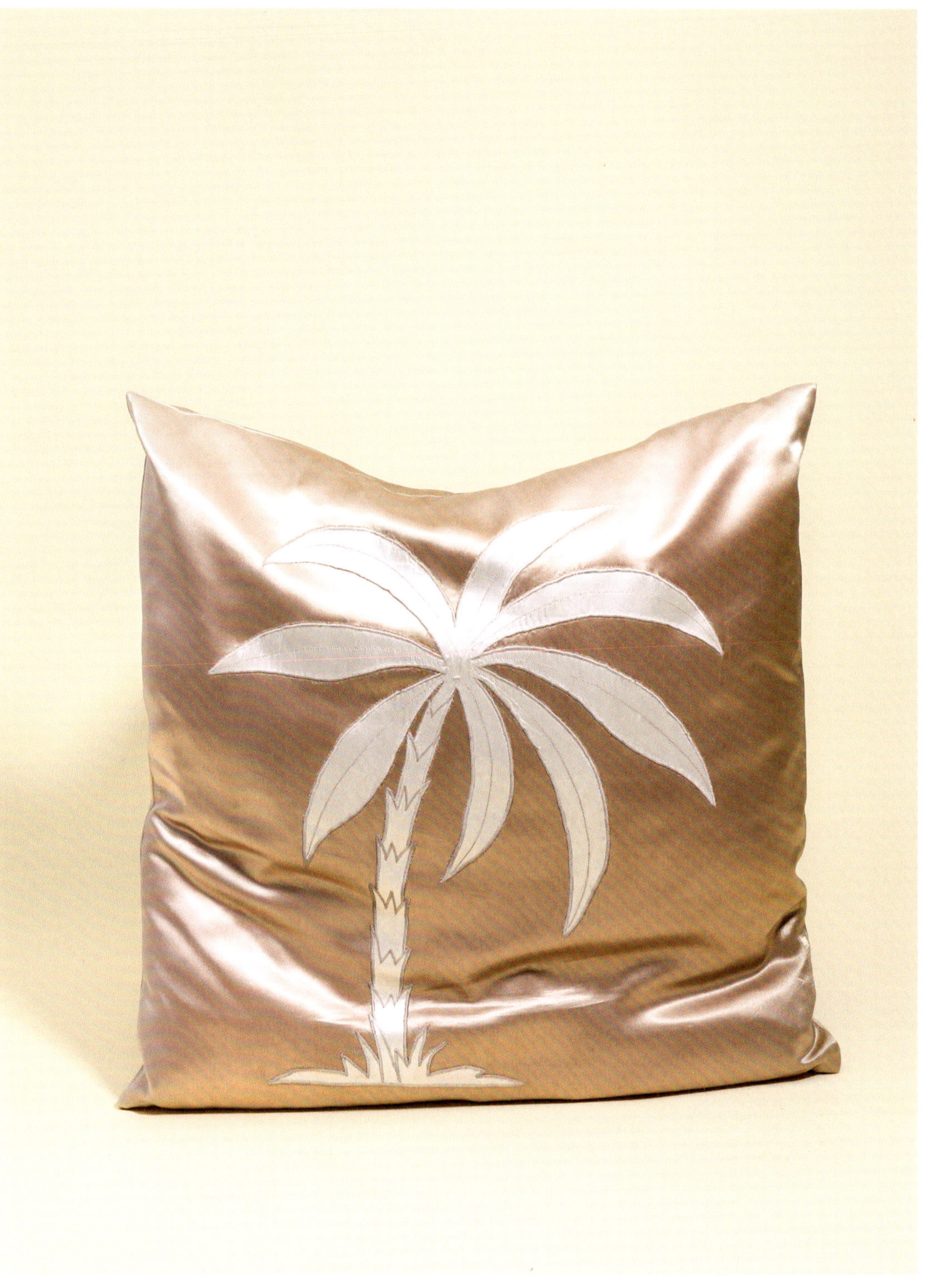

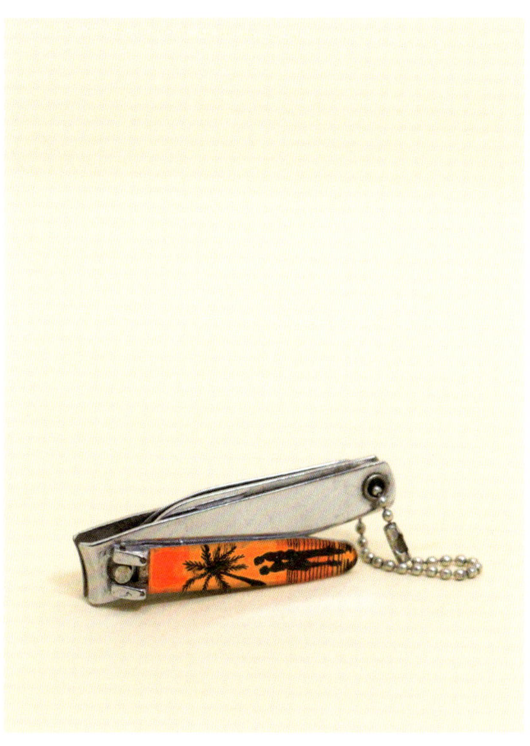

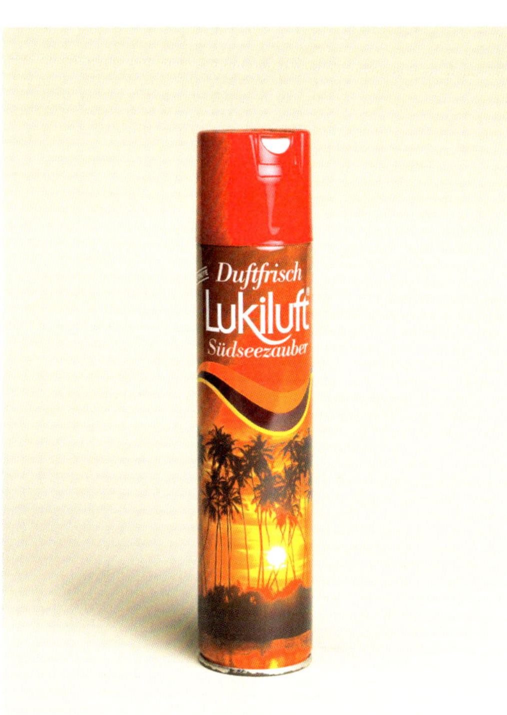

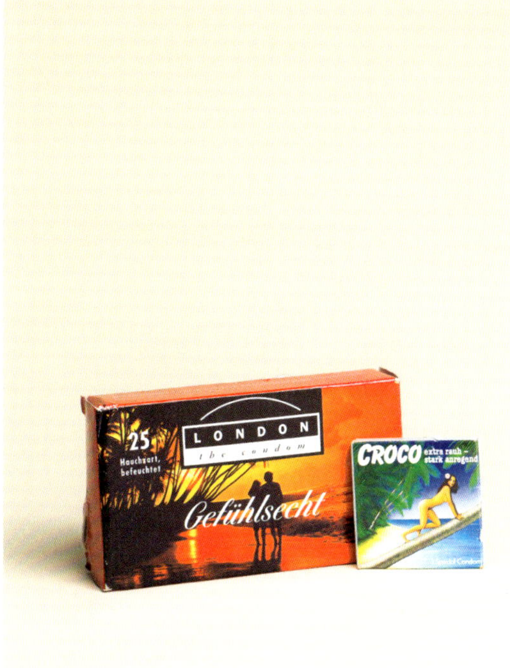

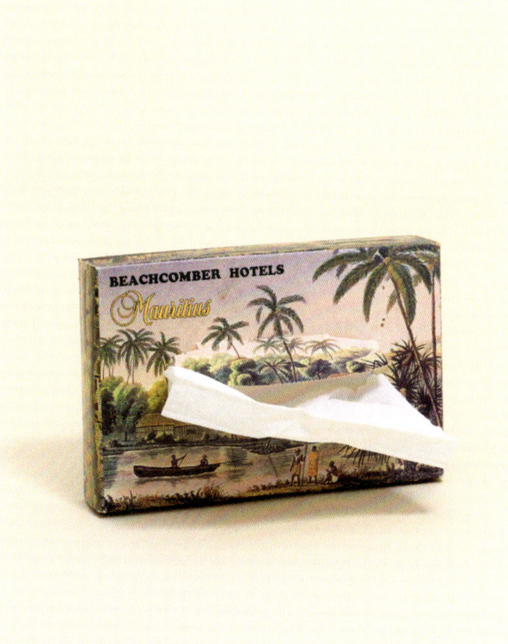

370
Nagelknipser mit Klappmesser und Feile (made in China), Metall, 6,9 × 1,4 × 1,9 cm, undatiert
Nail clipper with foldable knife and nail file (made in China), metal, 2.71 × 0.55 × 0.74 in, undated

371
Duftspray „Lukiluft Südseezauber“ Metall, 23,5 × 5 × 5 cm, undatiert; wird als Deko auf der Toilettenfensterbank genutzt, fast leer, in Besitz von Alf Trojan
Air freshener "Lukiluft Südseezauber" metal, 9.25 × 1.96 × 1.96 in, undated; used as window sill decoration in restroom, almost empty, property of Alf Trojan

372–373
London-Kondome „Gefühlsecht“ Karton, 7 x 12,2 x 3,6 cm, 1997/ Österreich; ohne Inhalt
London-condoms "True sensation" cardboard, 1.41 × 4.8 × 2.75 in, 1997/ Austria; without content

Croco-Kondom „extra rauh – stark anregend“ Karton, 5 × 5 cm, 1998/ Deutschland; leichte Gebrauchsspuren
Croco-condom "extra rough – strongly stimulating" 1.96 × 1.96 in, 1998/Germany; slight signs of wear

374
Taschentuchspender Karton, Papier, 11 × 17 × 3,1 cm, 1996; aus dem Beachcomber Hotel auf Mauritius, leichte Gebrauchsspuren
Paper tissue dispenser cardboard, paper, 4.33 × 6.69 × 1.22 in, 1996; from the Beachcomber Hotel in Mauritius, slight signs of wear

375
Aschenbecher „It's beter in Israel“
mit Zigarette, Metall, 14,1 × 14,1 cm, 2003/ Israel; starke Gebrauchsspuren, Flecken
Ashtray "It's beter in Israel"
with cigarette, metal, 5.55 × 5.55 in, 2003/ Israel; heavy signs of wear, stains

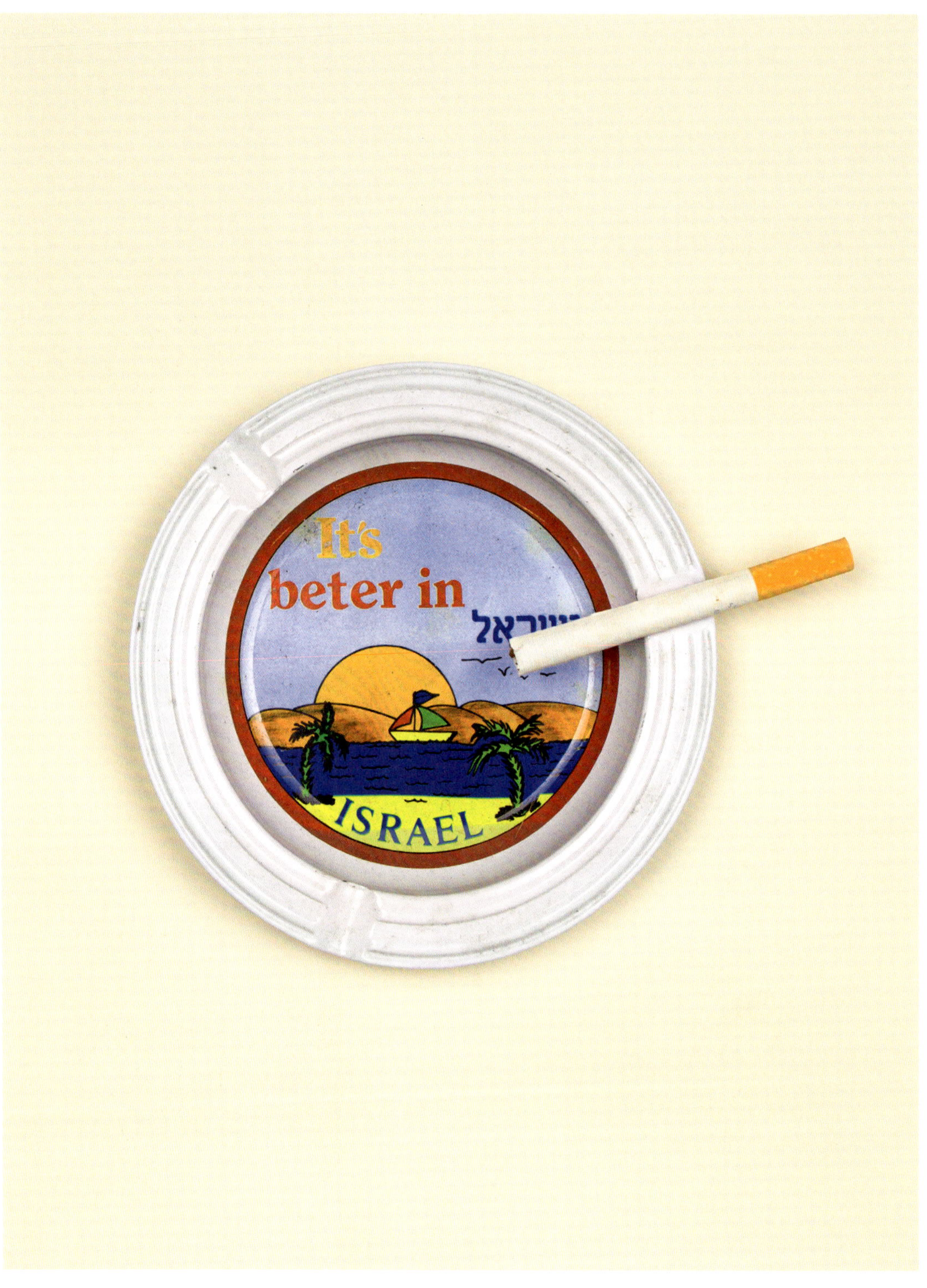

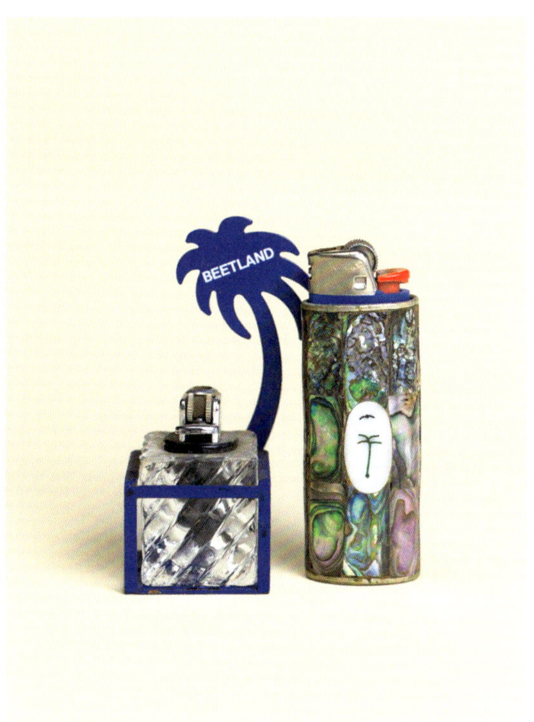

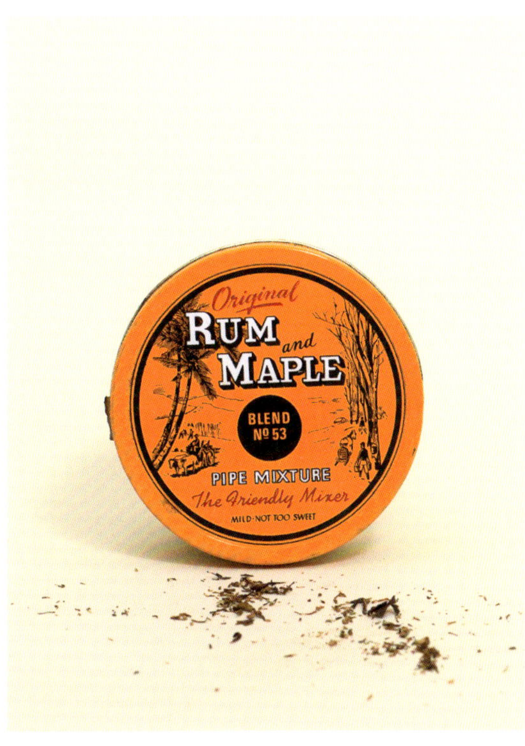

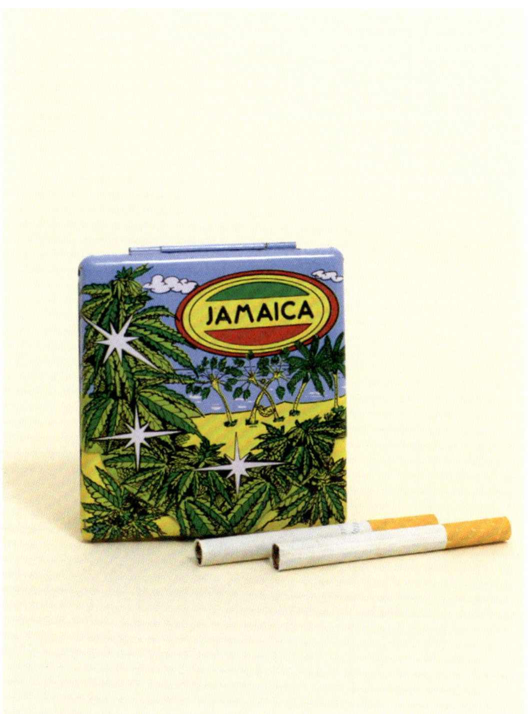

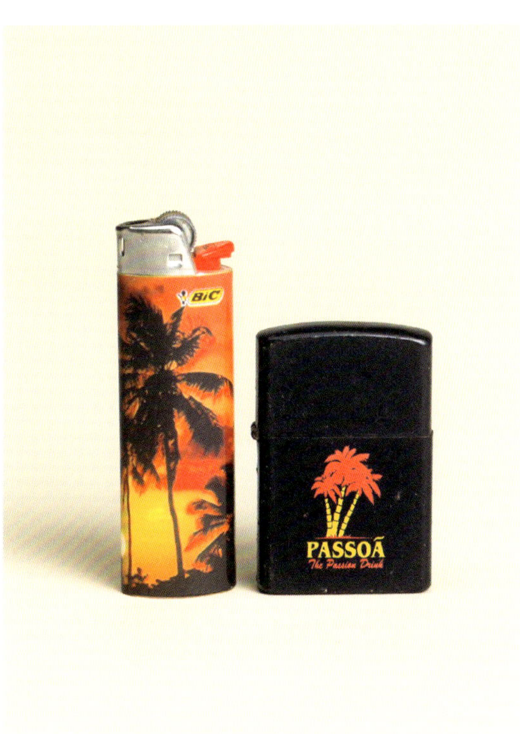

376–377

Feuerzeug „Beetland“ Metall, Glas, 8,7 × 3,6 × 3,6 cm, 1995/ Souvenir Japan; wie neu

Lighter “Beetland” metal, glass, 3.42 × 1.41 × 1.41 in, 1995/ souvenir Japan; like new

Feuerzeughülle mit BIC-Feuerzeug Metall, Perlmutt, Kunststoff, 8,2 × 3 × 1,8 cm, undatiert; wie neu

Lighter case with BIC lighter metal, nacre, plastic, 3.22 × 1.18 × 0.7 in, undated; like new

378

Pfeifentabakdose Metall, Tabak, 3,8 × 11,7 × 11,7 cm, undatiert

Pipe tobacco box metal, tobacco, 1.49 × 4.6 × 4.6 in, undated

379

Zigarettenschachtel „Jamaica“ mit sieben Zigaretten, Metall, 9 × 8 × 1 cm, 2008/Spanien; wie neu

Cigarette box “Jamaica” with seven cigarettes, metal, 3.54 × 3.14 × 0.39 in, 2008/Spain; like new

380–381

BIC-Feuerzeug Kunststoff, Metall, 7,8 × 2,4 × 1,3 cm, undatiert; wie neu

BIC lighter plastic, metal, 3.07 × 0.94 × 0.51 in, undated; like new

Benzinfeuerzeug „Passoá“ Metall, 5,6 × 3,7 × 1,2 cm, undatiert

Petrol lighter “Passoá” metal, 2.2 × 1.45 × 0.47 in, undated

382
Bettwäsche mit Druckknöpfen
2-teilig, Frottee, 70 × 70 cm/
174 × 132 cm; Geschenk der Ehefrau,
stark ausgewaschen
Linen with snap buttons
two parts, terry, 27,55 × 27,55 in/
68.5 × 51.96 in; gift from wife,
heavily washed out

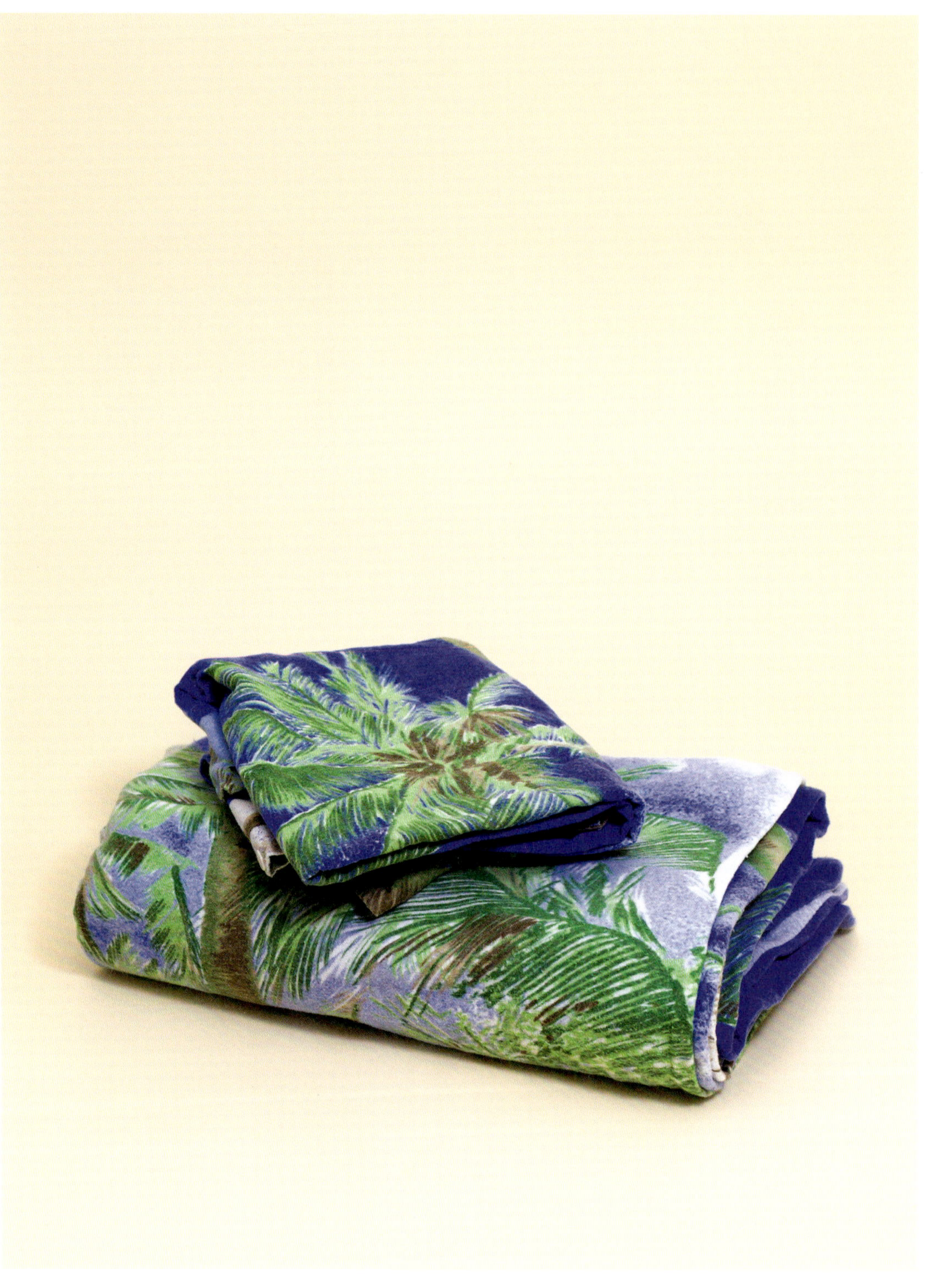

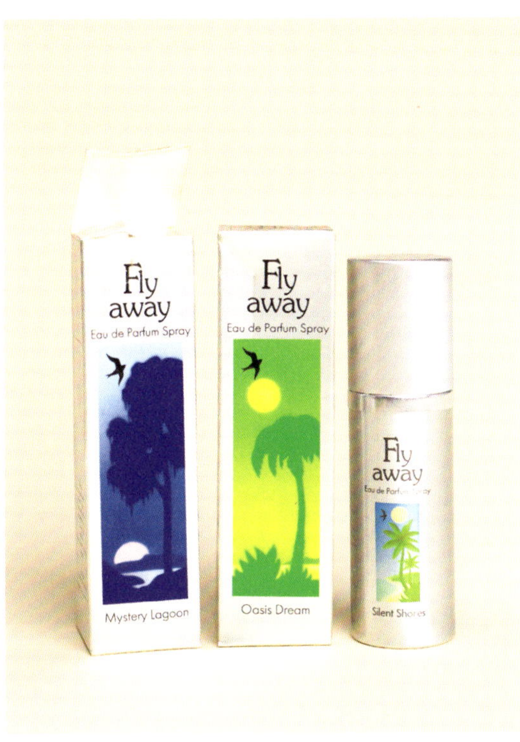

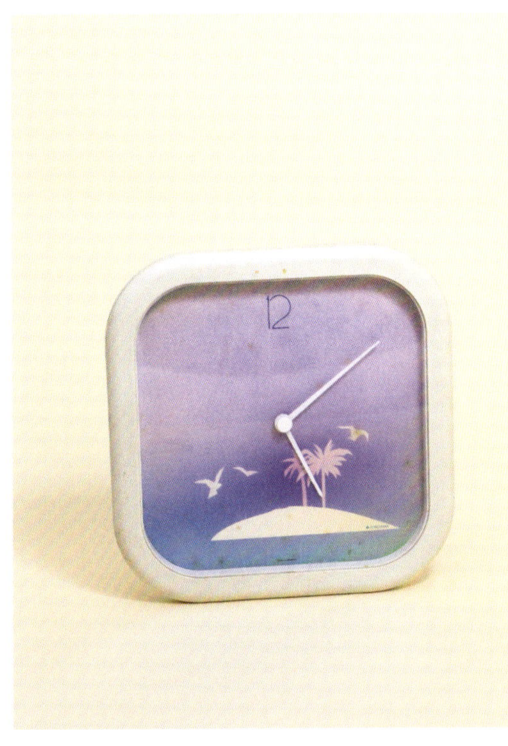

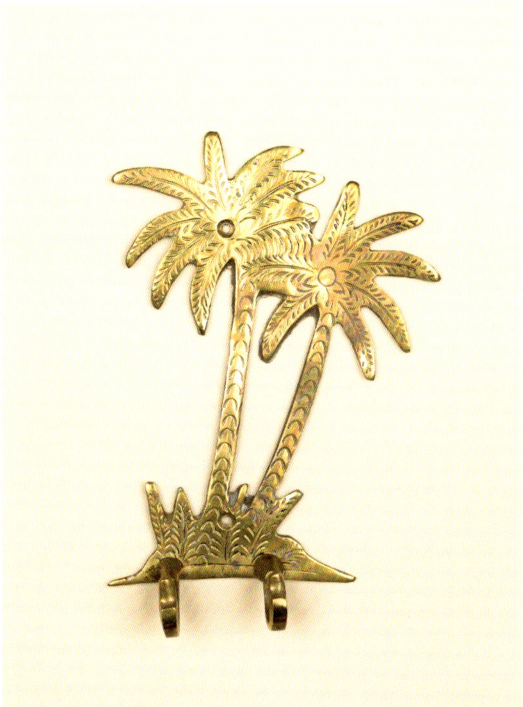

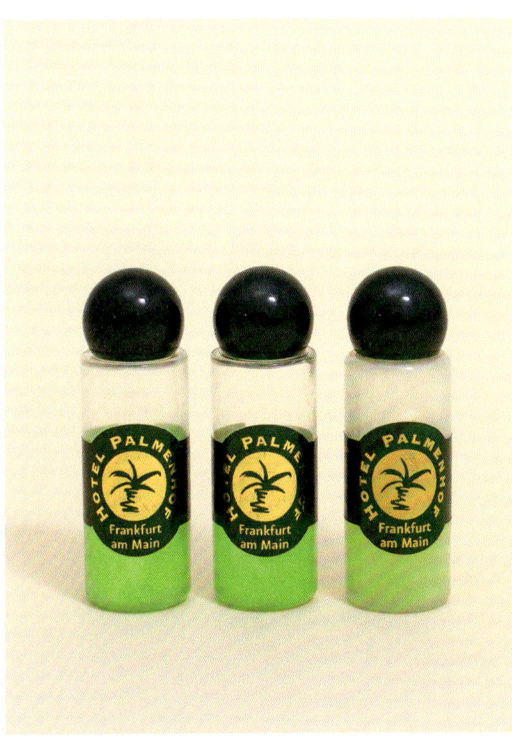

383–385
Drei Eau de Parfum „Fly away"
Karton, Glas, 13,2 × 3,7 × 3,7 cm, undatiert; Duftrichtungen Mystery Lagoon, Oasis Dream und Silent Shores
Three Eau de Perfume "Fly away"
cardboard, glass, 5.19 × 1.45 × 1.45 in, undated; fragrances Mystery Lagoon, Oasis Dream and Silent Shores

386
Wanduhr Kunststoff, 23,5 × 23,5 cm; starke Flecken, batteriebetrieben
Clock plastic, 9.25 × 9.25 in; heavy stains, battery run

387
Garderobenhaken für die Wand
Messing, 19,2 × 14,8 × 4,2 cm, 2010/ Marrakesch; Geschenk der Ehefrau, in Besitz von Alf Trojan
Wardrobe hanger for wall
brass, 7.55 × 5.82 × 1.65 in, 2010/ Marrakesh; gift from wife, property of Alf Trojan

388–390
Drei Shampoofläschchen
Kunststoff, Seife, 8 × 2,5 × 2,5 cm, 1991; Mitbringsel der Ehefrau aus dem Hotel Palmenhof, Frankfurt am Main, halb leer, in Besitz von Alf Trojan
Three shampoo mini bottles
plastic, soap, 3.14 × 0.98 × 0.98 in, 1991; souvenir of wife from Hotel Palmenhof, Frankfurt am Main, half empty, property of Alf Trojan

391
Dekopalme Papier, Karton, 25,2 × 28 cm, 2003/Dänemark; starke Gebrauchsspuren
Decorative palm tree paper, cardboard, 9.92 × 11 in, 2003/ Denmark; heavy signs of wear

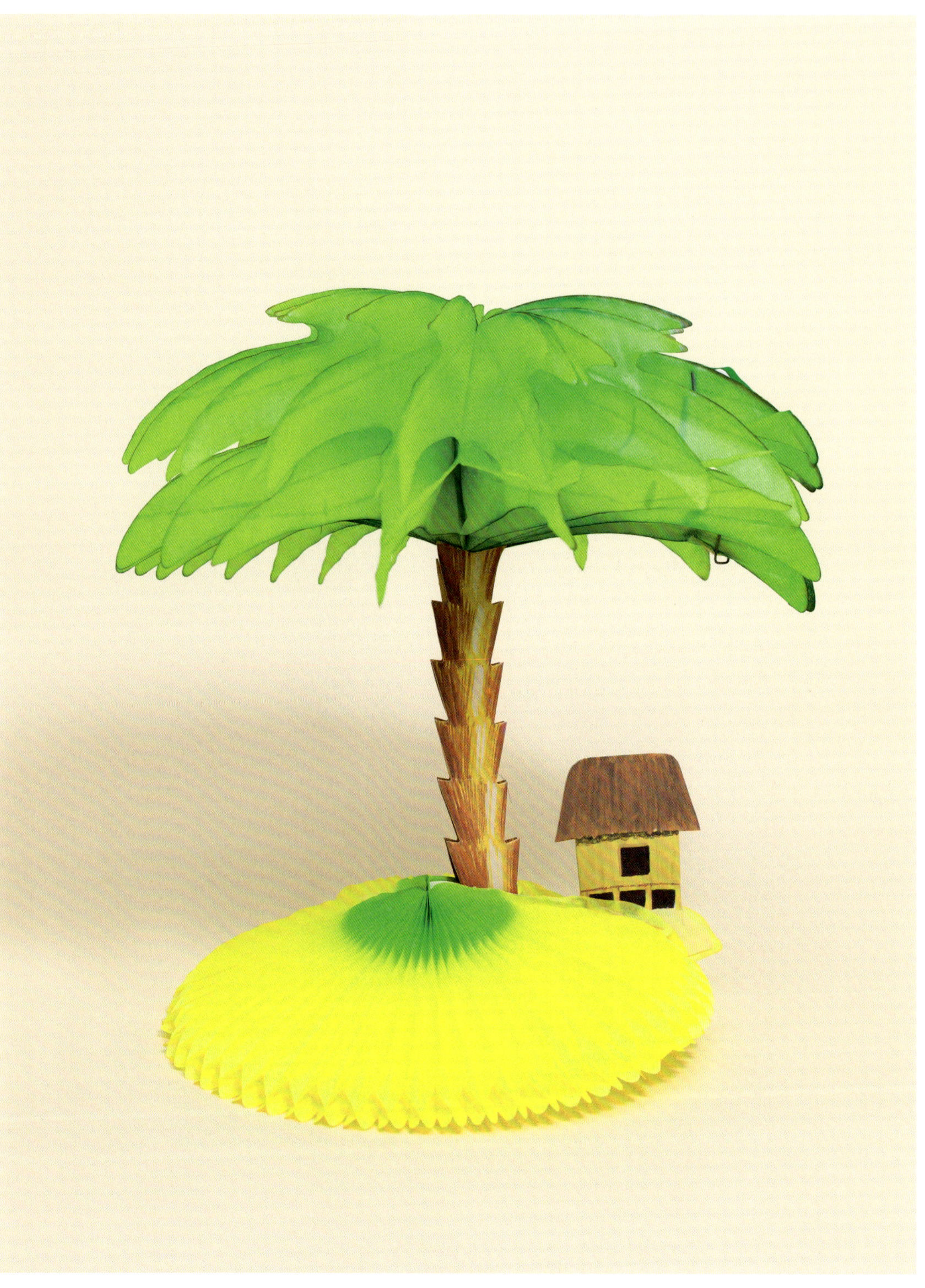

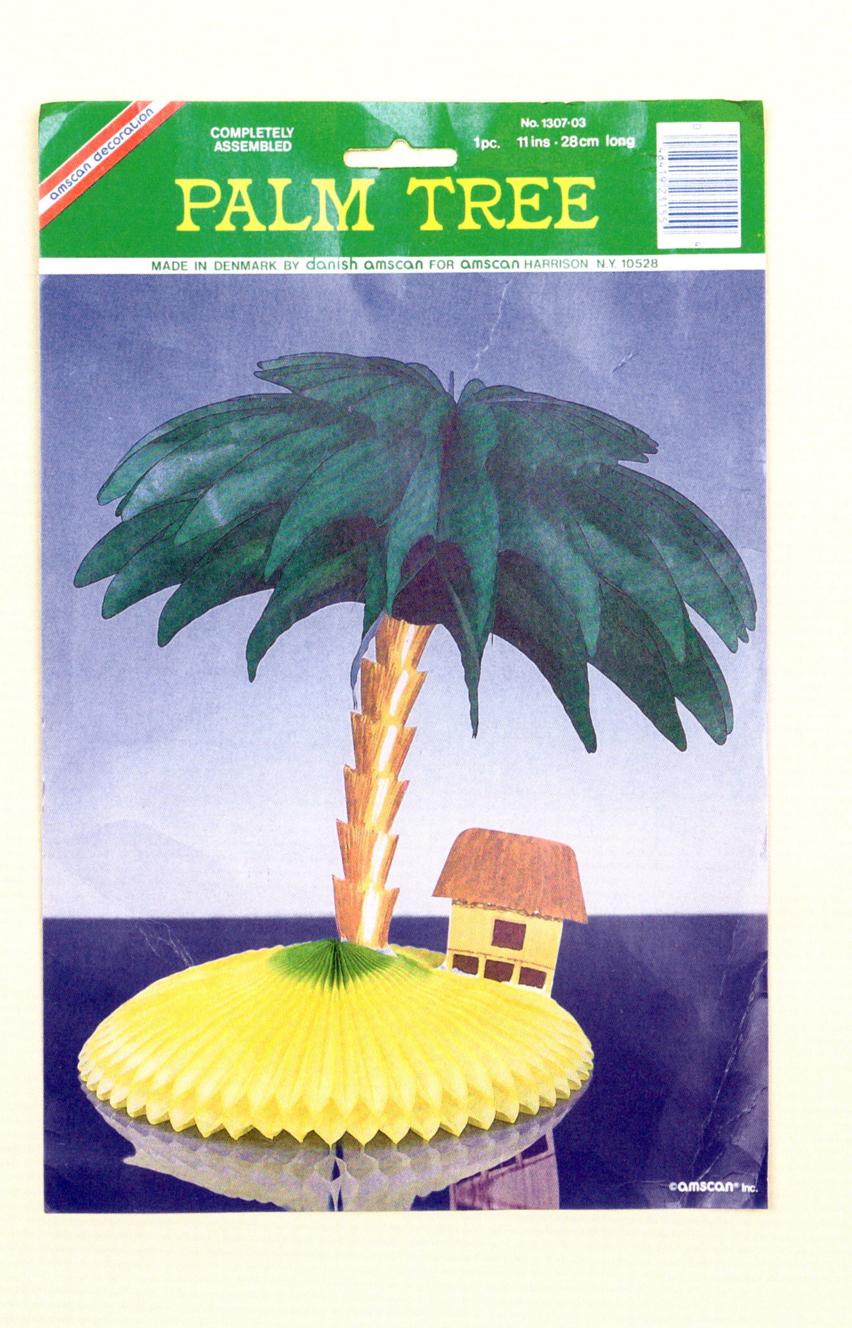

392
Dekopalme Papier, Karton, 25,2 × 28 cm, undatiert; starke Gebrauchsspuren
Decorative palm tree paper, cardboard, 9.92 × 11 in, undated; heavy signs of wear

393

Meditationskissen Samt, Sand, 18 × 33 × 33 cm, 2015; Geschenk der Ehefrau, erworben auf der Kulturellen Landpartie im Wendland, dient als Schlafzimmerdeko, in Besitz von Alf Trojan

Meditation cushion velvet, sand, 7.08 × 12.99 × 12.99 in, 2015; gift from wife, purchased at the Kulturelle Landpartie in Wendland, in use as bedroom decoration, property of Alf Trojan

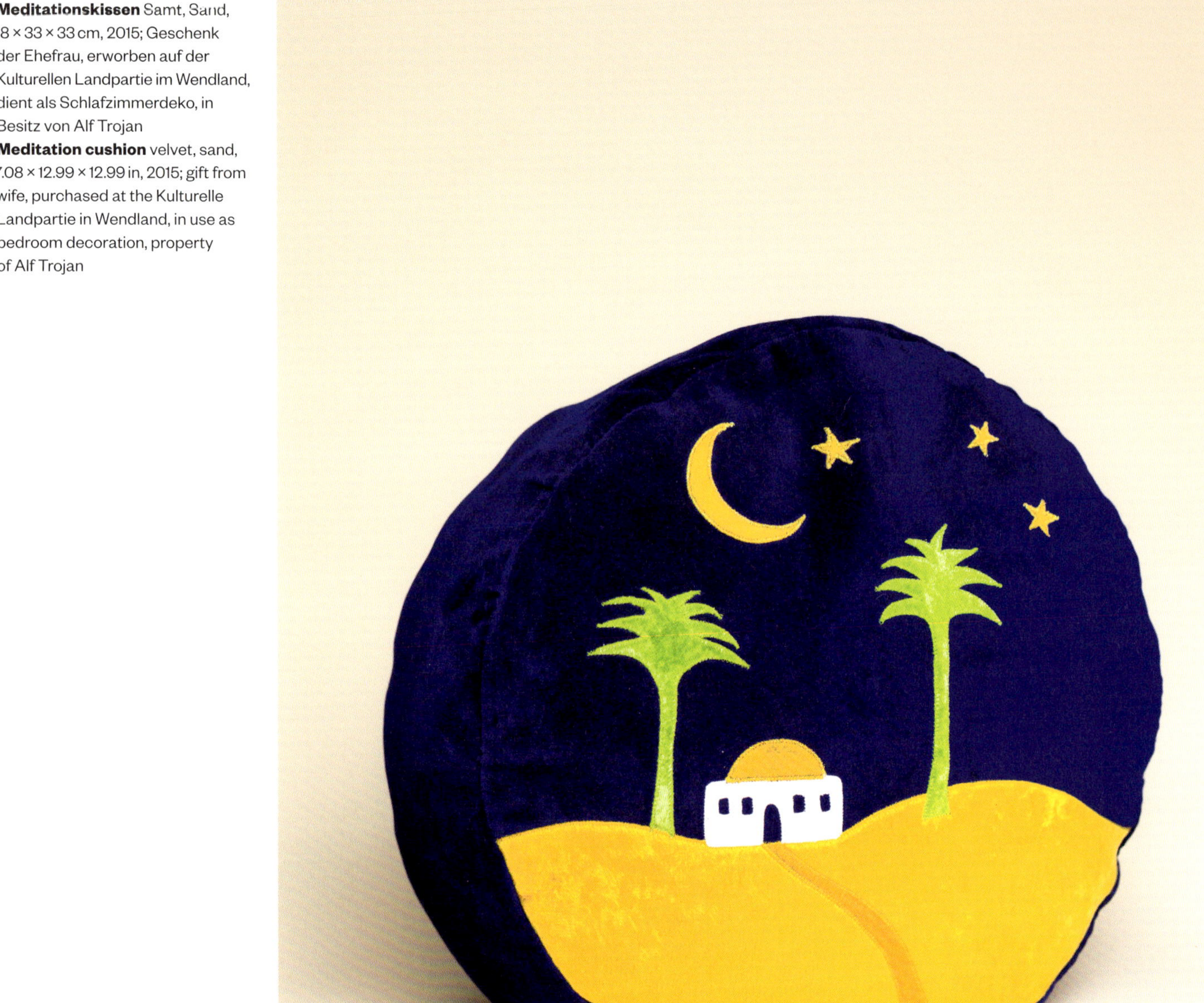

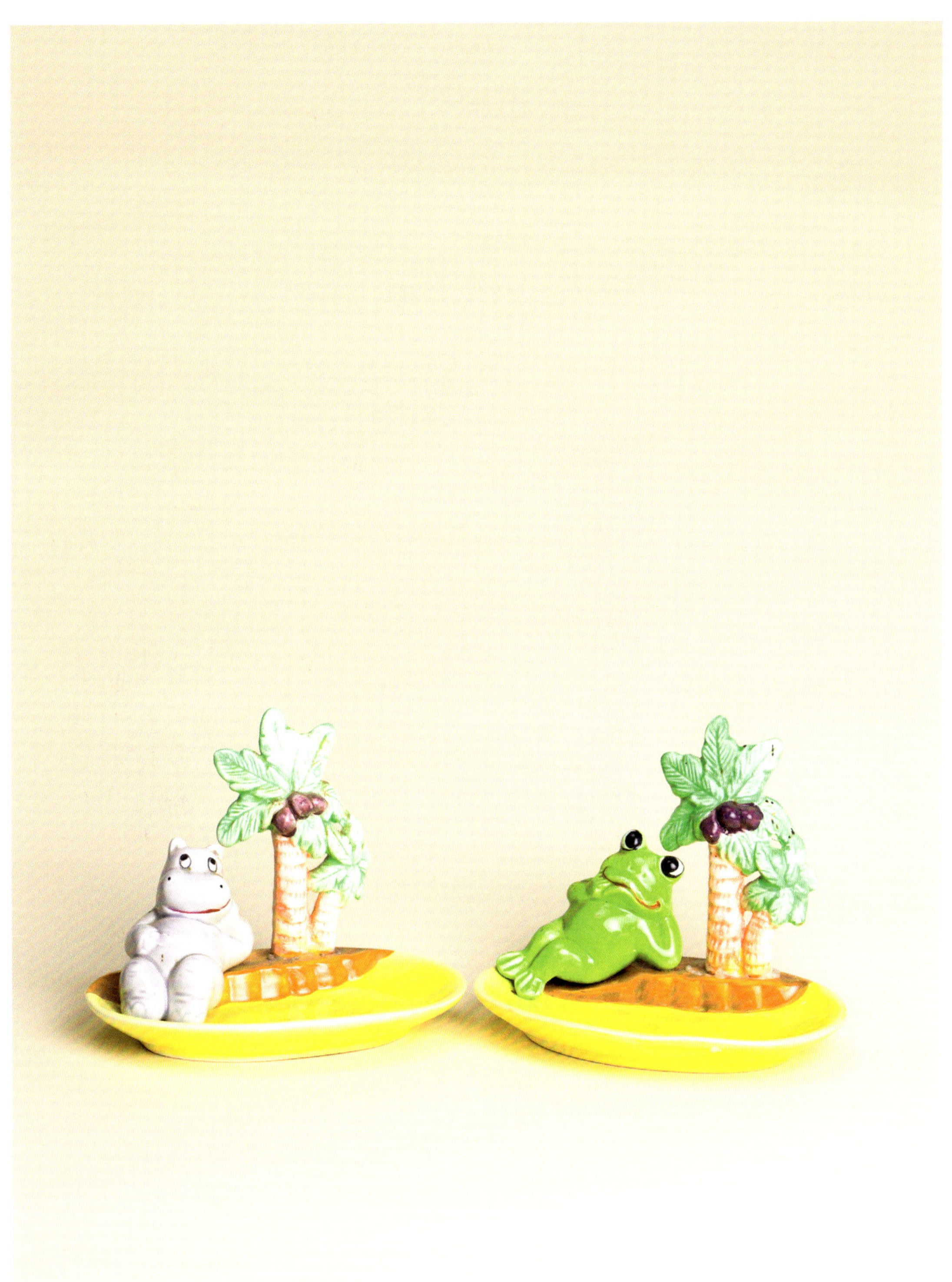

394–395
Zwei Seifenschalen Porzellan, 13 × 15,2 × 11,5 cm, undatiert; wie neu
Two soap trays porcelain, 5.11 × 5.98 × 4.52 in, undated; like new

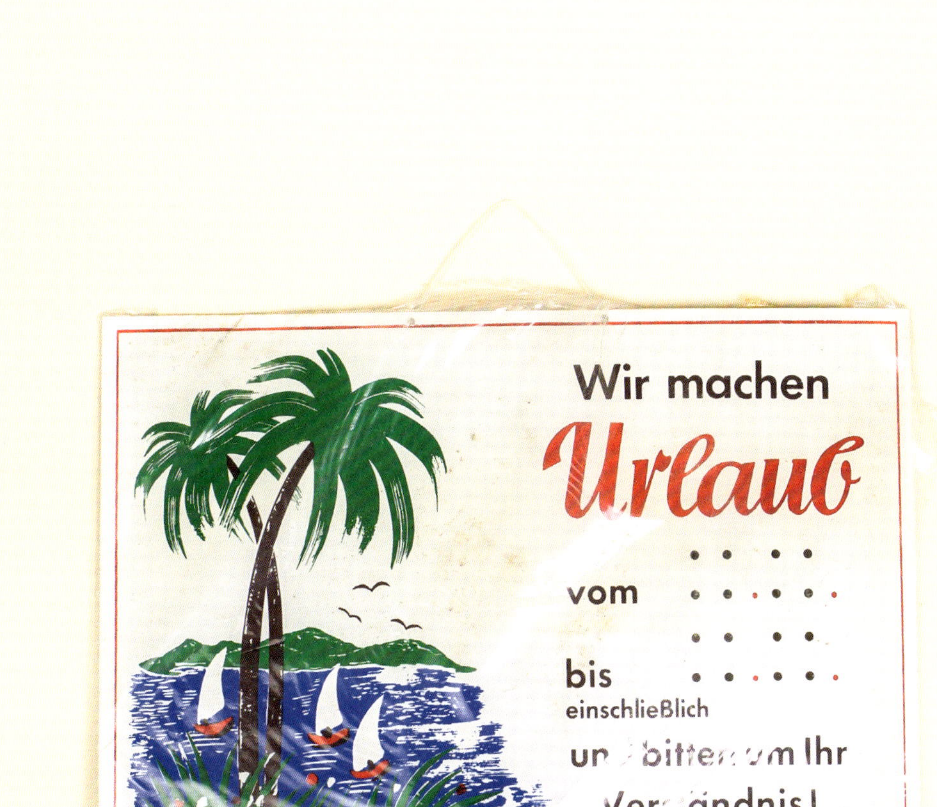

396
Schild „Wir machen Urlaub“ mit Kunststoffziffern Kunststoff, 20 × 30 cm, undatiert; originalverpackt, starke Flecken
Sign “We are going on holidays” with plastic figures plastic, 7.87 × 11.81 in, undated; original packaging, heavy stains

ALF TROJAN

Alf Trojan, geboren 1944, Arzt und Sozialwissenschaftler, ehemals Direktor des Instituts für Medizinische Soziologie des Universitätsklinikums Hamburg-Eppendorf, hat in den Siebzigerjahren begonnen, Gegenstände zu sammeln, die das Motiv der Palme tragen. Nachdem ihm auf einem Londoner Flohmarkt ein Palmenanstecker in die Hände fiel, entwickelte sich langsam, aber unaufhaltsam eine lebenslange Leidenschaft. Früh vom Sammeln infiziert, hatte er schon in seiner Jugend begonnen, Alben mit Briefmarken zu füllen. Das Motiv der Palme ließ ihn schließlich nicht mehr los. Über 40 Jahre lang häufte er zunächst Anstecker, dann weitere Objekte an. Bis er 2017 entschied, seine Sammlung mit über 1500 Objekten aufzugeben.

Alf Trojan, born in 1944, is a physician and social scientist, former director of the Institute of Medical Sociology, started collecting objects with palm trees in the early seventies. After he spotted a pin in the shape of a palm tree on a flea market in London, his lifelong passion for palm trees was initiated. As a devoted collector, his early passion for collecting objects focused on stamps since youth. Finally, it was the palm tree he focused on. In over forty years, he hoarded pins and all kinds of objects until he decided in 2017 to dissolve his collection of more than 1.500 objects.

DANK / THANKS

Alf Trojan, Alisa Karabut, Annelies Arp-Trojan, Antje Sauer, Barbara Tietze vom Höhbeck-Museum Vietze, Caroline Schubert, Charlotte Krauß, Christian Hornung, Clemens Cordes, Daniel Behrens, Daniela Hinrichs, Fotoclub Worpswede, Frederik Busch, Frederik Misch, Gesa Hansen, Hans Christoph Buch, Hanseatische Materialverwaltung/www.hanseatische-materialverwaltung.de, Ingo Taubhorn, Isa Schmidt, Janna Wieland, Johanna Zinecker, Julia Braune, Kay Riechers, Lia Darjes, Manu Dollt, Nik Antoniadis, Paula Markert, Petra Sommer, Sabine Danek, Silke Kämmerer, Steff Janotta, Thomas Ackermann, Thomas Ehgartner, Ute Mahler; meinen Freunden und meiner Familie/my friends and family

IMPRESSUM / COLOPHON

KONZEPT UND FOTOS / CONCEPT AND PHOTOS
Nele Gülck; www.neleguelck.de

GESTALTUNG / GRAPHIC DESIGN
Public; www.pblcdsgn.de

BILDBEARBEITUNG / PHOTO EDITING
Kay Riechers

TEXTE / TEXTS
Sabine Danek

ÜBERSETZUNG / TRANSLATIONS
Johanna Zinecker, James Rumball

LEKTORAT / COPYEDITING
Julia Braune

PROJEKTMANAGEMENT / PROJECT MANAGEMENT
Verena Simon, Kerber Verlag

Die Deutsche Nationalbibliothek verzeichnet diese Publikation in der Deutschen Nationalbibliografie; detaillierte bibliografische Daten sind im Internet über http://dnb.dnb.de abrufbar.

The Deutsche Nationalbibliothek lists this publication in the Deutsche Nationalbibliografie; detailed bibliographic data are available on the Internet at http://dnb.dnb.de.

GESAMTHERSTELLUNG UND VERTRIEB / PRINTED AND PUBLISHED BY
Kerber Verlag, Bielefeld
Windelsbleicher Str. 166–170
33659 Bielefeld
Germany
T: +49 (0) 5 21/9 50 08-10
F: +49 (0) 5 21/9 50 08-88
info@kerberverlag.com

Kerber, US Distribution
ARTBOOK | D.A.P.
75 Broad Street, Suite 630
New York, NY 10004
T: +1 (212) 627-1999
F: +1 (212) 627-9484

KERBER Publikationen sind weltweit in ausgewählten Buchhandlungen und Museumsshops erhältlich (Vertrieb in Europa, Asien, Süd- und Nordamerika).

KERBER publications are available in selected bookstores and museum shops worldwide (distributed in Europe, Asia, South and North America).

ISBN 978-3-7356-0551-1
www.kerberverlag.com

Printed in Germany

Diese Publikation wurde durch die Stiftung Kunstfonds gefördert.
This Publication was supported by Stiftung Kunstfonds.

STIFTUNG **KUNSTFONDS**